The American Deficit: Fulfillment of a Prophecy?

"America will spend herself out of existence"
Lenin (1917)

by Helen P. Rogers

WELLINGTON PUBLICATIONS
CARMEL, CALIFORNIA

First Edition

Library of Congress Catalog Card No.: 85-052235

ISBN: 0-915915-02-2

Printed in the U.S.A.

TO C-SPAN
The Cable Satellite Public Affairs Network
and all the wonderful people connected with it—
THE BEST THING THAT HAS HAPPENED TO THIS NATION IN A LONG TIME!

Laws, regulations, economic and social conditions constantly change, therefore the reader is urged to use this writing as only a beginning to his own investigation.

The information presented is believed to be correct and current at the time of this writing. The ideas presented do not pretend to be original with the author but are gratefully acknowledged as stemming from the many books and magazines listed in the bibliography, audio and visual news sources as well as discussions with colleagues.

Other Publications by Helen P. Rogers

Everyone's Guide to Financial Planning

Social Security: An Idea Whose Time Has Passed

The Election Process

Report Series
- Credit
- Risk
- Unemployment insurance
- Goals
- Investment
- Renovation & Recycling Real Property

"Germany will militarize herself out of existence, England will expand herself out of existence, and America will spend herself out of existence."

(Lenin 1917)

Contents

Preface

"If we fail to practice economy, if we do not balance the budget, then we shall have created a malevolent wheel which is revolving constantly in an adverse direction and which inevitably means the complete economic collapse of the United States. . . It would mean plunging the whole world into Darkness."

Those were the impassioned words spoken in 1932 by FDR's Budget Director, Lewis Douglas, a former Congressman from Arizona. Mr. Douglas was not only adamant in his belief that deficit spending must be curtailed, but that it must be curtailed *without* the benefit of increased revenue. As Arthur Schlesinger, Jr. put it, "A large tax burden he (Douglas) felt, would have economic effects almost as deplorable as deficit spending itself."[A]

One would hardly know that Franklin Delano Roosevelt and the majority of Democrats in Congress today were in the same political party! During his 1932 campaign FDR made a famous speech at Pittsburgh in which he proclaimed that "the one sound foundation of permanent economic recovery (was)—a complete and honest balancing of the Federal budget."

Most of us would agree that the deficit is an urgent concern, even today in this supposedly enlightened post-Keynesian era. On the surface the solution appears simple: cut spending or raise revenue or some of both. Simple means uncomplicated but not necessarily easy. Naturally, no group is going to object if government spending benefits them. There's a lot of truth to the saying that if you rob Peter to pay Paul you can always count on Paul's support. Our society is wonderfully full of diversity. Have you ever noticed how a liberal refers to redistribution as "sharing-the-wealth", whereas a conservative calls it "soaking-the-rich"? Chief Justice Earl Warren said some years ago: "Many people consider the things which government does for them to be social progress, but they consider the things government does for others as socialism."

Our tax dollars, although they may not be used as efficiently as we would like, go towards "What the people want", or so we are told. Who, after all, is against helping the poor, sick, elderly and very young? No one, of course. But "poor", "sick", "elderly" and "young" are what we call buzz words and are used to stifle opposition whenever tax dollars are wrested from us.

The Reverend Jesse Jackson and others, feel supply-side economics has not worked. He favors what he calls demand-side economics. Many people feel the poor, sick, elderly and young (those buzz words again) are entitled to whatever resources are necessary to fund programs which serve their needs. To those whose main concern is social programs, it is incomprehensible that anything could take priority or hold a higher claim on our national resources (Whatever "national resources" means?) They figure that deficits and higher taxes are a small price to pay in order to satisfy the needs of those who cannot adequately care for themselves.

On the other hand, Ayn Rand (wouldn't you like to have seen the late Ms. Rand and the Reverend Jackson on the same platform?) in her epic *Atlas Shrugged* maintains that "A morality that holds need as a claim holds emptiness—nonexistence as its standard of value; it rewards an absence, a defect. . ."

Before the advent of capitalism a portion of the human population had been doomed to extinction—it was capital in the form of new technology and machinery that made its survival possible.

It's a favorite pasttime of socialists to attempt to discredit capitalism by suggesting that the recognition of private property is a perversion of a primitive and more natural system of communal property. It is true that private property is a concept, first and only, given life by capitalism.

When Europe was steeped in feudalism, an elaborate system of rights and duties substituted for the centralized power prevalent before and after. Private property existed de facto, by custom, but not de jure, not by law. As man came out of the middle ages he substituted duty to the tribe (the common good) for duty to the tribal chief or nobleman. In precapitalist times wealth was believed to be an anonymous product of the tribe belonging to all members of society equally. Capitalists consider this notion as nonsense, believing instead that all wealth is produced by some individual and belongs to the individual that produced it. (No such thing as "national resources.")

The advent of machinery provided both the means and the opportunity for survival of what in the past had been a perpetual surplus of population doomed to early death. Man's inventions gave future generations the possibility of survival.

But central to the belief of Karl Marx and other opponents of capitalism was the idea that the rise of capitalism had been detrimental to the working classes. The reports of the early 19th century as chronicled in most history books (Charles Dickens added to the misinformation) tends to reinforce that supposition despite the fact that after the price fall of 1820–21 the purchasing power of wages in general was definitely greater than it had been just before the revolutionary and Napoleonic wars. Earnings increased and most men and women were better off even though protestations were louder than they had been in an earlier, supposedly more congenial, era.

However, Karl Marx was quick to admit that capitalism emerged because it offered more potentialities for mankind than was offered by feudalism and other forms of government. But he was equally quick to claim that wealth caused poverty as capitalists enriched themselves by exploiting workers and stealing the product of their labor. Capitalists, on the other hand, maintain that by doing well for themselves, risk-taking entrepreneurs created jobs and new opportunities for others as well.

In Book I of *Capital,* Karl Marx discussed the problem of finding an objective measure of the economic value of goods and services so that a just exchange of commodities would be possible. In the *Ethics,* Aristotle maintained a just exchange of qualitatively different things requires that they be of equivalent value and that this requires finding a way to measure that value. Aristotle decided that "demand" is the proper measurement for value. Equal demand will result in equal value as exemplified in trade. Demand, he says ". . . holds all things together; for if men did not need one another's goods at all, or did not need them equally, there would be either no exchange or not an equal exchange." Actually Aristotle was the first to admit that free competition is the only way to determine value—that everything else requires force. It seems that Aristotle and Marx are alone in proposing solutions to the problem of how to value different things in order to determine equivalents for a fair exchange, although the problem is being seriously studied by proponents of comparable worth today. Many years later Karl Marx explained the labor theory of value. Louis Kelso and Martin Adler in their 1958 book, *The Capitalist Manifesto,* declared that since capital produces wealth just as labor does, Marx's labor theory of value was incorrect. The universal cause of poverty, they claim, is failure of individuals to own sufficient productive capital.

The French Constitution included a clause which stated that "each of us places in common his person and his powers under the supreme direction of the general will." The American Constitution included no such sentiment and for good reason.

Some years ago Ralph Nader and Milton Friedman had a revealing disagreement. The issue was whether government had the right to require motorcyclists to wear helmets. (An issue heatedly debated also in 1987.) Mr. Friedman, quite naturally objected to interference with an individual's free choice, whereas Mr. Nader insisted cyclists be required to wear helmets in order to reduce their chance of injury. He reasoned that since taxpayers foot the bill for public ambulances, highway patrol and emergency medical facilities they have the right to make such a demand. The stupidity of refusing to wear a helmet was not to be tolerated in Mr. Nader's protective society.

In the words of Alexis de Tocqueville: "A government that provides total security for its people, foresees and supplies their necessities, manages their principal concerns, directs their industry, regulates the descent of property and subdivides their inheritance—what remains but to spare them all the care of thinking, and all the trouble of living."

I intend to show that government spending, instead of a "good" which we must stoically cut because of our immense deficit, is really undesirable and should be restricted even were it not for the deficit.

Helen P. Rogers
Carmel, California
July 23, 1987

Section One

The Great American Deficit

The Great American Deficit

SO WHAT ELSE IS NEW?

"It took 204 years to accumulate $1 trillion in debt and only 4 years (1981–1985) to accumulate the second trillion." The preceding sentence, once shocking, has now been widely quoted and calmly accepted. "By the spring of 1985 the United States had become a debtor nation for the first time since 1914." And you've no doubt heard that before too. "U.S. debt for all government, nonfinancial business and private households increased 14 percent in one year (1984)." And so what else is new? "All public spending in 1986 accounted for 36 percent of GNP." "Government has shown a deficit 25 out of the last 46 years." If you are like most Americans there are few facts you have not heard and beyond an initial indignation, few that will move you to action.

Because our system for gathering data is 25 years or more out of date, the data available to our public officials is inadequate, making economic policy even more speculative and uncertain than it needs to be. The Standard Industrial Classification code which organizes economic activity into major industry groups, has no separate classification for computers, software or microprocessors.

We have the situation where something like traffic congestion, because it causes more gasoline consumption can, on paper at least, increase our GNP. We can ooh and ahh over lower unemployment numbers, oblivious to the fact that they are due to a higher crime rate and the necessity of hiring more guards. The celebrated increase in GNP may be due to the stepped-up manufacture of iron bars and security systems. What looks like good news for the nation is an illusion created by numbers. The reality is most citizens would prefer a smoother traffic flow and less crime.

Since 1854 only two expansions lasted more than 58 months—June 1938 to February 1945 and February 1961 to December 1969. WW II kept the economy growing in the forties, Vietnam in the sixties. There are many that say it's done with smoke and mirrors in the eighties!

FANCY FOOTWORK

Headlines from the Associated Press on August 21, 1986 screamed "INCOME RISE BIGGEST IN 3 MONTHS" and as we read we found the increase was due to retroactive Social Security benefit payments and some fancy footwork with farm subsidies.

In September we heard retail sales were up 4.6 percent! Great news unless you consider the fantastic credit breaks given by the automobile industry which increased their sales for that one month pretty near 20 percent. Without the auto sales the increase in activity for all other retailers moved up only one tenth of one percent in the month of September, 1986.

In October we discovered the slowdowns in health care costs were little more than a failure to adjust for changes in the purchasing power of the dollar.

What is real, what is an illusion whipped up by policy makers for the purpose of manipulation?

GNP figures are geared to a smokestack economy while the real world is now service oriented. Service production, consumption and exports are under-reported at every stage. Things like the distribution of films, TV footage and financial services are hardly mentioned. There are numerous nonmarket activities which have been abandoned, hurriedly done or substituted as a result of women exchanging nonpaid work for wages. The list is long: home-cooked meals, housework, child care, chauffeuring, volunteering, gardening, painting, ironing, decorating, crafts, baking, sewing, on ad infinitum. With more and more women in the labor force there are many missed activities that have made the nation worse off but have not lowered real GNP as it is currently measured. In the past our method of GNP accounting tended to understate GNP, now GNP is probably overstated due to the omission of activities no longer being performed.

It is advisable to use caution in interpreting GNP statistics and all other statistics for that matter, but to be especially cautious in automatically relating rises in GNP to improvements in the quality of life.

Retail sales numbers are distorted by blanket coverage of auto sales. Mail order is also poorly reported. Yet these admittedly inaccurate untimely and unstable numbers are all our esteemed policy makers have at their disposal for making decisions which ultimately affect every one of us.

The Consumer Price Index (CPI) last revamped in 1979, has been brought more into line with the nation's current buying habits. The

CPI is widely used in determining COLAs (cost of living increases) and wage negotiations and may affect the income of as many as 60 million workers. It has been estimated that each one percent variation triggers a $2.8 billion change in U. S. income payments.

According to the Research Institute of America, the new CPI ". . . will continue to be compared with '67 prices equalling 100. As of last November (1986) . . . the CPI registered 330.8, only 1.3% higher than the same period a year earlier. The 1987 Index will climb by about 3.5% due to increased food and energy costs."[1]

The formula for the new CPI, effective the end of February, 1987 includes video cassette recorders, smoke detectors, personal computers, child and elderly care costs, etc., and is based on the following:

Housing	42.6%
Transportation	18.7%
Food & beverage	17.8%
Medical care	4.8%
Energy costs	5.2%
Auto fuel	4.8%
Apparel	6.5%

(Based on data from the Bureau of Labor Statistics)

On July 3, 1987, Janet Norwood, Commissioner of Labor Statistics while testifying before a Senate Committee was asked by Senator John Melcher (D-MT) what the results would be if a special CPI were used to reflect the experience of older Americans. Currently, there is a "CPI-U" which reflects the purchasing habits of *all* urban consumers and the "CPI-W" (the one in normal usage) which includes no retirees in its samplings. Ms. Norwood advised the committee that the issue of whether to use "CPI-U" or "CPI-W" had been raised back in 1978 and it is not certain that older citizens would benefit by a change in the CPI. Senator Melcher's apparent goal is to get the largest cost of living increases (COLAs) possible for those on Social Security, realizing that COLAs are indexed to the CPI. But as Ms. Norwood warned, a special CPI *just* for retirees, while it might reflect the higher cost of medicine and health care, would omit college tuitions, new cars and a host of other high priced items that would not normally be included in a CPI for retirees only. At any rate, the Commissioner assured the Committee that up to age 75 the buying habits of older people conforms to the rest of society and a different CPI would reflect the experience of a relatively small, but admittedly growing segment of the population, i.e., those over age 75.

Even though the Committee was advised gathering data to formulate this special CPI would be extremely expensive and there is doubt that the CPI would actually be used (discarded you can bet if it failed to raise Social Security COLAs faster than the old CPI), Senator Melcher pushed for its formulation. No thought of belt-tightening evidenced here.

GOVERNMENT SHUTDOWNS

The government shut down in November 1981 at a cost of approximately $65 million in paper work and time lost.

On May 25, 1983, Congress approved raising the national debt limit from $1.29 trillion to $1.389 trillion.

The government shut down again in October 1984, sending 500,000 employees home.

At the end of 1985 the debt limit was $1,823 trillion; up to $7,614,51 per man, woman and child.

In February 1986 the Congress went to work in earnest and cut $11 billion from the deficit and added $3 billion revenue from taxes. Normally that would mean a $14 billion reduction but the August 1986 deficit was $55 billion more than expected! (Oh well—they tried.)

During the first two weeks of FY1987, which began October 1, 1986, there were two stopgap measures and on October 17, 1986 the government shut down once again and this time 400,000 government workers were sent home.

Before the 99th Congress adjourned, it increased the Treasury's borrowing authority by $189 billion and noted that the new debt ceiling of $2.3 *trillion* was a 133 percent increase just since Ronald Reagan took office in 1981.

But if you think your elected officials on Capitol Hill have any kind of handle on our national debt you had better think again. In mid-July 1987 the 100th Congress OK'd a $245 billion increase in the debt limit—getting worse not better, isn't it? But that didn't phase our leaders and on September 29, 1987 the debt ceiling was raised still further to $2.8 *trillion.* What can I say?

Before there were trillions we used to explain billions. If you had a billion dollars you could spend $100,000 every day for 27 years and unless it was stashed in a cookie jar, it would increase by $70 million every year (at 7%). Now one year's budget is a trillion dollars! A trillion = 317 centuries of seconds. Phooey—I'll leave those illustrations to presidents.

DEALING WITH THE DEFICIT

Deficits are undesirable for many reasons. When financed by savings they restrict the capital available for investments; when financed from abroad they give foreigners a rain check on the future of our children; when financed by excessive monetary expansion (always that temptation exists) inflation may ensue and finally the greater the deficit the greater the interest cost burden and the need to raise interest rates as a hedge against inflation.

Let's look at our alternatives. We can continue to borrow, we can raise taxes, we can monetize the debt or we can curtail spending. The first alternative, borrowing, has found favor with our short-sighted leaders up until now. Postponing the day of reckoning may have been politically expedient at one time but citizens will no longer stand still for such shenanigans. Raising taxes has become more popular with those politicians who like to call themselves realists; I prefer to call them cowards. Unfortunately the third alternative, monetizing the debt, has historical precedent. But as Henry Kaufman has pointed out, the old solutions of deflation (bankruptcy) or inflation (making debt worth less to our creditors) won't work in today's world; it would only lead to massive dislocations.[2] The fourth and the only alternative that should even be considered is cutting back on government spending.

INFLATION

Keynesian economics was deficit on purpose. Today the deficit is a by-product of the collapse of inflation. The Reagan Administration predicted a decline in inflation. From 13 percent to 3 percent in two years is not a decline, it's a free fall. Budget assumptions were based on erroneous inflation estimates and as a consequence less revenue was collected, nevertheless money was spent as budgeted. Expand, contract, inflate, collapse; spending goes obliviously on, but it is a one way street—if prices fall money isn't returned to taxpayers, it is just spread over more things.

In the 1970s high inflation and relatively low real interest rates tempted those dealing with natural resources to expand, setting them up for the plunge which was to follow in the 1980s. All over the world, the race was on to boost production of oil, commodities, metals and all natural resources. But then the bubble burst.

Deflation is not so much a slowing down of inflation as it is an abrupt halt, making bankrupts out of once conservative borrowers. The falling dollar, a rising money supply and the huge deficit are keeping inflation expectations alive. Not surprisingly high inflation, which allows even marginal investments to recoup their cost, is seen as the way out for many.

The reason our debt is half of what it was at the end of the second world war was partially due to inflation. Inflation, which unfortunately for debtors, was brought under control so abruptly during 1981–82. On the other hand, falling inflation allowed the price of high-yielding Treasury Bonds to rise and interest rates to fall despite the rise in the deficit. That would have been the time to cut back on the deficit using spending restraint and encouraging economic growth. Unfortunately, the opportunity was missed because of the Fed's strong fear of inflation and consequent curb on the growth of the economy in 1984.

As creditors began to catch on they placed an inflation premium on the interest rates. Anything which fuels the expectations of inflation will raise inflation premiums on interest rates. Fed expansion or contraction can either raise or lower interest rates depending on which causal chain is stronger. In the early years of inflation, there was no inflation premium; in the later decades there was. It all depends on the subjective expectations of the public and this is one reason why economic forecasts can never be made with certainty.

Historically, the largest deficits are a result of war not government spending as such. Supply and demand get out of sync as goods are siphoned to the war effort. Then there is the large scale destruction of a nation's productive capacity which occurs when roads, factories and sources of power are destroyed. America gained a large advantage over the rest of the world because her capacity to produce was not interrupted during this century.

We experienced economic growth (2% range) in the 1980s even with high interest rates. True it was less than the 4 percent growth of the 1960s or the 3 percent growth of the 1970s, but it was growth. Policy makers point to the 1982–83 period, when deficits were accelerating and inflation was waning, as proof that deficits and inflation have little influence on each other.

As further proof that inflation is not caused by deficit financing we can look at the boom years, 1956–57 when the government ran a combined surplus of $7.7 billion but prices rose nevertheless 5 percent during those 2 years. An even better example, though somewhat more distant, would be the years 1897 to 1913. The government experienced a surplus during 7 of those years, the deficit was 3 percent lower in 1913 than in 1987 and prices rose 50 percent. Even the fact that the nation was on a gold standard didn't stop inflation.

The problem in 1963 was excess capacity and the challenge was to create demand to increase employment and put idle factories back to work. This was the type of situation that Lord Keynes told us could be helped by government borrowing—that government deficits under such conditions would lead to more production rather than inflation. Only when the economy is already producing at maximum capacity do deficits pose a real problem. Only when supply can't meet the increased demand does inflation have a chance. The solution in such an instance would be to raise taxes or restrict government spending. An increase in demand that can be filled is not inflationary at all.

When the public buys government securities there is no increase in the money supply but when commercial banks buy government securities brand-new money is created, a process referred to as monetizing the debt. Monetizing *is* inflationary. The Federal Reserve attempts to control the bank's lending capacity but the longer large deficits are allowed to continue the greater the pressure becomes to simply monetize them.

CROWDING OUT

Milton Friedman tries to rebut the crowding-out effect of deficits claiming that all government spending not just deficits equally crowd out private savings and investment. Taxes reduce public consumption as effectively as savings. Since funds for all federal spending ultimately come from the private sector, whether via inflation, taxes or government borrowing, it would seem clear that it is the spending itself which must be curtailed. But on Capitol Hill it is not only possible but probable that "cutting the deficit" be interpreted as a call to raise taxes. That's why we must make it clear to our elected officials that we want *spending* cut; not the deficit. The reduction of spending means ending some programs or contracting the federal outlays in other ways, like closing facilities and eliminating unneeded employees. Deficit reduction is the DC buzz word for revenue enhancement—known outside the belt way as a tax hike!

"WISE GUY RECIPE"

The following is what I call the wise-guy's recipe for ending the deficit: cut both defense and domestic spending, raise taxes and encourage savings and other stimulants to the growth of the economy. That would do it all right, but it would take a genius not merely a wise guy to know how much of each ingredient is required. Some "cooks" insist that certain of the above ingredients would ruin the outcome and should be eliminated entirely. Practically no one in the country agrees upon the proportion of all the ingredients.

John Makin of the American Enterprise Institute is one of many economists who suggest it may be unduly harsh and indeed harmful to the economy to aim for a zero deficit by 1991 as mandated under Gramm-Rudman (G-R). They warn of overkill and suggest the budget should only be cut until the ratio of debt to GNP is stabilized and that perhaps a target of $135 billion deficit in FY1988 might be preferred to the established G-R target of $108 billion. Drastic cuts could, they fear, exacerbate the deficit problem by slowing economic growth. As stated earlier, an obsessive desire for a balance budget could have unpleasant consequences for an economy where consumer and investment demands are inadequate to provide full employment and maximum output. Problems arise only when debt is created beyond the nation's capacity to produce wealth. For example, look at the troubled years 1930–1935 when there was an overall decrease in the nation's debt:

	1930 Debt	1935 Debt
Corporate	$ 89 billion	$ 75 billion
Consumer	59 billion	41 billion
State & local	14 billion	16 billion
Fed. Govt.	17 billion	34 billion
Total	$179 billion	$166 billion

Compare 1930–35 with the boom years 1950–55 when debt skyrocketed:

	1950 Debt	1955 Debt
Corporate	$251 billion	$403 billion
Consumer	97 billion	172 billion
State & local	21 billion	38 billion
Fed. Govt.	219 billion	232 billion
Total	$588 billion	$835 billion

The increase in government spending in 1930–35 couldn't make up for the decrease in corporate and consumer spending.

On the other hand, James Miller III, head of the Office of Management and Budget (OMB), who prefaced his remarks in defense of the Administration FY1988 budget with the observation that he used to teach economics, felt a $63 billion reduction in one year would be stimulative and not a contractionary policy.

REDUCING THE DEFICIT WITHOUT RAISING TAXES

A NBC/WSJ poll taken in January 1986 showed 62 percent of the people polled thought the deficit could be reduced without a raise in tax revenue (but what do the people know—right?) and yet Congress is unwilling to try. If the Grace Commissions's recommendations had been implemented in 1983 we would have been $242.4 billion to the better by now. Instead we are playing around with sales and fees to raise additional revenue hoping no one will notice. Certain foreign airline passengers will be assessed $5 a head to help finance the Immigration & Naturalization Service; additional court fees will help out the Justice Department; sales have been proposed for Export-Import Bank loans, the Naval Petroleum Reserves and Conrail. In November 1985, by a vote of 358 to 60, the House of Representatives passed a $20 billion water construction projects bill stipulating that partial funding come from a new tariff on cargo entering the United

States. Not only is that a form of protectionism but it amounts to a back-door tax on U. S. consumers.

The Reagan Administration's deficit reduction package for FY1987 consisted of so-called non-tax revenue as well as cutting spending. Revenue was anticipated from the addition of state and local government employees into the Medicare system (whether they liked it or not) and also a .22 percent tariff on imports, called a Customs Service user fee (more name games) as well as a tougher crack down on citizens by the Internal Revenue Service.

BLAMING THE REAGAN TAX CUT

It is important to note that the increase in our national deficit is not due to a decrease in revenue. I heard Robert McNamara make the claim recently that the 1981 tax cut was the source of our budget deficits.[3] The truth about the 1981 tax cut is that any revenue shortfall was due only one-third to tax reduction and two-thirds to the edge of a recession.

The cuts were not carried out according to plan and then blamed for not working. I'm referring to the phasing in rather than giving the economy the planned jolt of a 30 percent cut in personal tax rates in one full swoop. As it was, the five percent cut in October 1981, was wiped out by the January 1982 increase in Social Security taxes. The 10 percent cut in the summer of 1982 was undermined by the redesigning of the IRS's withholding tables and TEFRA (Tax Equity & Fiscal Responsibility Act) which took back 71 percent of the cut (ERTA—the Economic Recovery Tax Act). It was the tax reductions that brought us out of that recession and set us on our way to 5 years of expansion. The 1981 cut was our salvation not our downfall as Mr. McNamara and others would have us believe.

TAX INCREASES

Although tax increases could conceivably balance the budget, they have historically added more fuel to the government's spending spree. Tax financed spending is no better than government borrowing as to its effect on economic growth—both pre-empt private funds. Not only are tax increases no cure for the deficit, the earnings of hard working citizens are confiscated for the benefit of a bureaucracy that adds insult to injury by using part of that confiscated money to push the public around.

In the sixties the predominant belief was that economic growth and inflation would continue to increase, pushing citizens into ever higher tax brackets. Bulging coffers would permit redistribution of wealth with no strain and little harm to the nation. With the higher inflation of the 1970s, bracket creep forced taxpayers to hand over approximately an extra $127 billion in federal income taxes.

It has been estimated that indexing taxes saved rises of $7.6 billion in 1985, $18.1 billion in 1986 and $30.3 billion in 1987 and $43.9 billion in 1988. Usually, you hear those statistics phrased as "cost the government. . .".

On NBC's MEET THE PRESS on April 12, 1987, former deputy Treasury Secretary, Richard Darman said that the Reagan Administration might be willing to negotiate with Congress over the FY1988 budget, possibly in the areas of new excise taxes and middle class entitlement cuts. (No one dares mention Social Security—the "S" word—and cuts in the same breath).

Senator Bentsen, on the same program, favored a new fee on imported oil but was against any broad-based tax on energy. (P. S. Senator Bentsen is from Texas.)

Many people are against new taxes, of any type, fearing that the money won't be used to reduce the deficit but only to expand programs. There is a built-in system within the bureaucracy which feeds upon itself, discouraging efforts of efficiency. On the other side are the citizens who use "There is no free lunch" as a slogan to enlist support for more taxes; the idea being to "tax *us*" so grandchildren will not be saddled with our free and loose living; an emotional appeal.

The question becomes: Are government operations a stimulant or a burden? The answer is a matter of philosophy and politics *not* economics. I agree with Senator Phil Gramm of Texas who claims the budget debate is not so much about numbers as it is about the future of America. "Those of us who want to control spending want to let the working men and women keep more of what they earn, because we want America dominated by opportunity. Those who want to raise your taxes so that government can keep growing, want an America that's dominated by government. That's the real choice."[4]

SAVINGS

Some hard line Keynesians believe excessive savings and inadequate consumption were the true cause of the Great Depression. Since then we have had little to fear from either. (The understatement of the year!)

A financial newsletter in Arizona predicts that the personal savings rate in 1987 will fall to 3.6 percent of disposable income, the lowest level since the 3.1 percent rate registered in 1947 when the nation's pent-up war time sacrifices erupted in a full-blown buying spree. During WW II when consumers had little to buy, the savings rate in this country was over 20 percent. In a recent effort to stimulate savings, the government instituted All-Savers Certificates, expanded Individual Retirement Accounts, improved Keogh Plans, lowered tax rates and deregulated interest rates on savings and checking accounts.

Net private savings is the number most bantered about and calculated to cause concern. It treats the purchase of durable goods as consumption, even though everyone knows you do not consume a washer and dryer when it is purchased but rather its services are consumed over a period of years.

The savings rate averaged close to 8 percent during most of the seventies but as income growth cooled and families attempted to maintain their living standards, the savings rate dropped to around 6.5 percent where it hovered through 1984, falling again in 1985 to 4.6 percent. However, in 1985 consumer spending was up in real terms by 3.3 percent and GNP grew (only 2.2 percent but better than nothing) making a minority of economists suggest an increased savings rate could hurt rather than help the economy. They claim if Americans saved more, the economy might suffer from lack of investment.

A developed nation like the United States, according to these economists, simply doesn't need the same capital commitment that a lessor developed country might. Savings are very important to an underdeveloped nation that is attempting to build up its productive capacity. Such countries need to increase capital because there isn't enough otherwise for business to invest in equipment and technology and for government to use for roads and schools; all things necessary to increase productive capacity. Others argue that is exactly where America is now—needing to improve all those things as if it were a lessor developed nation.

In the United States, little was done to discourage borrowing until the 1986 tax reform (ACT) which denied deductions for consumer interest. But a coherent tax plan was too much to hope for and even as the 1986 reform discouraged borrowing it also took away some of the incentives to save by making Keoghs and IRAs less attractive. The new tax changes put a 15 percent surtax on anyone whose total income from pensions, including IRA's exceeds $112,500 a year in retirement. Gary Strum of E. F. Hutton refers to it as a "communist tax" because it penalizes investment success.

It's wrong to compare our savings with Japan. Noble prize economist Franco Modigliani's life-cycle theory offers another explanation of why countries such as the United States save less than generally poorer but faster growing countries. He postulates that most people try to maintain a fairly level standard of living by circumventing ups and downs whenever possible. The purpose of saving early is, he says, to spend later, usually in retirement. (You can see how the advent of the Social Security system skews things also—but more of that later). This leads Professor Modigliani to the conclusion that countries with high productivity (Japan fits) and younger populations (Japan doesn't fit) save more than those with older more stable populations and relatively lower economic growth.

I recently heard a radio commentator say the Japanese are successful *because* they save three times what we do. Baloney! But few dispute the fact that personal savings are less efficient than business savings which go directly into capital stock. Although a good portion of personal savings are eventually used for investment in equipment, research and increased business productivity, many economists believe reducing taxes on business would give the biggest impetus to the economy. In an attempt to encourage consumers to save, Professor John Shoven of Stanford, has proposed "consumption deferral accounts". People could save as much as they wished, tax deferred and they would be able to withdraw any amount at any time with the tax due as the money is spent. With compound interest working, there would be a powerful incentive to leave those dollars alone, benefitting the individual saver and the economy as a whole.

CONSUMPTION

Some 24 million 13 to 19 year olds will spend $30 billion of their own money this year. On top of that, many do the family shopping for working parents which means they have control over an additional $40 billion. Many teens are disciplined about acquiring money and extremely goal oriented. However, there has been a major change in the work ethic; it's no longer work hard and save for a brighter future, it's work hard and get what you want *today*!

DOES SPENDING HURT?

Our self-indulgent ways may be starving the country of the physical capital it needs to grow; at least that's the way the media myth goes. But let's look at some facts.

Over the last 35 years or so, our GNP has tripled and our standard of living has doubled. Of course not all government spending is the same, some government spending is an investment. Under President Eisenhower a good portion of government spending went to create resources such as bridges, dams, highways and to finance education and research. Such spending spurred new industry and the interstate highway system reduced shipping costs for business and profits increased. These capital investments carry a return as they make citizens more productive. Unfortunately, the majority of current spending by government is for interest on the debt, transfer payments and defense, none of which increase productivity nor add to our collective resources.

FOREIGN FUNDS

But facts take off where theories end and as a nation, we have thus far been saved from our spending follies by the fact that United States government securities are still the most popular investment in the world. Those who purchase our government securities are buying future tax collections in this country.

By the 1980s both Germany and Japan had surplus capital to invest. Both countries had earlier lent surplus capital to third world nations but by the eighties these nations were no longer living up to their commitments. Investing in the United States seemed the logical solution to the problem of excess capital.

Foreign funds have made it possible for us to continue domestic investment despite the government's need for credit. Foreigners are financing the deficit and disproving the theory that said interest rates would soar because the federal deficit with its insatiable appetite for domestic savings would force the private sector into a capital shortage. Foreign financing freed domestic savings and as the fear of scarcity was dispelled, interest rates fell. Nevertheless, money that is made in this country doesn't necessarily stay here and some observes fear that what we produce in the 1990s will go to pay for the extremely high level of consumption in the eighties. Eventually international investors will call it quits and our savings will have to switch from domestic investment to servicing the federal government's appetite for funds.

WHO CAN PREDICT?

David Stockman, former OMB Director, was quoted in the December 1981 issue of the Atlantic as admitting "None of us really understands what's going on with all these numbers. You've got so many different budgets out and so many different base lines. . . People are getting from A to B, and it's not clear how they're getting there."

Some of the overruns are due to errors in forecasting business cycles. Greater than anticipated unemployment rates and less economic growth mean higher expenditures in the form of food stamps, insurance benefits, etc., coupled with less revenue than anticipated. However, the majority of the overruns are due to the failure to accurately anticipate Congress's love affair with spending.

The OMB midsession review on July 30, 1982 predicted the deficit would jump from $100 billion to $115 billion in FY1983 before falling to $74 billion in FY1985. Of course the actual FY1985 was just short of $212 billion. (You can stop laughing now!) So what do you expect when $734 billion comes in and $946 billion goes out?

Had the economy grown as anticipated (the FY1983 receipts were 16 percent lower than estimated), the deficit would be half the size it attained in 1983. However, interest rates were higher and inflation lower than expected which made the cost of financing the debt just that much higher also. The lower inflation meant less revenue because taxpayers were not pushed into higher tax brackets as the soothsayers had assumed they would be.

Similarly, as FY1987 began there were many reasons to anticipate a boom in the economy. Lower interest rates, lower inflation, lower energy prices, lower value of the dollar. But these were offset by the realities of higher unemployment in the areas of manufacturing, energy, commercial real estate and agriculture. An all out recession was averted only by some Federal Reserve policies and propitious use of the government's automatic safety nets, including food stamps, welfare and unemployment and social insurance. Of course greater use of services coupled with lower revenue (thanks to lower employment) increased the deficit.

FEDERAL SPENDING AS A PERCENTAGE OF GNP

Figures on government spending vary depending on what is included. In 1981, total spending (by government, business and consumers) amounted to 98 percent of GNP, the other 2 percent ($65 billion) was invested abroad. In 1985 the federal government was spending $600 million more a day than it was taking in, or put another way, it was collecting 80 cents and spending a dollar. According to OMB predictions, if nothing were done, by 1989 the debt would amount to $2.5 trillion and interest alone would demand 50 percent of our income tax revenue.

Less than 50 years ago, federal spending was only 10 percent of GNP. (See chart I) For those whose religion recommends tithing, 10 percent to God and 10 percent to the state makes sense. (The rest of us could probably live with it too.)

Between 1970 and 1979, federal outlays rose consistently at a rate of about 1.8 percent per year. Then suddenly in 1979 the spending rate skyrocketed 4.6 percent in one year reaching 23 percent of GNP. Ronald Reagan campaigned with the promise to bring spending down to the 19 percent range again. But after only three years of the Reagan Administration, federal spending had risen to 25 percent of GNP.

But why the fuss? As Chart I shows, we have experienced even larger percentages of government spending to GNP with no ill effects; in fact some of these have been boom years and this is true also with regard to debt as a percentage of GNP. The problem is the recent acceleration of the debt. Since 1981 publicly held debt has been compounding at 16 percent a year which is twice as fast as GNP has been rising. According to the Federal Reserve Board, all government debt (federal, state & local) has grown 14.4 percent per year whereas GNP has been growing at a rate close to 8.6 percent. When debt grows faster than GNP, interest costs (not rates) rise faster than revenue. In 1980, the national debt (not annual spending but accumulated debt) was $930 billion or approximately 35 percent of GNP and interest cost

$53 billion or 2 percent of GNP. By 1986, the publicly held debt was $1.7 trillion or 41 percent of 1986's GNP and despite the lower interest rates, the cost of interest on that debt was in the $140 billion range or about 4 percent of GNP.

Chart I
Debt & Govt. Spending as % of GNP

	GNP	Outstanding Gross Debt as % of GNP	% Govt. Spent of GNP
1940	$ 100.0 billion	53.4%	10.0%
1945	212.4 billion	119.9%	42.7%
1950	286.5 billion	96.9%	16.1%
1955	400.0 billion	72.1%	18.0%
1960	506.5 billion	58.4%	18.5%
1965	691.1 billion	49.0%	17.9%
1970	992.7 billion	39.5%	20.2%
1975	1,549.2 billion	36.8%	22.5%
1980	2,631.7 billion	35.5%	22.9%
1985	3,992.0 billion	47.6%	24.8%

(All figures from Bureau of Census Statistical Abstract of U.S.)
Source: U.S. Office of Management & Budget

You can see how it might not be such a good idea to have the national debt doubling and redoubling every four or five years. Interest on that debt would soon eat up all tax revenue. If, on the other hand, over the next five years real economic growth could be maintained close to 3.5 percent, unemployment could be held at 6 percent, inflation permitted to rise no higher than 4.5 percent, all accompanied by a drop in interest rates to 5 percent, then perhaps in this best of all possible worlds, we could ignore the deficit. But, as we have seen, growth in the eighties has thus far been in the 2 percent range. If we had now the 4.4 percent growth that occurred in the sixties, we'd have a surplus. If elephants had wings, they'd fly.

GROWTH

In any anti-deficit strategy, growth becomes the key. A 1984 Congressional Budget Office (CBO) study found a one percentage point increase in economic growth contributes almost twice as much to deficit reduction as a spending freeze. Chart II shows a spending freeze would save only $185 billion whereas a one percentage point increase in annual economic growth over the same time period would result in a savings of $322 billion.

Chart II
Effect Of Freeze & Growth On Deficit

Fiscal Year	1986	1987	1988	1989
		(billions of dollars)		
Baseline deficit	$195	$216	$238	$263
Spending freeze	-17	-38	-56	-74
Faster growth	-36	-61	-94	-131
Deficit	142	117	88	58

(DATA: CONGRESSIONAL BUDGET OFFICE)

Unfortunately, as the government's share increases, economic growth tends to slow.

Between 1965–74 Western Europe spent 37 percent of its GNP and economic growth was 4.3 percent. Between 1975–84 Western Europe spent 47 percent of GNP and economic growth was 1.8 percent, plus there was 152 percent increase in unemployment as an added bonus. (OK, so there was a world recession in the early 80s and before that the huge increase in energy prices. I admit it's not so easy to determine cause and effect).

The U. S. Chamber of Commerce discovered some useful trends, however. In OECD countries when 15–25 percent of GNP was spent by governments, maximum economic growth occurred. When 45 percent or more was spent the countries experienced the lowest growth. The U. S. government is currently spending 36 percent of GNP.

IS THE DEFICIT REAL?

Robert Eisner, Professor at Northwestern University, claims in his new book, HOW REAL IS THE FEDERAL DEFICIT, that we are not measuring the federal deficit accurately. He contends that inflation and resulting higher interest rates eat away at the market value of the national debt and what appears on the books as deficit of some $1.1 trillion, accumulated from 1946 to 1984, is less than half that amount in real market value. Subtracting tax revenue from government spending yields either a surplus or a deficit but then, according to Eisner, that number must be adjusted to reflect the decline in value caused by inflation in that year. Sometimes a recorded deficit turns out to be a surplus. For example, he estimates that the reported deficit in 1980 of $61 billion was actually an "adjusted surplus of $7.6 billion". Professor Eisner believes that reducing the deficit in line with Gramm-Rudman mandates could create a surplus of about $100 billion once the effects of expected inflation are considered.

The Professor's critics, on the other hand, say he is adding apples and oranges. The decline in the market value of the national debt, which is held by the public and which Eisner subtracts from the recorded deficit, does not reduce income, it reduces wealth. They claim Professor Eisner is giving the same weight to a change in people's income as to a change in their wealth. Numerous studies show that a dollar of added income will boost spending far more than an increase in wealth.

Peter H. Bernstein of New York[5] also found surpluses where others see deficits. He claims if we subtract interest payments the government was in surplus from 1959 through 1970. The raw figures show deficits in 8 of those years. Interest payments are significant only when they are paid to foreigners, according to Mr. Bernstein, otherwise interest rates paid by government to its own citizens go into the pockets of individuals, lending institutions and simply add to savings. We should see federal debt as a portfolio of Treasury and other federal obligations which the institutions and individuals that hold them consider to be the safest of investments rather than a huge burden to be borne by the taxpayers.

Society is made up of young people with potential whose financial assets are small in relation to their income and older people living off interest and dividends whose assets are large in relation to their income. The first group pays more taxes than it earns in interest while it is the reverse for the second group. If interest rates were to fall because the deficit were paid off and the government was no longer a borrower the incomes of the older people would slump.

HISTORY OF THE DEFICIT

Senator Don Riegle of Michigan, rather calmly observed before the Senate Finance Committee (1/15/87), "Our national debt is growing $1 billion every 2.5 days." Ho-hum!

How times have changed! We have increased tax revenue pretty near 200 times since 1931 when our deficits first began. Allowing for the inflation which was largely a consequence of those deficits, our tax burden has increased more than 30 times in real terms. During those deep depression years, FDR never had the courage to run more than a 5 percent of GNP deficit. In 1983, Reagan ran a deficit of $195.4 billion which amounts to a 6.1 percent of GNP. Back in 1960, our national debt was $291 billion which was well over half our entire GNP. It more than tripled by 1980 to $914 billion but was then less than one-third of GNP. Numbers are tricky!

The Kennedy Administration was the first to invoke the wonders of Lord Keynes and his prescription for deficit spending as a means to manage the economy. The late Walter Heller, Chairman of the President's Council of Economic Advisors, had suggested a tax cut which was enacted in order to stimulate the economy during the early days of the Johnson Administration. The deficit received perhaps its greatest impetus in the seventies when the federal government began picking up the tab for state and local government expenses. Between

1973–1983, three-quarters of the increase in the federal debt was due to a transfer of federal funds to state and local governments, a fact not as widely publicized as the infamous increases in entitlements and later defense, but which boosted the debt nevertheless.

By 1978, federal aid accounted for 26.8% of all spending by state and local governments. President Reagan was rebuffed in 1981 when he argued that urban roads were not a federal responsibility and should not be included in funding for the interstate highway program. If Congress had listened, billions of federal dollars would have been saved. Funding local transit systems is not only an improper function of the federal government, costs billions of dollars we have not collected, but also has the perverse effect of discouraging transit authorities from monitoring expenses. (see pp 69–71)

During his 1984 campaign, President Reagan promised no tax increases and no tax cuts in Social Security, yet he promised to bring the deficit into line. Perhaps such thinking makes sense in a world where tax cuts raise the revenue, where spending increases are represented as savings and where mounting deficits are seen as the road to a balanced budget—and I'm not being facetious in all instances! However, economic growth can only be an insurance policy against larger deficits.

The idea that growth would fix everything encouraged the expansion of benefits and increased leniency in eligibility requirements in all social programs. Defense spending fell from 9.1 percent of GNP in 1960 to only 5.2 percent of GNP in 1980. That freed up a huge financial dividend that Congress was quick to spend by extending programs such as Social Security, student aid, health care, food stamps and nutrition. Domestic federal spending soared from 9.4 percent of GNP in 1960 to 17.7 percent of GNP in 1980 just before Ronald Reagan took office. (See Chart III—OMB 1987). Food stamps went from $4.6 billion in FY1975 to $10.3 billion in FY1982 as Congress automatically increased the amount of funds according to the rise in demand for veterans benefits, especially pensions and medical care, and civil service pension which in 1982 were three times their 1975 level.

Chart III

Federal Spending as Percentage of GNP

	1960	1965	1970	1975	1980	1985
Total Spending	18.5	17.9	20.2	22.5	22.9	24.8
Defense	9.1	7.7	8.4	5.8	5.2	6.6
Non-defense	9.4	10.2	11.8	16.7	17.7	18.3

(All figures from Bureau of Census Statistical Abstract of U.S.)
Source: U.S. Office of Management & Budget

FACTS AND FICTION

It's time to stop listening to rhetoric and face some facts. Granted the numbers aren't precise and vary greatly depending on the source, nevertheless, the trend is unmistakable. Under Kennedy, the government spent 18 to 19 percent of GNP, under Reagan 23 to 25 percent. Economic growth was 4 percent a year in the 1960s and 2.4 percent in 1986. The Reagan Administration had predicted 4 percent growth and spent according to those predictions rather than reality. The FY1984 budget allocated two and a half times more, in real terms, for programs to benefit low-income persons than was spent in 1970. By 1984, there were five million more people receiving food stamps than received them in 1975, a recession year.

The nation has actually experienced an expansion of about average size in output and employment during the Reagan years. Defense expenditures in 1986 were about back to the levels envisioned by the Carter Administration and the growth of nondefense has slowed only to be replaced by the rapid growth of the interest on the debt. However, the 1986 slump was somewhat offset by the boom in the service sector. The number of service jobs has increased gradually over the last 20 years but it has become fashionable to remark on it lately. The service oriented work force constituted 64 percent of the entire work force in 1965 and was up to 75 percent by 1985.

The FY1986 budget actually saved, (it decreased the already planned increases) only $18 billion because the budget wasn't passed until the fiscal year was half over and the money that was going to be saved had already been spent. (Oh!)

Forget all the talk about the Congress giving the President what he wanted. Considering the regular appropriations and other direct spending bills, the President actually signed into law $40 billion more in domestic spending and $30 billion less in defense than he had initially requested for FY1986.

BUDGET PROCEDURE

Our budget problems accelerated with the passage of the Budget Control and Impoundment Act of 1974, whereby the legislative branch quite emphatically won a separation-of-powers dispute with the executive. Formerly, presidents had the power to impound money which had been voted by Congress, simply by not spending the appropriations for budgetary reasons. The 1974 Act ended impoundments, substituting an executive recision-power.

Established procedure calls for 13 separate appropriation bills but under the Budget Impoundment and Control Act of 1974, all that went by the board. In a gigantic effort the 99th Congress came up with *one* continuing resolution authorizing $576 billion in outlays.

According to Senator Mark Hatfield of Oregon, "the Continuing Resolution is a horrible way to conduct business."[6]

Most everyone else agrees. It is a testimony to an incompetent Congress unable to make the necessary choices to come up with the 13 required annual appropriation bills. To others, the problem is the 1974 Budget Control Act itself, in Senator Goldwater's words, "the most G-d-awful thing we ever did".

All presidents, beginning with the venerable George Washington, have fought against having to either accept or reject budgets presented by Congress. During the Civil War period, vote-swapping among politicians to ensure passage of special interest legislation was practiced to the point of abuse so that the framers of the Confederate Constitution provided Jefferson Davis with line-item-veto authority as an improvement.

In 1873, President Ulysses S. Grant asked Congress ". . . to authorize the Executive to approve of so much of any measure passing the two houses of Congress as his judgment may dictate, without approving the whole" claiming a line-item-veto would ". . . protect the public against the many abuses and waste of public moneys. . .". Presidents Hayes and Arthur echoed this recommendation as did FDR, Truman and Eisenhower. Theoretically, the president has the same power to veto appropriation bills as he has to veto other measures, but in actuality the presidential veto has been reduced to a nullity.

The majority of states have given the line-item-veto to their governors but the "sacrifice" is comparatively minor when one considers the states are unable to print money to cover their over-runs.

Currently, when a president receives an appropriations bill loaded with "pork", his alternatives are to veto the entire bill—condemning the good along with the bad—or bite his tongue and sign. According to Norman Ornst of the American Enterprise Institute, "It is both repulsive and immoral for the legislators of this or any government to say that programs they enacted into law *must* spend hundreds of billions of the public's money every year because programs are 'uncontrollable'. This is the public morality of Marie Antoinette."[7]

On the other hand, many observers (including Benjamin Zycher in his writing for the Wall Street Journal, and Congressman Edwards of Oklahoma), believe a strong president is more to be feared than a pork-barreling Congress. Apparently the founding fathers agreed because they allocated the final say on taxing and spending to Congress, the branch of government they felt would be least likely to over-tax or over-spend. Of course it all depends on who is in office. There would seem to be less opportunity for disaster by relying on 535 Congress-persons as opposed to one Chief Executive, at least in an offensive mode. But the line-item-veto is a defensive tool to keep collusions in Congress from holding the taxpayers hostage. It has not been employed as a weapon for blackmail by the governors and it is highly unlikely Congress, the press and the American people would allow any president to use it in such a manner. Not too long ago, a gallup poll showed that 67 percent of Americans favored granting the presidential line-item-veto power, 25 percent opposed it and the rest didn't have any opinion.[8] Since more than half the budget now goes for nonappropriated entitlements and interest on the debt, if defense is also removed very little would be left to discretion and the line-item-veto. Therefore, although it might be an improvement over our present situation, the issue is, at the moment, a tempest in a teapot.

Although the president has consistently and emphatically been denied the line-item-veto there are still two means Congress created for the executive to make narrow changes in the budget—recision and deferral. The trouble is each recision vanishes just like Cinderella's coach, after 45 days without the approval of Congress. (You didn't think Congress would give a *real* tool to the executive branch now did you?).

As for the ability to defer, President Reagan was sued after requesting that $251 million for Urban Development Grants be deferred in 1986 and the House Appropriations Committee had voted to kill his deferral authority. (Even useless gifts can be reclaimed by a fickle Congress!)

Senator Daniel Quayle of Indiana hopes to change all that with his "Pork Buster".

The Pork Buster was originally known as the Federal Spending Control Initiative first introduced by Senator Quayle on September 17, 1985 and again early in the 100th Congress. It permits a recision of spending authority to be enacted if the President and both Houses agree. The legislation would guarantee Congressional action on executive proposals to reduce or eliminate line-items in specific appropriation measures. It does away with the 45 day automatic lapse used by Congress to shirk their duty to review presidential recision proposals. In the last two budgets President Reagan has included 327 recissions equal to $12.6 billion in potential spending. Most were simply ignored by Congress.

The Gramm-Rudman (G-R) legislation provided for an April 15th deadline for enacting a federal budget for FY1987. On March 19, 1986, a bipartisan majority of the Senate Budget Committee approved an $18.7 billion tax increase, claiming the G-R target of $144 billion couldn't be reached without it. The Senate wouldn't hear of President Reagan's proposed domestic cuts but instead voted to raise $300 million in taxes for education programs. The President had proposed eliminating 44 domestic programs but the Congress just couldn't stomach the cuts. Everyone fought like cats and dogs, nothing much passed and the G-R target was not met by a long shot. Who calls that nonsense trying?

In August 1986, both the Office of Management and Budget (OMB) and the Congressional Budget Office (CBO) saw the handwriting on the wall and estimated the deficit for FY1987 at $163.4 billion. Remember, $144 billion was the target deficit for FY1987 under the G-R legislation. It means Congress threw up their usual smoke screen of talk vowing to reduce to G-R levels and then just failed to do it! The actual FY1987 deficit was close to $175 billion. They have the nerve to pat themselves on the back because that was lower than the unconscionable $221 FY1986 deficit! Agggh. . .!

SENATE BUDGET COMMITTEE, JANUARY 1987

Let me take you to the Senate Budget Committee, chaired by Senator Lawton Chiles of Florida held on January 7, 1987, to hear OMB head, James Miller III defend the Reagan Administration's FY1988 budget—the one that was dead *before* arrival.

Mr. Miller seemed proud that although there had been a 4 percent growth in programs this budget proposal would trim that growth to only 1 percent. (Didn't you think they were supposed to be cutting not slowing the growth? Someone's not communicating!) The Administration's FY1988 proposal would have trimmed $6.7 billion from the medical area, $3.4 billion from entitlements and $8.6 billion from non-defense discretionary spending with cuts totalling $18.7 billion, $8 billion would have been added for defense leaving net cuts of $10.7 billion. Then $22.4 billion from increased revenue (asset sales, user fees, etc.) was to be used for further reductions. ($10.7 + $22.4 = $33.1 billion in total reductions).

Mr. Miller showed with charts that outlays for major medical expenditures by the federal government have spiraled since 1976. As for Medicare Part B, Medicare recipients have been paying a mere 25 percent of the real cost of premiums; finally the Administration found the courage to request that new recipients pay 35 percent of the true cost of premiums. They still won't dare ask those already accustomed to that lovely 75 percent subsidy. (*subsidy, subsidy*—we all enjoy our *subsidies*!)

Senator Chiles made a point of objecting to FHA user fees saying they could increase costs to every home buyer by as much as $1,600. In defense of user fees in general, Mr. Miller explained that they reveal what government programs are really worth to beneficiaries and that user fees do not involve compulsion as a tax does. The Senator countered that selling assets would result in an overall net loss to the government. (No more revenue once the assets are sold). Mr. Miller's argument, for the Administration, was that the government should not be in the business of competing with private business and should not do what the private sector is able to do. (Hip hip hooray!)

Senator Charles Grassley of Iowa asked Mr. Miller how the country could take the Congress and Administration seriously when they recommended pay increases in the midst of what was supposed to be budget austerity. Mr. Miller answered that studies have shown the pay increase was warranted in order to maintain parity with the private sector. The President, by compromising those pay recommendations, was sending a signal of austerity to the country by cutting even legitimate demands in the spirit of belt-tightening. Although a lot of people in the public eye were affected the amount was modest overall—less than $40 million according to Mr. Miller.

Officials who think this way are misled because in such an instance people are concerned with integrity not amount. They should understand no signal of serious austerity was received even though the administration may wish to claim it was sent!

Senator Terry Sanford of North Carolina asked: "Doesn't the President feel any compulsion to present a balanced budget"? Senator Stanford suggested that proceeds from the sale of government assets go to reduce the national debt and not to ease current budget constraints. Mr. Miller agreed that was good business practice and should be looked into at a future time.

Senator Jim Sasser said, "The President proposed and the Congress disposes", re-emphasizing Senator Sanford's criticism of the unbalanced budgets presented to Congress by the President over the years. Pointing to the user fees in the Administration's FY1988 proposal, Senator Sasser was quick to see an opening in which to propose tax hikes. He said those fees were evidence that the administration acknowledges a *need* for more revenue and he saw it as a hopeful sign for a bid to raise taxes.

This faint hint that the Administration might be receptive to a suggestion to increase taxes was jumped on by others. Senator Chiles tried to get Mr. Miller to commit the Administration by having him repeat the sentiment that taxes to decrease the deficit would end when the deficit ended. However, Mr. Miller side-stepped smartly when he retorted that more efficient government is what we're after in the long run and that can only come from reduction of government's functions (not continuing to manage oil fields, publishing entities, loan collections, etc.) and adding revenue would not tackle this core problem.

Senator Don Nickles of Oklahoma was too lavish in his praise for what he repeatedly observed was a decrease in the increase of government spending. (At least he was honest enough not to call it a cut.) He did ask how the G-R target ($144) that everyone was assured six months ago would be met, had in that time grown by $30 billion to a deficit of $174 billion. Mr. Miller said the main reason was an undetected deterioration in economic growth (They never seem to learn from these mistakes!) "$10 billion is small", he had the nerve to say, "when talking about a trillion dollar budget". (Just one more reason to get those number down!)

Senator Wyche Fowler of Georgia asked what happened to the biblical precepts of "justice and mercy"? Miller intimated that the Administration felt that it would be most merciful in the long run to encourage expansion of the economy so that there would be jobs and dollars for private programs. He said cutting back the low interest loans made by the general revenue taxpayer to the REA (Rural Electrification Administration) was a manifestation of justice; the REA had completed its job for rural America. Subsidized or free lunches will continue for poor children (mercy) but children from families whose incomes are twice the poverty level would not get lunch subsidies under the FY1988 Administration's proposal and that too can be viewed as a manifestation of justice.

Mr. Miller had charts which showed an estimated increase in revenue of $74 billion over FY1987 with outgo remaining fairly steady. (So where's the cuts?) The charts Mr. Miller exhibited showed revenue increasing over the years with no allowance made for the possibility of a recession and less revenue. By the summer of 1987 it was apparent the President's FY1988 budget would produce a $135 billion deficit instead of the projected $108 because the GNP turned out to be about $16 billion less than estimated and re-estimates and new federal outlays such as the water and highway bills accounted for another $11 billion of deficit.

Senator Phil Gramm of Texas, a month after the Budget Committee hearing, took Mr. Miller at his word and elaborately showed the readers of the February 5, 1987 edition of the Wall Street Journal an easy foolproof way to reduce the deficit. ". . . a moderate level of economic growth generates about $70 billion of additional revenue a year"—ala Mr. Miller's estimate—so forget cutting (way too hard) or raising revenue (folks don't take kindly to that) and sit back and let growth do it! (Excuse us—we seem to have heard this one before. . .)

During the hearing, Senator Conrad of North Dakota baited Mr. Miller over cuts in farm price supports and Mr. Miller replied that it is imperative to break the link between subsidy and the market. He argued against Senator Conrad that restraints on production and cartels is the way to go; it would penalize the consumers according to Mr. Miller.

Senator Don Quayle of Indiana had some good concrete ideas such as having a budget every two instead of every single year and adopting a recision measure (since a line-item-veto is not forthcoming), which would let the President identify pieces in a large legislative package and take them before Congress demanding an up or down vote. The President could be defeated by 51 percent in either House since it would not take the 2/3 vote required by the line-item-veto (if he had it).

"GEORGE" WON'T DO IT!

BORING!! Why did I take you to a committee hearing? So you'll know what goes on in Washington D.C.—so you will stop sitting back and hoping "George will do it"—just listen to what some of your elected "Georges" are saying:

"We're talking charades in this whole business." (budgets)
Mark Hatfield (OR)

"We've been lying about the deficit every year."
Ernest Hollings (SC)

"Any process we've come up with we've found a way to get out of. We slip the noose."
Lawton Chiles (FL)

"Trying to reduce the deficit without taxes is like trying to put out a fire without water."
Jim Wright (TX)

Under the leadership of new House Speaker, Jim Wright of Texas, there appears to be less hope of reducing the deficit than ever before. He claims certain programs are so vital to the nation's welfare that wondering how to pay for them almost amounts to a sacrilege. He is busy backing bills to pour money into the homeless problem. "Reward an activity and it will increase" (sort of like feed a cold, starve a fever). Right up there on the compassionate list of wants are dollars for AIDS research, retraining for unemployed and the regular litany of education and welfare necessities.

A PHILOSOPHICAL PROBLEM

No doubt these programs would benefit certain individuals but at whose expense? The expense of other individuals. But, as the argument shamelessly goes, the individuals who are being forced to pay for these programs are *saving* money. (When were you *asked* what you wanted to pay for?) Policy-makers decide for you and bill you via the coercive IRS. The illogical thought pattern here is that if you were not made to pay for such programs the problems would expand and the cost you would be forced to bear later would be even worse. But why should you be forced to pay for these programs now or later? The most popular answer is "the programs are good for society—the "common good argument". Not a very satisfactory explanation because a part of society may be harmed by the forced contributions rather than benefitted. Obviously it is good for *certain individuals*—or is it? Because *these individuals* are supposedly being taken care of by government, wealthy philanthropist-A might not step into the picture, nor will organizer-activist-B bring his efforts to bear, rallying creative loving concern from a compassionate community. Instead *certain individuals,* thanks to policy-makers' omnipotent view of things, may find they are filling out myriads of forms and waiting long periods to receive impersonal and less than adequate help. If there is a question as to the good *certain individuals* are to derive from political decisions, it is even less likely that the remainder of society or the common-good will benefit. The rest of society, after all, had to first produce the dollars in order to turn them over to fulfill political plans for *certain individuals*. If the rest of society were slaves to either *certain individuals* or the state there would be no philosophical problem. But in the United States the rest of society consists of free men and women which presupposes control over private property. These "free" men and women no doubt have problems of their own and have prioritized needs that are already too many to fill. If they were consulted as to their priorities there would be less of a philosophical problem and a number of men and women would voluntarily contribute to the needs of *certain individuals* (high on their list of priorities). Since, however, American citizens are neither slaves nor asked if they wish to contribute voluntarily there very definitely is a problem. A moral ethical problem which for years has been swept under the rug and which we will only note for now and come back to later in our discussion.

FINE TUNING

Policy-makers can be relied on to take credit for what would have happened sooner or later without their interference. One of the most arrogant believers in government's destiny to "fine-tune" is Patrick Moynihan. "An information rich society by it's own dynamic learns about matters that make government goods and services either economically, or morally mandatory, as in medicine."[9]

According to the Senator, knowledge, generated and disseminated by government was responsible for the ability of only 3 percent of our population (farmers today) to feed the other 97 percent of the population. (And to think farmers wouldn't have progressed *but for* government!)

"Anti-poverty programs became a moral choice only after we learned how to measure poverty".[10] (As to the measurement of poverty, we're not one iota farther along on a consensus there than we are on how to reduce the deficit—but more of this later.)

As Professor Paul Craig Roberts has said, "By placing confidence in individual initiative and private property, supply-side economics devalues the fine-tuning expertise of policy makers".[11] And guess who doesn't like that?

NO WAY TO CUT

Representative William Natcher of Kentucky, during a Congressional hearing regarding the FY1988 budget in the spring of 1987, expressed his displeasure with the Administration's proposal to substitute loans for educational grants and to let the state and local governments and other already existing training programs take over the funding for vocational education. He went on criticizing all efforts to cut without listening to ascertain if there were logic to any of the reasons. "How can you cut funds for the handicapped?" the Senator asked James Miller, who happened to be visiting this committee on his rounds before the FY1988 administration budget was buried for good.

SPECIAL INTERESTS

There is no doubt but we have become a government of special interests. It is only natural that government would grow as special interest groups bargained among themselves, each in search of government outlays to their own benefit and willing to OK benefits to other groups in exchange.

On April 9, 1987, Congressman Ron Dellums spoke eloquently on the House floor on behalf of the Congressional Black Caucus (CBC) budget. He suggested there were four ways to lower the deficit; (1) expand the economy, (2) raise revenue, (3) reduce spending, or (4) a combination. He pointed out that without a tax hike and with entitlements and military spending frozen, 83 percent of the budget would be accounted for right there with only 17 percent left to cut. Mr. Dellums reminded his colleagues of the need to cut $63 billion in order to reach the FY1988 Gramm-Rudman (G-R) target of $108 billion.

The freeze itself, he said, would only offer an $11 billion reduction; $52 billion in cuts would still be necessary to hit the $108 G-R target. Now you will remember Senator Gramm counted on economic growth for $70 billion in extra revenue but Mr. Dellums was significantly less optimistic, and many would argue, more reasonable in estimating the role of economic growth in reducing the deficit.

The Congressman from Berkeley, California attempted to soothe potential opponents by also appearing reasonable in his approach to military outlays, insisting that the CBC believed Congress should spend whatever is necessary in this area. Then he proceeded to show that really not much was necessary. He saw how we could save a lot by basing our military budget on the capability to deter instead of fight. (But he somehow didn't consider the Strategic Defense Initiative a deterrence—whose surprised?) He found considerable savings in the budget by substituting food for arms in our dealings with the third world countries. (Bread not bombs—the kind of stuff bumper stickers are made from.) Then he started talking about saving even more money by reducing troops in Europe and Asia (because a conventional war would probably deteriorate into nuclear anyhow), swearing off third world interventions, and the one that really saves the big bucks—just forget about nuclear war capabilities because "to make it possible is to make it inevitable."

Breaking tradition with three generations, I moved from Berkeley because one can't listen to such logic over prolonged periods of time.

It's difficult to understand the fuss about President Reagan cutting back on domestic programs. He's wanted to allright, but hasn't gotten to first base. Employees and beneficiaries of any given program fight like wildcats not to give it up. It is almost impossible to rouse 20 million people to prevent a $1 increase in taxation but 20 people will do just about anything to get their hands on a bonanza of $1 million each. General interest has little chance of prevailing over special interests. Special interests are motivated and sustained according to the degree of benefits either promised or threatened. For example: there are 11 thousand sugar farmers in the U.S. who receive what amounts to a government subsidy equal to 4 to 6 times the world price of sugar. The sugar users far outnumber the growers but the users' sugar expenditures are only a tiny fraction of their overall budgets and therefore the incentive for the average sugar user to campaign for lower sugar prices is very small compared to the high per capita incentive the growers have to campaign to limit foreign sugar imports.

BURYING THE REAGAN FY1988 BUDGET

On May 6, 1987, the administration's FY1988 budget—the one that was dead before arrival—was buried on the Senate floor with the help of Senator Patrick Moynihan from New York. The Senator offered what he believed to be an appropriate quote from David Stockman's book in an eloquent effort to malign the President of the United States. Then, as if more were needed, he used his own words: "(The Reagan Administration) destroyed the fiscal ability of the federal government—they did it as a conspiracy—did it as a deliberate design. History will despise. . ." WOW! (That's my not-so-eloquent word for his!)

Senator Robert Byrd of West Virginia then saw that the President's budget got a warm reception and a fair hearing and put it to a vote with these words, "It is a calamity for America! Let's put it where it ought to be—in the file of rejection!". The vote was 81 to 18 against—that's rejection!

The whole sorry episode, according to Senator Moynihan who longed for greater media coverage in view of his earlier eloquence, was witnessed by four people in the press box.

AND NOW YOU KNOW THE REST OF THE STORY. If you are still in favor of a strong centralized government *trying* to do a myriad of things a government has no business doing, read on and let me try to change your mind.

Section Two

We Spend It On What?

"A LITTLE HERE AND A LITTLE THERE AND PRETTY SOON . . ."

PARKS & RECREATION LAND

Although the Reagan Administration called for a moratorium, Congress over the last few years has appropriated in the neighborhood of $300 million a year for park and refuge land acquisitions. Recently the President's own Commission on Americans Outdoors recommended the federal government spend a minimum of $1 billion a year for such land purchases. The $1 billion annual subsidy would be funded by a trust fund maintained by receipts from off shore oil leases. I mean, what else could we possibly do with the money anyway?

THE STATE DEPARTMENT

Don't say bureaucrats lack chutzpah (please)!

When the State Department requested $33 million (twice the cost of the nearby British embassy) to erect a terrorist-proof embassy in Belize in 1985, the Senate Foreign Relations Committee refused. Belize after all, is a tiny central American country with little money, few people (1985 population = 152,000) and so far, no terrorists.

But the Belize request pales when compared to the $190 million (so far) spent on our *unusable* embassy in Moscow.

U.S. FISH & WILDLIFE SERVICE

If you are keeping a tally on government spending, not simply additions to the deficit, then don't forget the $9 million spent by the Fish & Wildlife Service on a survey to determine how Americans *view* wildlife. I'm only happy to report the $9 million came from an excise tax on fishing and hunting equipment and not from all taxpayers and therefore did not add to the deficit.

DEPARTMENT OF JUSTICE

In 1985 the Justice Department appropriated over $734,000 of its budget to finance a study of pornography and child exploitation. The media had a good time ridiculing the project which surely must have consisted of more than the reported reading of Playboy, Penthouse and Hustler magazines. The price tag and the demands of the job somehow don't match. We all know many people who would have read the 660 issues without pay. Aside from the exorbitant cost of the study, the question of purpose remains. What would the Justice Department do with the results of such a study?

Columnist Jack Anderson reported in April 1986 that "A high Justice Department official has actually admitted that it was a mistake to pay a consultant to read sexually explicit magazines and report on their treatment of children in articles and cartoons."

An apology of sorts is well and good, but what about the $734,371? Would anyone over at the Justice Department like to pass the hat to show the taxpayers that some trusted officials believe in putting their money where their mouth is? It just may have to come to something like that sooner or later.

STATE EMPLOYMENT SERVICES (ES)

The federally funded State Employment Services (ES) were accused of holding poor people hostage in order to preserve their own inefficient jobs by James Bovard in his September 5, 1986 article for the Wall Street Journal. A report by the Government Accounting Office found that ES employees refused to refer low-income clients to private employment agencies even though they knew these private agencies could place a significantly higher percentage of welfare recipients in jobs, because they feared that by doing so they would be putting their own jobs in jeopardy. The U. S. Employment Service (ES) is a $740 million program that distributes federal dollars raised from employers through the Federal Unemployment Tax Account to ES agencies. It was started in 1933 and works as a labor exchange. A Government Accounting Office study found that ES exaggerated the number of its placements by 75 percent. ES often places the same person in short term jobs many times during the year, is inept in what it does do using wrong and outdated information in many instances, according to Mr. Bovard, and it duplicates other government programs. Sometimes, according to a 1982 Labor Department funded study, ES finds people lower paying jobs than they would have found on their own.

Since ES has not been successful at placing low-income people it has recently gone after the engineers, doctors and accountants. In 1986 it helped GM find 2,500 workers. Mr. Bovard rightly asks, "Should the government be paying for routine corporate operating expenses?"

It would be easy with today's computers to run a community job bank with no federal aid. Mr. Bovard claims, "The central data base could be accessible by computer monitors to welfare and food-stamp offices, county court buildings or any private business. In the majority of cases this would provide as good or better service than ES currently provides, at a fraction of the cost."[1] Poor people should not be kept out of jobs so that government clerks can draw salaries for shuffling paper in their behalf.

The State Employment Services (ES) is one more example of the government doing poorly what it has no business doing in the first place.

RURAL ELECTRIFICATION ADMINISTRATION (REA)

The Rural Electrification Administration (REA) was created in 1935 to bring electric power to rural America. The job has been effectively accomplished. 99 percent of all farms now have electrical power. Today the REA makes loans at interest rates of just 2 to 5 percent to hundreds of utilities, many serving affluent and definitely non-rural communities such as Dallas, Texas; Atlanta, Georgia; Ft. Myers, Florida or Vail, Colorado.

Over the past decade more than 80 percent of the more than $9 billion in subsidized REA loans have gone to urban and suburban utility customers. President Reagan has proposed a gradual substitution of the subsidies with new loans for utilities in the neighborhood of 1 and 1/8 percent over the T-Bill rate.

How can *any* continued subsidy be justified?

TIMBER SUBSIDIES

National forests are poorly managed in at least one aspect, to the detriment of the environment, the timber industry and last but not least, the taxpayer. The Forest Service continues to rely on an obsolete pricing system that fails to recover the cost of growing and selling trees. The General Accounting Office (GAO) found sales in two regions in the Rocky Mountains were more than 88 percent below cost in 1981 and 96 percent below cost in 1982. That year the U. S. Forest Service lost $740 million selling timber. The trend continued in 1983 with the finding that 37 percent of all timber sold was below cost. In Alaska, the return was minus 98 percent. Who in the world made the decision to spend $1 harvesting for a 2 cent sale?

The Forest Service harvests timber on millions of acres of public land where timber values are so low that private land owners would never consider building roads to do the job. Yet unless something is done to prevent it, over $3 billion of your dollars will be spent on 60,000 miles of new timber roads over the next 15 years. This despite figures that show the road fund has been nothing but a bottomless pit gobbling dollars faster than a fat man in a pie eating contest. $44.6 million was paid by the Forest Service in 1985 to help private timber companies remove the trees. So what did the Forest Service get for such an investment? $209 thousand dollars in fees for the trees harvested by bargain hunting entrepreneurs.

One more cliche is born: GOVERNMENT SERVICE MEANS NEVER HAVING TO MAKE A PROFIT!

Why do we allow this? There is an alternative. The government should encourage better use of untapped timber growing capacity on private lands. In 1980 the Forest Industry Council estimated that private forests alone could supply all domestic timber demands by 2030. However, the below-cost timber sales in the national forests retards this development. Below-cost timber should be tolerated only if there is a proven overriding benefit to other forest uses.

Just as agriculture policies in other regions have upset what would otherwise have been prudent farming practices, the government may now need to assist communities dependent on national forest below-cost timber in a transition to new areas of employment.

FREEDOM OF INFORMATION ACT

It costs the Food & Drug Administration (FDA) $4.5 million to process requests received by pharmaceutical companies seeking information concerning competitors. According to columnist Jack Anderson, the FDA recovered 5 percent of the processing cost for a 95 percent loss—large enough to make that all time "throw-it-down-a-black-hole" champ, the Forest Service, sit up and take notice!

ARTS

In his FY1988 budget the President once again asked Congress to reduce federal spending on the arts and humanities. The National Endowment for the Arts and the National Endowment for the Humanities are both independent federal agencies with access to taxpayer dollars which last year (1986) amounted to a combined $300 million plus. Congress has its own priorities but are they yours?

The National Endowment for the Arts coughed up $50,000 to finance the exhibit at the Guggenheim Museum in NYC of an artist whose specialty is "mud circles" and "lines of stone", (And you thought mud pies were only for the nursery set!) $274,500 was provided to aspiring composers, one of whom may come up with a break through in music for electronically altered tubas.

But perhaps we shouldn't be so harsh on our federal officials since local governments behave no differently. We have a display of large granite stones in ascending sizes at a local park. The artistic merit is not the issue; one person's monstrosity is another's art. The issue is priorities. Everyone has limited personal resources and unlimited desires. Why then are American citizens not given the choice to do what they want with their own money? A young couple might prefer to have their muffler repaired or purchase grass seed for their backyard rather than provide tax dollars to mud-circle-artists.

Art is highly subjective and should depend upon the private sector for its support. If an artist cannot get private underwriting why should all taxpayers be forced to do what they would not otherwise choose to do, i. e. subsidize such an endeavor?

For most of our history it was well settled that government was divided into three levels. The federal government was to concern itself with defense and clearly national issues such as currency, interstate commerce, foreign affairs, postal regulations and issues of law arising between the states or concerning the Constitution itself. The states were to take care of education and roads and mediating disputes among its own citizens. Local governments were to be responsible for the lower courts, and fire and police protection.

The question supposedly answered by our Constitution that had been asked for centuries was under what, if any, conditions can a society (group of individuals) impose its will on another individual or group of individuals? The question was answered by using negatives. Society was to have no right to demand that an individual do (active) anything but only that he refrain from doing (passive).

Making certain that people refrain from harming one another is a negative concept of law, like defining good as the absence of evil. It does not tell one what to do (doesn't define "good") but instead enumerates what one must not do (evil). Our Constitution was based on the Mosaic laws as specifically enumerated in the Ten Commandments. Not "Thou Shalt" but rather "Thou Shall Not".

Defining law in terms of positives substitutes the will of a small group for the will of individuals. This is how the welfare state works. Individuals helplessly put their lives in the hands of a chosen few; the leaders. They no longer need to plan or care for themselves; intelligence is no longer necessary nor sufficiently rewarded. Without challenges to face and a life to live (master of one's soul and all that type of thing) men cease to be human. A world which denies to an individual the right to choose the all-important means and methods of his own livelihood is a world without moral content. Freedom and the exercise of one's will are aspects of the same thing. I would argue with those who would claim that having the government take care of necessities such as food, shelter, health, education etc. frees citizens for higher pursuits. For even when a subsidy is neither needed nor desired, officials insist on controlling.

Musicians playing in the NYC subway stations and on downtown streets across the country are often subject to fines for soliciting, loitering, begging or vagrancy. One Julliard trained violinist makes in the neighborhood of $20–30/hour playing in the NYC subway stations, which shows the commuters enjoy his music. So why the government fines?

The New York Metropolitan Transit ran a four month experimental program in the fall of 1985 called "Music Under the City". Musicians were given permits to play at one of eight designated subway stations during predetermined hours. Cost= $75,000! I guess it's the normal price to pay to have bureaucracy triumph over spontaneity.

THE SECURITY EXCHANGE COMMISSION

There's little doubt the Security Exchange Commission (SEC) could use an electronic system to replace the torrents of paper now generated by corporations in an effort to meet SEC requirements, but the fear is that the agency may be heading towards the same type of computer-procurement fiasco that has befallen the Social Security Administration, the Pentagon and other federal agencies.

Under the current system a non-government contractor processes and copies disclosure reports and sells microfiche copies to the public to recoup its costs rather than charging the SEC. Although everyone would prefer an almost paper-free computerized system it would be so expensive that demand for the data base by the public wouldn't cover the costs and so contractors are not interested. Even if the demand were there government information can't be copyrighted so tapes could be duplicated and sold by competitors at rock-bottom retail prices. But by the end of 1986 the SEC was undaunted by logic and offered to provide $46.5 million dollars over an eight year period which is more than half the present estimated cost of the project. Where is this money to come from? Don't worry, those at the SEC feel confident Congress will appropriate it.

I think it's safe to say the people who take budget cutting seriously live outside Washington D.C.

THE PATENT OFFICE

The Patent Office showed the same audaciousness when in 1983 the overseeing Commerce Department turned down an expenditure approval because of lack of documentation. Not letting a little thing like that stop them, officials at the Patent Office went right ahead without approval. That bravado cost the taxpayers plenty even though the official in charge attempted to deflect criticism by pointing to frequent inaccuracies inherent in cost-benefit analyses (since they're so often inaccurate why bother to get one or if it looks bad ignore it).

But as Jack Anderson pointed out in his March 23, 1987 column, there was more to criticize here than inaccuracies: "The effort to computerize the Patent and Trademark Office is two years behind schedule and $159 billion over budget—yet the official who presided over the disaster was given a bonus and put in charge of computerization of the Census Bureau."

Reward incompetence and . . . THERE WE GO AGAIN!

SOCIAL SECURITY

Many people blame the President for not using his tremendous personal popularity for launching an attack on entitlements during his first term in office. Senator Pete Domenici in October 1981, offered a plan to cap Social Security COLAs (cost of living increases) which President Reagan then failed to push through Congress—or even attempt to do so.

Senator Robert Dole, one of the more consistent workers in the effort to reduce the federal deficit, was deserted by the President also. Soon after Ronald Reagan took office, Senator Dole started pushing a three year $150 billion deficit reduction package. It included a hike in taxes and cuts in federal programs including $28 billion from Social Security. Near the end of 1984 Senator Dole had 35 to 40 Republicans willing to back the GOP plan to cut the deficit but the President backed down. In the summer of 1985 the Senator tried suggesting an adjustment to the COLAs and tax indexing on a two year cycle but the President never did his part to bring this plan to fruition either.

President Reagan often appears to be long on rhetoric and short on political will. Unfortunately if anyone in government was to have a chance at reducing entitlements it was Ronald Reagan during his first term. The "Teflon President" would have had the best and perhaps the only chance at successfully leading such an attack. Instead he went along with the recommendations of the 1983 Commission on Social Security Reform who were spoonfed their information not by an objective outside party, but by one of the Social Security Administration's own. Robert Myers, a former chief actuary and definite insider, prepared the booklet which defined the Committee's agenda. It's no secret that the reform and "saving of the system" was accomplished, not by creative negotiation and bold imagination buy by a tax increase. Employers were made the fall-guys and payroll checks for working Americans shrank once again.[2]

SMALL BUSINESS ADMINISTRATION

The President, who has a long recognized reputation for loyalty, has uncharacteristically deserted his own party on the Hill on other occasions.

In 1985 an agreement was reached between the Republican leaders in both the House and Senate with the White House to preserve the Small Business Administration (SBA) for 3 years while reducing its $400 million annual budget. These leaders understandingly felt betrayed when the President targeted the SBA for elimination again in 1986.

The President could not bring himself to tackle Social Security and Republican leaders could not bring themselves to eliminate the SBA even though statistics show SBA lending programs cost far too much and serve too few.

FOREIGN AID

Since when have American taxpayers given aid to advanced industrial nations? Since 1986, thanks to some fast talking leprechauns in both the House and Senate.[3] Oddly enough President Reagan started the whole thing by responding to some blarney by Irish Head of State, Garret FitzGerald and Britain's Prime Minister, Margaret Thatcher, asking for "international support" for their November 15, 1985 agreement to settle the political strife between Britain and Ireland with economic and social development. Assuming "support" meant dollars, Ronald Reagan proposed giving these first-world-countries $20 million American taxpayer dollars per year over a five year period and an additional $150 million in loan guarantees and credits. Generous? "Enough" is just not an easy word to say, so Congress upped the largesse to $50 million cash per year over a five year period.

On April 26, 1985 Senator Bradley of New Jersey expressed a certain indignation on the David Brinkley Show. He said, "We have more and more young people who don't feel they have a responsibility to support the legitimate functions of government." Is it any wonder when so many of the so-called "functions" are so obviously *not* legitimate? Not that helping to stem further bloodshed in Ireland isn't a worthy cause, but aren't they all (except maybe the "mud circles")? Nevertheless to extend our concept of foreign aid from the third-world to include countries such as Britain and Ireland is incongruous especially in this era of supposed belt-tightening and especially if you remember the pleading Corozano Acquino had to do to extract the promise of $100 million in aid for the troubled Philippines. Yet as of February 24, 1987 less than a third of the $10 million in medical aid that we pledged to give the Philippines back in September 1986 had arrived. This was supposed to be *emergency* aid, yet like some cruel joke the United States sent parkas designed for use by ski troops and heavy wool blankets to troops who operate in tropical jungles. Tuberculosis is a leading killer among Filipino soldiers but boxes from the good 'ol United States labeled tuberculosis capsules were found to contain Anacin tablets.

How does it go—with friends like us, who needs enemies? To explain it away a senior official of the Joint U.S. Military Assistance Group in Manila told the press that the aid was authorized under a section of the Foreign Assistance Act of 1961 that requires that all supplies shipped come from existing U.S. military stocks. In other words, we promised the Philippines our leftovers, whatever they might be and they just happened to consist of ski parkas, wool blankets and Anacin tablets. How true the saying that experience is the hardest teacher because you take the test before you learn the lesson. Now what do you suppose the Filipino people learned?

In attempting to cut back to foreign aid Congress may have cut off its nose to spite its face (again). In the FY1987 budget the largest cut came in "security assistance, which includes FMS (foreign military sales) loans. Supposedly $1.7 billion was cut in FMS financing but in reality there was a shift to the much more expensive (to the American taxpayer) concessional financing. Concessional credits are offered at subsidized rates, sometimes 3 percent below the cost of money to the Treasury. According to Harry Shaw, former chief of the military-assistance branch of the Office of Management and Budget, the cuts may ". . . look good in the short run since total outlays are reduced and the budget balance is helped, over the long run deficits will be larger because of lower receipts."[4] Since the Reagan administration has been thwarted by Congress in the amount of aid it can give to other countries it is attempting to make up for quantity by increasing the quality—that is offering loans on better terms than our own Treasury can obtain.

Unfortunately the same short-sightedness that has been practiced by our policy-makers domestically, is beginning to carry over into foreign affairs. In searching for a debt-relief formula to help countries who have borrowed at high rates in the past, policy-makers have begun to consider the possibility of restructuring that debt, leaving borrowing countries to face balloon payments down the road sometime when our current "do gooders" have retired. No one wants to face the heat but each adds a little more fuel leaving an even bigger fire for those who come after to put out. Those in a position to make the hard changes are also, unfortunately, in a position to receive tough criticism. Few are courageous enough to douse the fire themselves but would rather hold their ground until their present position becomes more treacherous than the changes would be.

THE AMERICAN INDIAN

It is not that too little attention has been given the American Indian and his problems but that too little wisdom has been given.

Look at the Indians' plight: 58 percent of males are unemployed vs 8 percent of the nation—41 percent live below poverty levels vs 12 percent of the nation—27 percent have less than elementary education vs 10 percent of the nation—22 percent receive public assistance vs 8 percent of the nation. 1.4 million Indians are among the nation's most disadvantaged minorities—ill-educated, unhealthy and poor.

The Department of Commerce's Economic Development Administration (EDA) came up with some strange ideas. Building vacation resorts and putting Indians to work in them was one such scheme.

(Not so "strange" if it had worked!) The idea cost $61 million to put into practice and when the projects collapsed the promised jobs disappeared. EDA's industrial park program was another failure. Between 1966–85 $784 million was spent in constructing 55 industrial parks and to guarantee start-up loans and grants. Tenants never came. Social planners failed to consider what any businessman could have told them; that the locations were wrong, transportation costs were too high and that the low-skilled workers in the area wouldn't make up for the lower wages businesses might be required to pay.

The tribes are quasi-independent states within the U.S. free of state, local and sometimes even federal jurisdiction. They can impose taxes and exploit their territorial status by selling gasoline and cigarettes and have recently introduced Bingo and gambling onto their reservations. According to a 1984 Bureau of Indian Affairs study, 12 tribes take in over $1 million each year, but more often than not they are cheated by fast-talking advisers.

The tribes themselves have tried one business venture after another but they lack entrepreneurial spirit—they want to run a business by committee like a communist country. (Ask the Soviets why it doesn't work!) Resources belong to the tribe rather than to individuals and are shared equally among the membership. The welfare programs the government poured onto the reservations served only to strengthen these patterns as entrepreneurs were co-opted by government interference. The tribal mentality is something that affects underdeveloped economies everywhere. Bureaucracy, wherever it is found, at the tribal level or in Washington D.C., is a barrier to the entrepreneurial spirit. We must not continue to ignore the American Indian but rather do an "about face" in our policy to date. I am suggesting an upheaval that will require educating the Indians as to the advantages a new policy would hold for them as well as educating our legislators in Washington D.C. (Sorry—we're fresh out of quick easy solutions!)

UNITED NATIONS

According to a Wall Street Journal article written by Kishore Mahbubani, Singapore's ambassador to the United Nations, in the fall of 1986, the United States is being subsidized at the United Nations by the other member countries. U.N. assessments are made on a complicated set of calculations based on a country's GNP and population. As "the richest nation in the world" the USA should be shouldering 28% to 29% of the U.N. budget, says Mr. Mahbubani, instead of the 25% actually assessed because of a ceiling written into the charter.

In 1986 the following assessments were made on the five top contributor nations:

USA	$210,000,000
Japan	76,000,000
Soviet Union	71,000,000
West Germany	58,000,000
France	45,000,000

Mr. Mahubani's logic was curious. Apparently he wants us to believe a ceiling on the amount required of the largest contributor (USA) amounts to a "special preference". Indeed, I would imagine all other nations already enjoy the protection of that same ceiling so there is no preference.

The USA is one of 159 members. In 1946 there were 1,546 employees. Jose S. Sorzano, former deputy U.S. representative to the U.N. says, "The entire Secretariat (now) employs 52,000 civil servants, compared with a total of 4,500 in the State Department."[5] Salaries are about 80% of the U.N. budget. There are 28 under secretaries-general; the sort that retire with a lump sum of $350,000 after serving 30 years, all the while enjoying plush salaries.

Talk about waste! According to columnist Jack Anderson (10/7/86) because each page of output must be translated into six languages each page ends up costing $558 each. And, as in all bureaucracies, employees are eager to churn out the paper work in order to justify their high salaries and in some instances, their very existence.

The regular budget has more than tripled in the past ten years thanks to the proliferation of smaller less developed countries whose goal is to use the U.N. as a political channel for economic assistance. These countries, as a matter of course, inflated the organization's outlays by voting expensive add-ons with no special regard to those larger developed countries who supply the cash. Growth without proper coordination meant costly duplication of programs. (Does this sound familiar?) More boards, more committees, more commissions inevitably mean more documentation, more employees, more meetings. More, in the words of a member of the Secretariat for 18 years "people running around doing nothing."

It's little wonder then that Congress thought the U.N. would be a good place to get serious about our budget deficit. The U.S. has been supplying about one quarter of the U. N's funds. On October 25, 1986 the Congress decided to ignore a little more than half our bill and allocated only $100 million towards our assessed dues of more than $210,000,000.

American critics of the United Nations feel we are purchasing the rope and letting the U.N. hang us with it. We supply the most money and reap the most criticism. The U.N's Department of Public Information publishes two periodicals and over two million documents on an annual basis, operates 66 information centers and broadcasts on

Radio Perspective to 167 countries in 25 languages. Studies have shown a distinct anti-American bias in all this information. As James J. Kilpatrick asked in a 1985 column "Why pay to be trashed?" On the other hand, supporters point out that the U.S. has highlighted violations of human rights by Cuba and by the Soviets in Afghanistan and the leadership in Iran.

Senator Kassenbaum of Kansas wants the U.N. to give consideration to countries who contribute the most by adopting a form of weighted voting as opposed to the current one country one vote. We must have gotten their attention because on Friday December 19, 1986 the General Assembly passed new legislation regarding budget proposals. The CPC (Committee on Programs and Coordination) is a 21 member committee charged to provide recommendations on the size and limits of the U.N. budget; the priorities of the U.N. and the problem of "add ons". Major donors to the U.N. will have an influence on CPC. Since decisions must be unanimous each member in effect has a veto.

It's nice to know the Secretary General is taking his job seriously. In order to curb expenses the fountain in front of the Secretariat building has been shut off and no more pitchers of ice water are available at the place of members in their meeting rooms. I don't know what kind of a dent that has made in the U.N.'s budget but I'll bet it has boosted the cause of water conservation in New York City.

CIVIL SERVICE

In August of 1985 our local paper carried a grievance "letter to the editor" from a civil service worker at nearby Ford Ord who lamented the 5 percent cut in civil service pay urged by the President at that time. I'm afraid his cries of anguish fell pretty much on deaf ears and I offer the following by way of explanation:

Most of us get our idea of government workers via the media. We are constantly reminded of the dangerously bloated federal budget that hangs like an ominous cloud over the heads of all Americans. We are told that in 1932 government employees patriotically took a 10 percent pay cut "to help the nation". About the time of the Ft. Ord employee's letter I found this item in our local paper: "Washington officials could not recall when there had been a year without a pay increase."

Wages and benefits rose by just 3.2 percent in FY1986, which was the lowest private-sector gain in ten years. However, public sector wage-benefits, always higher than private, increased by 5.2 percent.

But just as food stamps, housing subsidies and other non-cash benefits are not included in determining who is below the poverty line, "benefits" are discounted when compensation of government employees is considered.

A 1986 Labor Department study found that federal workers were paid 23.79 percent less than their counterparts outside government. A spokesman for the Office Of Management and Budget said that the 23 percent figure was so huge "because it was based on the accumulated effects of the survey over an eight-year period."? 1.4 million workers hadn't had a payraise since 1985 (Wow—a whole year!) so a 2 percent increase was suggested by the President (yes, the same President who urged a 5 percent cut a year earlier) for January 1987. There are 2.8 million non-uniformed federal workers—all get the raise but half through an administrative process rather than through Congress. The 2.1 military will get even more. The House recommended a 3 percent hike and the Senate a 4 percent hike for military personnel. Oh yes, the House and Senate had wanted to give civil service workers 3 percent instead of the 2 percent proposed by the President whom it seems was trying to tighten the belt after all. But guess who prevailed—AGAIN?

PENSIONS

The biggest cost of running the government is not a bloated, over indulgent bureaucracy but is rather a pension system that provides benefits which in the private sector would only be reserved for top executives. In 1984 the Congressional Budget Office (CBO) estimated that $5.2 billion in outlays could be saved over the next five years (1984–1989) by slowing the rate at which benefits accrue, reducing the COLA escalator (cost of living increases) and adding penalities for nondisability retirement prior to age 62.

Big savings could also be achieved by making changes in the military retirement system according to the same CBO report. It was estimated that between 1984–89 $2.6 billion could be saved by making employees who retire after 20 years of service wait until they reach age 62 before granting full benefits. It was also suggested that military retirees still of working age be given only half the normal COLA.

Government pension benefits are so generous that the Treasury has to make huge annual supplements to the pension contributions made by federal employees and the agencies for which they work. These supplements amounted to over $22 billion in FY1984 and are estimated to cost $30 billion by 1989.

The Office of Personnel Management (OPM) estimates that the government's total liability to current and future retirees totals $514 billion and is rising at the rate of $100 million a day not counting the military retirement system, which would mean a rise in pension costs of $1 trillion over the next 30 years.

In addition to the $24 billion that could be cut from pensions, $12.4 billion more could be saved over five years by shrinking the bureaucracy and bringing it more into line with private sector employees. For instance, comparable private sector employees get an average annual vacation of 9 days as opposed to the 13 days allotted government employees. Little wonder between 1946 and 1984 the number of government employees soared from 1.5 million to 2.1 million.

Contracting-out-work, now done by government employees, could eliminate 180,000 jobs and save approximately $1 billion over a five year period and those people could do something that adds to the nation's productivity once they join the private sector. And if we're talking simply dollars, another estimated $3.7 billion could be saved over the same time period through automating office procedures—if done competently. (A risk!)

Current practice is to grant civil service employees automatic promotions whether or not their abilities and responsibilities have increased. The OPM has estimated that almost 14 percent of all civilian workers are classified in grades higher than they merit. But merit is subjective and we, the taxpayers who pay public salaries, continue to elect the incompetent as evidenced by congressional approval at the end of FY1986 of the 3 percent pay increase for federal workers *without* the appropriation of the necessary funds.

ABUSE AND FRAUD

We hear about abuse, fraud and unbelievable perks, and we fail to distinguish between those on the higher and lower end of the GS scale.

We are told chauffeured limousine service cost taxpayers $35,000 per year with approximately three fifths of the trips unauthorized. Examples like that of the Environmental Protection Agency employees' use of government cars "for lunch" at a cost of $45 a trip compared to cab fare at $5 a trip, tend to stick with us because we can identify. It is harder to identify with the exploits of those who use military aircraft to shuttle back and forth even though the numbers are so much larger and should elicit even more outrage from us. Such planes can cost anywhere from $1,000 to $7,000 per hour.

The most publicized and possibly the saddest showing of abuse by the State Department and the U.S. Information Agency (USIA) has occurred in the area of travel. Apparently many employees assume first class cruises on luxury liners are just one of those perquisites of serving abroad. The State Department allows its people to travel to and fro by sea whereas the USIA only permits its employees to use ships one way.

According to official records, from 1982 to 1984, 260 persons connected with these agencies spent $400,000 more than necessary to get to and from destinations in an effort to take advantage of these perks. A mere "drop in the bucket" as government spending goes but "A LITTLE HERE AND . . ."

The trip which triggered a series of investigations took place in 1982 and was made by a State Department employee and his family who returned to Iowa from an assignment in Uruguay via a 600 mile 12 day luxury steamboat trip up the MISSISSIPPI RIVER!

Records show thousands of Foreign Service officers have used ships as opposed to airlines at a cost of five to ten times as much. But airline flights aren't necessarily inexpensive either. In an early 1983 column, Jack Anderson gave an example of a flight between Detroit and Washington D.C. in a T-39 costing $1,578 as opposed to a commercial fare of $95. If the plane had chauffeured 16 muckamucks it might have made sense, but apparently the expense was incurred for only one extravagant muckamuck.

Even more colorful and therefore easier to remember, are things like the "picture-frame perks" or the full time fine-arts coordinator (with a government salary of close to $40,000) who arranges art displays in the entrance and hallways leading to the Federal Reserve governor's boardroom. In fact the perks accorded government workers at the Federal Reserve, such as weight-rooms, squash courts and "more private dining rooms per capita in Washington"[6] all tend to prejudice the average citizen against even the poor guy at the lower end of the GS scale.

COSTLY CONGRESS

Most people don't necessarily like it, but nevertheless accept the folk wisdom that it costs taxpayers about a million "to keep" each Congressman. Hard to prove maybe, but not so hard to believe, especially when one considers travel and housing allowances right down to the much publicized free art, haircuts and unnecessary doormen and elevator operators. Many of these wasteful, abusive expenses have been documented.

In 1985 three out of five members of the House of Representatives traveled abroad at *least* once. The 1985 tab was more than $4 million, not including transportation; that's right, I said WITHOUT THE COST OF TRANSPORTATION!

2 weeks to S. Korea, Taiwan, Hong Kong & China for 26 people = $70,360
10 days to W. Germany, Spain & the USSR for 23 people = $42,966
5 days in Ireland for 17 people = $118,331 and this one *does* include transportation costs of $106,651.

Transportation is often via military aircraft (more costly than civilian) and when included, can be seen to easily be the most expensive item of any trip.

An example from 1986 doesn't show much improvement over 1985 with $300,000 spent by 13 congressmen, their aides and spouses on just one trip to Buenos Aires (where, incidentally there was an attempt on the part of at least one congressman to undermine the Reagan Administration's policy in Central America).

Under a 1985 law, Congress devised a unique way to avoid voting itself pay raises. If it simply refuses to vote against it, any new pay scale will automatically become effective 30 days after it is presented to the legislature. A 1986 presidential commission recommended increases for the top 3,000 federal officials as high as 74%:

Cabinet members from $88,800 to $160,000
Congress members from $77,400 to $135,000
District court judges from $81,100 to $130,000

Not having attained the presidency without a certain degree of political astuteness, Ronald Reagan took the deficit-cutting mood of the country into consideration and trimmed the recommendations to:

Cabinet Members = $99,500
Congress and District Court Judges = $89,500

The Senate, aware no doubt of a December 1986 ABC poll that showed 5,800 constituents in agreement with the pay raise and 167,600 against, voted on February 4, 1987 to rescind the increase. Not a very noble thing to do when one considers the pay raise cannot be blocked unless the House *also* votes against it. It was apparent the House had no intention of even bringing the matter to a vote, so although it was a safe move, the Senate didn't fool John Q. Public for a moment. However the public's wrath was turned on the House, which showed its disdain for the average citizen by waiting until the pay raise took effect automatically, then ineffectually voting it down a day late. The voice vote was nothing but an ill conceived smoke screen which revealed slyness and cunning unbecoming a Congress person.

Of course there were those who felt a pay raise was long overdue. (I mean besides the Congressmen themselves and the 5,800 polled.) The purchasing power of our top public officials had dropped 41% over a 17 year period and this despite the efforts of the 99th Congress to care for its own by voting themselves a $3,000 tax deduction on housing costs and pocketing an automatic $2,500 pay increase on January 1, 1987.

The two main arguments for a pay raise were not believed by most Americans. I call the first the "Extra Expense Argument". It went like this: "Members of congress must keep two home; one in ultra-expensive Washington, D.C." The second argument I refer to as the "Brain Drain Argument": "In order to attract and keep the best people, private and federal pay scales must be brought closer together. It would be dangerous to have Congress made up of millionaires or incompetents." (It may be too late.)

As for the first argument, I heard a talk-show listener call-in what I consider to be a very acceptable and creative solution. He suggested a set of condominiums be set aside in Washington, DC for the use of Congress. He pointed out that churches provide rectories for their ministers; the military provides base housing and off-base living allowances. No one is denying the expense of housing but it can be borne by the taxpayers (who ultimately must bear it no matter how you look at it) in a more cost-effective manner.

I would agree the "Brain Drain Argument" is compelling when it comes to judges who receive their appointments for life, barring unseen circumstances. Elected representatives however, are another story.

Representative Downy from New York told a C-Span audience on January 11, 1987 "I would do this job for $20,000. If I could pitch (baseball) better I could be making $800,000." I'm not suggesting the Congressman would be willing to leave an $800,000 private sector job (which he didn't have so it couldn't be put to the test) for $20,000 and the privilege of being a U.S. Congressman, but there is no doubt many citizens would do so—in a flash!! Some for patriotic reasons (but those would be your nasty 'ol millionaires who nobody wants or trusts anyway) but most for darn good economic reasons. Many a medical or law student will tell you about living on peanut butter and tuna temporarily for the big payoff once that degree is in hand. Congressman Downy spoke of retiring Congressmen being snapped up by the private sector for three times their government salaries. Tip O'Neil would be earning $100,800 as Speaker of the House had he stayed on in the 100th Congress, but instead, according to an account in the January 26, 1987 edition of Time magazine, "he stands to rake in as much as $400,000 this year." He has apparently been offered $1.5 million for his autobiography, $20,000 per speech, invitations for TV appearances, commercials and that's on top of his federal pension of $83,000!

A lot of folks feel that's worth waiting for and would probably beg, borrow and steal for a chance to say "ex-Congressman" or "ex-Department Head" in a few years. There is not a better investment to be made from a purely economic point of view.

Members of the House were never meant to serve for twenty or thirty years at a stretch. The "sacrifice" was to be for two or at most four years. I would like to see the law changed to ensure that is the case. It's nonsense to insist we'd be giving up "valuable experience" or that "it takes at least eight years to learn the DC ropes". I say phooey; and a lot of other citizens join me. Get in there—do your thing and leave it for the next guy to have a go at it. The deplorable record in costly ineffectual legislation over the past decades reinforces my point. The worst that could happen, according to past experience, is we would be trading incompetence for more incompetence and there's always the chance we're going to get some fresh ideas and new blood and even guts now and again. I'm all for increasing the odds. How about you?

HOUSING

THE PROGRAM

How can there be an acute need for low-income housing in a capitalist society based on a free market economy? What happened to supply and demand? You know the answer by now. "Government stepped in with its mandates, restrictions and regulations". Unbelievably many politicians and well-meaning activists are looking to government to solve the very problem it created. (Sound familiar?)

Housing prices have risen 4 times faster than incomes! Does anybody ask why? Apartments are being converted to condominiums. Again, why? As renovations are made to existing housing-stock rents are raised. Why? Congress voted to close off the federal housing construction programs. Do activists bother to find out why and if they know do they tell you? Federal housing assistance has been cut from over $30 billion to under $8 billion under the Reagan administration. Do you ask why? Local zoning restrictions are wrecking havoc with the housing market. Do you know why? It is less profitable to invest in housing than it has been in the past. Why? Do you know what happened?

PUBLIC HOUSING

Public housing began in the 1930's as a temporary solution to the need for shelter for the unemployed who were supposed to eventually find work and save money to purchase better private-sector housing. In other words, the original housing units weren't built to last.

In 1981 the federal government's long term housing commitments amounted to almost $240 billion. Because of excessive costs and wasteful management Congress, in 1982, brought a halt to all federal construction programs. However funds appropriated during the Carter years have produced units during the Reagan administration, as many as 76,000 just in 1987 (251,000 units in FY1981). But that fact didn't stop Samuel Pierce, Secretary of HUD from appearing before the National Press Club in early January 1987 and attempting to take "credit" (I use the term loosely) for programs the Reagan administration has vowed to wind-down, stating that "We now have 4.3 million assisted housing units and one quarter of that amount came about during Ronald Reagan's six years."

At the beginning of 1986 there were approximately 3,000 independent public housing authorities (PHAs) operating 1.3 million dwelling units. About 700 of these PHAs received no federal money, whereas about 50 (2% of all PHAs) took 75 percent of all operating subsidies. To be fair, it is necessary to add that these 50 troubled PHAs embody almost half of all the PHA housing units in the nation.

Overstaffing PHAs is a problem. It seems the more inflated the PHA staff, the more tenants are apt to be shortchanged. Almost as troublesome are the HUD regulations which often make it difficult for authorities to make necessary repairs.

William Celis III, writing for the Wall Street Journal (12/15/86) told of a lady who sued the New Orleans Public Housing Authority because the Child Welfare Department threatened to place her six children in other surroundings if repairs weren't made to her $56 a month four bedroom apartment. Government got her both ways—coming and going! The suit was no big-deal to the New Orleans Authority which was reportedly sued three times a day in 1986. Budget cuts have been responsible for low or non-existent maintenance in public housing around the country. HUD spokesmen suggest a thousand units a year are demolished because it is cheaper to abandon than repair them. In contrast, deteriating and unsavory accomodations for farm workers in Monterey County, California go for as high as $500 per month for a one bedroom unit. (What's that about New Orleans again?) High land costs and restrictive zoning, intended to control growth and protect agricultural land, are the greatest obstacles to new housing developments for farm workers. Even when cooperatives have been able to purchase old labor camps in this area, they are often faced with restrictive modern building codes regulating density, sewer, water and electrical requirements.

HOUSING VOUCHERS

In his FY1987 budget, President Reagan requested $2.5 billion in housing subsidies; a far cry from the $33.2 billion requested by the Carter administration at the start of FY 1981 (Oct 1980). In keeping with its commitment to free choice whenever possible, the Reagan administration has opted for housing vouchers at the expense of virtually all other housing subsidies. Vouchers cost taxpayers half as much as new construction, which incidentally subsidizes developers more than tenants. According to the OMB, tenants in government subsidized construction projects receive 34¢ worth of benefits for every one dollar spent whereas they receive 84¢ for every dollar spent in a voucher program. Vouchers are given to qualifying families to make up the discrepency between 30 percent of a family's monthly income and the so-called reasonable rental payment authorized for the area in which the participating family chooses to live. The Reagan administration has eliminated many of the restrictions inherent in earlier voucher programs. Under current plans voucher recipients can supplement vouchers from their own incomes and move to better neighborhoods as their particular priorities dictate. On the other hand, if they are able to rent acceptable dwellings for less than the value of their vouchers, they can keep the difference. The system is designed to replace paternalism with individual choice, flexibility being the key.

RENT CONTROL

Another book might well look into the arguments that led up to rent control being declared constitutional in 1921. New York City has the oldest and strictest rent control laws in the nation, the lowest vacancy, lowest new housing starts, lowest inclination to lend by residential lenders and lowest profit to residential investors (all understatements!) In fact in 1983 average rents were $78 a month below operating costs. No wonder so many landlords continue to lose money.

Carolyn Lochhead, writing for *Insight* (4/13/87) told of an 87 year old gentleman who had been given property in Harlem, by an employer for whom he worked as a plumber-handyman for 23 years. The property owner reportedly spent over $40,000 heating a building for two years which is and was frequented by squatters. Nevertheless, he was sent to jail three times "for failing to supply heat to squatters." He has boarded up the building at night only to find squatters there in the morning. You can understand his indignation at being told he must take care of these squatters. "The judge strictly told me that regardless of who it is, I'm supposed to give them heat and hot water."[7] At the time of the interview with Ms. Lochhead this 87 year old property owner was almost bankrupt, yet he was forced by NYC rent control laws to rent out a five room unit for $55 a month. (Ok—I remember 4 br for $56 but NYC isn't New Orleans!)

Another example cited by Ms. Lochhead was a steelworker who lost $11,000 in 1986 because half the units in a 35-unit apartment house had to be rented for under $100 a month. (We're still talking about NYC) Neither property owner could sell at other than a loss. If this isn't robbery by a government entity (taking by force) than I don't know what else to call it! Over and over the constitutionality of such statutes has been challenged. A new knight on a white charger is emerging to do battle once again, this time from San Jose, California. In Pennell v City of San Jose the issue is whether property owners can be forced to subsidize low-income earners by linking rent increases to tenant income. I hope you will agree the idea is preposterous!

In many instances it has been determined that housing shortages didn't exist before rent-control and if they did it was thanks to the hinderance of zoning and other restrictive municipal statutes.

When rent-control moves in, developers, investors and lenders all move out; few capital improvements are made from then on and maintenance begins to wear thin. Tenants report code violations and if there are none they often create them in order to get the upper hand. Under rent control there is a subtle but speedy shifting of valuable rights from owners to old tenants. The poor—those folks supposedly helped most by rent-control—actually benefit least as they are most likely to move around and rent-control always reduces the number of units available in a community. Powerful political constituencies emerge and feed on people's desperation. Black markets develop as old tenants demand tribute for access to their lease rights. Ownership rights become a drag on the market—a losing proposition under rent control—but lease rights are in great demand. Vacancies are communicated via the underground, necessitating the payment of more tribute to the bearers of news about possible vacancies. In a condominium conversion property owners are forced to buy-out old tenants. Payments run as high as $40,000 and sometimes more in New York City. Old tenants are the special interests enjoying privileges at the expense of new tenants, property owners and the housing market in general.

A study by the Center for Community Change found the money saved by rent-control (remember it has been shown that the poor benefit least) goes to subsidize gourmet restaurants and the fancier more exclusive retail stores in the area. We should all question the appropriateness of landlords involuntarily subsidizing the increased consumption of luxuries such as liquor, gourmet foods and other non-essentials.

1986 TAX REFORM

Recent tax legislation has left real estate investors with a feeling of uncertainty. Thanks to the 1986 reform (ACT) many saw the value of their write-offs decline and investments that fail to yield intended benefits will not be repeated. The bond and tax rules were changed because various Congress persons thought developers had been getting too good a tax break. (That's what "they" call it when they let you keep some of your own earnings.) By law, rents charged to low-income tenants can equal only the operator's actual expenses plus a maintenance reserve which effectively does away with cash flows. Rent control diminishes the chance of rapid appreciation and a profit on resale. That leaves large write-offs as the only incentive to attract investors to low-income housing. When the 1986 tax revision reduced the top bracket from 50 percent to 28 percent those write-offs suddenly became worth a lot less.

Congress, not necessarily out of sympathy for investors who, afterall can always put their money someplace else, but realizing the losers could be millions of low-income people who have trouble finding decent, reasonable and secure places to live, decided a tax credit was in order. But nothing too simple; one where the size of the credit depends on the *kind* of low-income housing. If the units are not financed via government subsidies the maximum credit to build or rehabilitate is now 9 percent of the purchase price taken each year for ten years. If the property is ten years old or more and the construction or rehabilitation is government financed, the maximum credit drops to 4 percent each year. One more stipulation; in order to qualify for the rehabilitation credit, the owner has to spend at least $2,000 for renovating each unit.

Just qualifying a project as low-income housing can be a job. Either 20 percent of the units must be rented to people with incomes below 50 percent of the median income for the locality, or 40 percent of the units must be occupied by tenants with incomes below 60 percent of the median. Owners must also meet state and federal guidelines in setting the rents charged to below-median-income tenants. If this were not enough, there are contradictory rules between the Treasury Department (this is the first housing program to be administered by the Treasury Department rather that the Department of Housing and Urban Development) and government lenders.

Although the tax credits apply to federal income tax they are administered by each state according to its unique rules. Every state is allowed $1.25 of credit per resident per year, 10 percent of which must be allocated to non-profit organizations.

But nothing is as straight forward as it may seem (and if this seems straight forward so far, my hat's off to you!). The Spring 1987 American Bar Association Bulletin of the Special Committee on Housing and Urban Development Law detailed 30 "intracies" to be discussed at a meeting in Washington DC on May 15, 1987. Intricacies to lawyers can hardly be understood by the average investor. Projects must be held and managed to qualified low-income housing for a minimum of 15 years although the tax credits run out at the end of ten years. There's more; if at any time during those 15 years the percentage of low-income tenants drops below the minimum requirement, the tax credit taken in previous years is subject to recapture. Since voucher-holders can move at will, it's all too easy to fall below the minimum and trigger recapture.

Before the second world war less than half the housing units in American were owned by their occupants. Easy homeowner financing and the housing boom which followed the war brought home ownership within reach of more and more Americans and by 1980 65.8 percent of all units were owner-occupied. But soaring prices, high interest and a decline in inventory has recently resulted in fewer people participating in the dream of home ownership and owner-occupied units had dropped to 63.9 percent of the whole as 1987 began.

In an attempt to change this situation the Reagan Administration is attempting to substitute loan subsidies for rent subsidies—home ownership for public housing. Rent for federally subsidized housing is based on income which means the more a person makes the more he pays. Not exactly an incentive for more work or a formula for getting ahead. Low interest loans often bring mortgage payments down to the level of rent and offer a family a real chance to get ahead. Home ownership not only enhances net-worth but enhances self-worth as well.

In an effort to discourage borrowing the 1986 Tax Reform Act made interest on home mortgages and home equity loans the only interest still deductible. To have done the job correctly Congress should not have given into the real estate lobbyists as it did. Lenders are tempting the vulnerable American consumer, long accustomed to living over his head, with revolving lines of credit against equity in his home. Being able to draw against this equity via a credit card has lured an unprecedented amount of homeowners into jeopardizing their own interests and their ability to pass home equity on to their children as previous generations of homeowners have generally done.

MAKE "THEM" DO IT!

On December 8, 1986, the housing situation was the subject of the Phil Donahue Show on network television. The prevailing sentiment was a "get the rich, the landlords, the developers and *make* them put profits into helping others" type of attitude. Mr. Donahue, as devil's advocate, brought up the fact that non-owner occupied property is often "trashed". He wondered about incentives (especially relevant in light of the preceeding discussion regarding loss of write-offs and uncertain tax credits) to build low-income housing. A lady in the audience saw no problem. "Why can't we build more shelters instead of one more nuclear bomb?", she asked. Her "we" presupposes a government solution and why not?

WHY NOT?

It seems to me "why not" was emphatically answered in the December 15, 1985 issue of TIME magazine which reported on Chicago's Cabrini-Green, 23 high rise buildings which have been home to generations of low-income blacks. The article compared the housing project to Belfast or Beirut; a battlefield between opposing gang members where innocent bystanders are frequently injured, sometimes fatally.

On the other hand we have "Cochran", hailed by many as an inspiring success story. Cochran is the tenant-managed public housing complex in St. Louis which was highlighted by the popular television show "60 MINUTES" on November 30, 1986. Conditions were once so bad that Cochran was referred to as "Little Nam". In 1976 management was transferred to its 2,100 residents who not only hired private security guards but began evicting trouble makers and instituting strict regulations.

We learned of one lady who knew her friends were going to evict her so she sent her family away. Apparently an entire family can face eviction if only one member violates the rules. According to Cochran resident and president, Bertha Gilkey, the "tenant is managed" at Cochran. Some people may find that a little harsh. Cabrini-Green and Cochran are opposite sides of the same coin—that coin being a government solution. A better solution might be to eliminate dependence on and interference by government through a gradual transfer of ownership to the tenants. Ms. Gilkey believes Cochran may be completely in private hands by 1991.

Private ownership of currently government owned housing projects has been advocated by many politicians including presidential hopeful Jack Kemp (R-NY) who has suggested that government owned units be sold to tenant groups at 25 percent of market value.

PRIVATE SECTOR HORROR STORIES

But the private sector has its own horror stories. Perhaps you read the newspaper account (Associated Press 12/26/86) of nineteen families who had been paying $40 per month to live in delapidated structures referred to as "Slave City". The property owner said it would cost more then $40,000 to extend water lines, install proper bathrooms etc. and that his tenants could hardly afford the $40 per month rental fee let alone what the rents would have to be raised to in order to cover the expense of making repairs. Although the lady in the Donahue audience might have wanted to see the owner *made* to renovate and keep the rents low, the AP story related a government solution she would have liked. Even though the shameful housing was located outside the Selma, Alabama city limits, Selma's mayor arranged to have the more than 80 residents move to Craig Field, an Air Force base that closed in 1977. The move was accomplished under a little known law enacted by Congress in 1983 which orders the military to make unused space at military facilities nationwide available for use by the homeless. The government facilities are said to have central air, refrigerators, stoves, running water and indoor bathrooms. Somebody paid more than $40 per month for all this. *Guess who!*

In Bethel, Alaska, there are 117 subsidized housing units but the wait to get into one is anywhere from six months to a year. In the meantime, those who can't afford the unsubsidized $1,300 per month average rent for a two bedroom house can rent rusted, patched metal boxes, once used for freight, for only $200 per month. Tenants use plastic pails for toilets and dump their dishwater outside where it freezes immediately. Many of these 8′ × 24′ container-homes have broken windows and sagging plywood doors which are a menace in the sub-zero climate.

One man's deprivation is another's opportunity. Should these tenants be forced out for "their own good" and perhaps have to leave the area, or should other Alaska residents be forced to foot their neighbor's bill?

In April, 1987, a San Francisco architect designed and built a couple 8′ X 4′ hinged boxes with foam mattresses (City Sleepers) in order to provide inexpensive shelter for homeless persons who otherwise curl up on the hard sidewalk or damp grass at night. The architect has located 500 potential spots on public land for more of the "Sleepers" but it seems unlikely he will be able to talk the city into endorsing the idea. What would it look like? City Sleepers have no plumbing, are possible fire hazards and cost $800 each to build. San Francisco, the compassionate city by the bay could be accused of treating a segment of its population as if they were dogs. (Sorry—no air conditioning.)

ONLY CHUMPS PLAY BY THE RULES

New York City has 175,000 families waiting for low-income housing and yet they are giving publicly owned property to squatters; people who unlawfully occupied and in some cases renovated city owned property. ACORN (Association of Community Organizations for Reform Now) is an example of how not to handle our housing problems. They advocate anarchy—disregard for law—because their cause is just and above law. Such arrogance was met by an unbelievable mealy-mouthed response from a New York City official quoted in the January 12, 1987 issue of *Insight;* "The government has to show some flexibility in looking at individual cases. To take a hard-line position across the board against people who in good faith invested in the renovation of those buildings would be a mistake."

Where in the world was the "good faith"? These people were willing to invest money and labor and occupy these buildings under the threat of jail. They knew full well they were breaking the law and opted to accept the consequences in hopes of changing the law. All well and good—there is a time for arrogance and civil disobedience but there must be consequences to suffer. Hard decisions were not made by the city of New York whose officials tried to duck the issue and give it a different name. In doing so they fostered a disregard for law and broke faith with the 175,000 families on the low-income housing waiting list who were playing by the rules. According to the

Insight article the squatters and city ended up working together with a member of ACORN's staff saying "We really feel this is a model for low-income housing." Is *anyone* thinking clearly in this nation or is the problem confined to New York City? I understand in Queens a health code violation is needed to qualify a property for a reduced rent so a prospective tenant can move in with a promise "to fix it". Now what would you do? We say we want one thing and we continually encourage the opposite!

THANK YOU, THANK YOU ALMIGHTY BUREAUCRATS

But to be fair to New York, the Nehemiah project in Brooklyn demonstrated how well private and public sectors can compliment one another. The City donated 30 blocks of vacant land and interest free second mortgages to help make the 1,000 new low-income residences a reality.

In San Francisco the Bay Area Residential Investment and Development Group (BRIDGE) obtained special favors from the local government which made it possible to erect 2,400 low-income housing units.

But apparently taxpayers are required to subsidize only those that show little or no ambition and creativity. Not long ago a couple and their four children were accused of defrauding the Monterey County Housing Authority because they lived in a publicly subsidized apartment for four years while they skrimped and saved to better their condition by building a house on a country lot, purchased with unacknowledged and disqualifying funds.

What is it about G-d helping those who help themselves? That's good because taxpayer funds don't and won't—and I'm not saying they *should* but only how necessarily unfair it is when bureaucrats oversee taxpayer dollars and play G-d with other people's money and lives as they preside over the redistribution. In the Authority's favor, however, is the fact that in return for the subsidized portion of rent plus interest (slightly under $6,000) the family was not prosecuted. If private sector groups had dollars to distribute things might be arranged according to different criteria and there would be no need to cheat. We want to see people get ahead but in this case the bureaucracy rewarded fraud. What's to prevent others from helping themselves to a loan to make saving for that dream house a little quicker and easier?

THE POWER TO . . .

Those with the most power over us gained control via the purse strings. ("Wallet" just doesn't have the same ring to it.) But lesser officials without direct authority to use taxpayer money may nevertheless use dollars to make us obey, either by threatening us with fines or seducing us with incentives.

Many developers would happily provide low-cost housing in exchange for a right to build more offices or homes on any particular site. (The right to build might be defined as blackmail.) Policy makers, not the market place control their profits. In some areas of Monterey County developers of senior citizen homes are given twice the number of units afforded ordinary developers for market-rate developments. Taking their power to heart, certain county bureaucrats saw an opportunity to artificially encourage the development of more units for the elderly and began advocating the allowance of 3 senior-citizen-units where only 1 non-senior-unit would be allowed. This is not the free market at work. This is the raw power found in fascist governments. The POWER is saying "My way be done or . . .!"

If there's a need it will be filled, but apparently not by the free-market. The more committees, commissions, authorities, boards, forums, task forces, coalitions, panels—whatever we call them—the more power we give other people over our lives the more inefficient, frustrated and dependent we will become.

Monterey county may or may not be typical, but it *is* regulated. Some supervisors have let power go to their heads, requiring permission in the form of permits and inspections for everything and anything while collecting fees to support a bureaucracy which tells owners of supposedly private property what they can or cannot do with it.

The power-crazed mayor of one local community (no, I'm not referring to Mr. Eastwood) attempted to revoke the building permit of a developer. Why? Because in preparing the developer's privately owned land to build 37 sorely needed dwellings, 10 trees along the perimeter of the acreage were inadvertently bulldozed along with the other trees where removal *was* permitted. The city attorney told the council its options were to "revoke the use permit, withhold approval of the final map for the project, withhold architectural approval, refuse to issue a building permit, fine the developer or sue in civil court."[8] WHEW! In what appeared to be a groveling gesture of appeasement, the developer (producer in society) was held hostage to the bureaucrats (non-producers) and in this case attempted to secure his freedom by offering to make amends for the 10 downed trees by planting 153 new ones along the perimeter of the land at a cost of $20,000. (And oh what a good boy was he!)

A Monterey county supervisor was quoted as saying "I'm, heartened to hear someone tell me that it took them several months to get a permit for something."[9] Heartened because it showed a willingness to go through the oppressive, socialistic, inefficient process. Rather than heartening, I find it shameful. County bureaucrats express horror when violators (read private property owners) ". . . try to avoid the expensive conditions the country sometimes tacks on to permits."[10] Monterey county has hired three investigators to track down "violators". I'm certain my pioneer grandparents who came to this state in 1840 would not believe it—the U.S.——?

THE LANDOWNERS' BILL OF RIGHTS

The "Landowners' Bill of Rights" was approved by voters in Tehama County, California in November 1982. The ordinance included provisions prohibiting county government from imposing requirements related to the type of housing that could be built or the size or location of any commercial business within the county. After a series of appeals it was finally decided that many provisions of the ordinance were invalid since they conflicted with both the California Government code and state land use law. The final ruling reiterating the need for just compensation for declaring any private property a set aside as open space or as a historical site was in the voters' favor.

California's constitution gives cities and counties the authority to make and enforce "all local police, sanitary and other ordinances and regulations not in conflict with general laws". A conflict exists if the ordinance duplicates, contradicts or enters an area fully occupied by state law. Preemption is a principle of law full of imperfections and inconsistencies. Nevertheless the trend in California was to presume a local regulation is not preempted as long as there are significant local interests to be served, and these naturally differ from one locality to another.

In June 1987 the U.S. Supreme Court ruled in a case from Los Angeles County that land-use restrictions, even temporary ones, are inverse condemnations for which property owners must be compensated.[11] Formerly California's Supreme Court had prohibited suits for "just compensation". In his dissent Justice John Paul Stevens lamented that "Much important regulation will never be enacted. . ." Now it will presumably be too costly. All I can say is "AMEN!"

IDEAS

Government waivers, financing or any discriminating legislation is a subsidy; a favoring of one citizen above another. We are so used to allowing the end to justify the means that it is almost impossible to see the situation objectively. There are plenty of ideas however, with some imported from abroad. 35 percent of the housing built in West Germany since WW II is mutually owned by government and tenants.

Chester Hartman of the Washington Institute for Policy Studies proposes the U.S. government provide capital grants to build 200,000 units of new social housing (he's got to mean subsidized low-income housing or public housing with a fancy new name) and 400,000 units of rehabilitated housing *annually!* It would cost $24 billion a year. Once a unit of "social housing" was built it would never fall into private (for profit G-d forbid!) hands, but it would be operated by nonprofit associations (nonprofit means the good guys) and tenant co-ops. The accomodations would not have mortgages to pay off so the tenants' monthly payments would cover taxes, maintenance and refurbishing. You can bet there would never be enough money to do everything *they* want and since low-income tenants can only be allowed to pay a limited amount *they'd* be back demanding more funds to protect the *taxpayers investment* claiming the economy just didn't behave *as planned.* (So what else is new?)

James Rouses, renovator of downtown Boston and Baltimore's harbor, is founder of the Enterprise Foundation which provides funds to nonprofit housing groups across the country. The Foundation has drawn up plans for a 10-year program to upgrade low-income housing in Chattanooga, Tennessee. The program, estimated to cost about $200 million, is counting on non-profit local volunteers and neighborhood groups for its success. Mr. Rouses favors a national network of low-income housing backed by federal funding. He would probably support the resolution adopted by the U.S. Conference of Mayors on June 13, 1987 to urge Congress to establish a trust fund which would provide $5 billion annually for low-income housing. They suggested the funds come from interest on tenants' security deposits, a federal real estate transfer tax (guess whose going to be fighting against that one?), interest on mortgage escrow deposits or assessments on financial institutions.

CDCs and LISC

But aren't Community Development Corporations (CDCs) one step better? The CDCs first appeared in the late 1960s and caught on because they involved local residents in planning and managing developments. In 1979 when Franklin Thomas became president of the Ford Foundation, he founded a group called Local Initiatives Support Corporation (LISC) with $34 million of Foundation money. The LISC was designed to cut the risks of CDC projects by demanding rigorous lending and management standards. The MacArthur Foundation, Metropolitan Life Insurance Company of America and Cigna Corporation were all charter investors, along with the Ford Foundation.

The Reagan administration predicted the vacuum created by the withdrawal of the federal government would be filled by church groups, foundations and corporations such as the LISC. In 1986 the LISC had more than $100 million in capital from more than 300 corporations and foundations and three government bodies. By the end of 1986 it had funded 400 community groups in 27 cities. Chicago, for example, lost 90 percent of its federal housing subsidies but about half that amount was replaced by LISC funded housing projects.

As increasing amounts of money become available to non-profit organizations, their role in the housing industry will automatically expand. The tax advantage (more influence by government) they enjoy makes them logical players in the housing market. "Habitat for Humanity" is a Christian group which raises funds from churches and local organizations around the country. In 1987 it had an $11 million budget and was operating in 170 cities across the nation.

Nearly 80 percent of 66 projects studied by the Kennedy School of Government at Harvard produced the financial returns the CDCs and LISC predicted. They have been successful in areas where efforts by other organizations have failed. In December of 1986 LISC announced the creation of a $10.5 million fund to purchase more than forty loans made to CDCs by LISC and others who have lent money to LISC projects. This will create a secondary market guaranteeing decent returns to participants and making the entire concept that much more stable. The emphasis is on providing local solutions and involvement to urban problems.

OUR RECALCITRANT CONGRESS

Over the Reagan administration's opposition ("Remember the deficit!"), the Senate passed a bill March 31, 1987 providing $18.8 billion in FY1988 and $19.8 billion in FY1989 for federal housing programs. Again the Republicans brought up the matter of the budget deficit only to be trounced by the budget-busting Democrats who know everything I have written here—surely enough to convince all but the most closed minds that subsidized housing does not work.

Younger V. Turnage, a suit brought by 2 homeless veterans, the Vietnam Veterans of America, a homeless shelter and the National Coalition for the Homeless, which alleges that the Veteran Administration has an obligation to homeless veterans, no doubt influenced the Senate. On the same day, (March 31, 1987) it passed a bill requiring the Veterans Administration to turn over foreclosed VA homes to veterans' service organizations and other non-profits organizations so that they might be used to shelter homeless veterans and their families. (This is beginning to sound like a chapter out of *DR. ZHIVAGO!*) Total cost estimates: $10 million in FY1988, $34 million in FY1989 and $7 million in FY 1990. Easy—mere millions instead of the *billions* they had voted to spend minutes earlier.

SHADOW MARKETS

Professor William Baer of the University of Southern California has coined the phrase "shadow markets"—referring to a conversion of previously uninhabited buildings such as old schools, abandoned buildings, churches and in some cases illegal accessory apartments to legitimate residential housing. As Virginia Postrel, assistant editor of Reason magazine said, "Communities need only make relatively modest changes in their zoning and building codes—to help people who already live in their neighborhoods do things they already want to do. How willing local governments are to loosen their controls will provide an excellent measure of the nation's true concern about the much-discussed housing crisis."[12]

FROM RENTER TO HOMEOWNER

In the fifties approximately one third of the nation's renters paid more than a quarter of their incomes on housing; by 1980 half were doing so. Naturally as incomes decrease, percentages increase, as there are fewer discretionary dollars. In Monterey County, California in February 1987, prospective buyers began camping out in their cars in order to secure a place in line to purchase the last few homes "permitted" (by whom do you suppose?) to be developed in a certain coastal area. February in central California is not February in New Hampshire but it is not exactly camping-out weather either. Nevertheless there is little choice when demand outpaces supply thanks to zoning laws and other restrictions. "Favors" in such an atmosphere become a way of life and the environment becomes fertile for blackmail and underground activity.

When government enters the picture with its threat of force, words take on whatever meaning the policy-makers desire. In the United States of America in 1987 "low-income household" means a household (naturally to qualify the fewer income-earners in the "house" the better, and folks catch on to that quickly enough) which received less than 50 percent of the region's median income, or at most $21,000! Check this HUD definition: "overcrowding = more than one person to a room." Knowing the correct definition is the key to qualifying for most government programs. You can then *make* things fit!

Alan Reynolds remarked that it requires great statistical imagination for which PhDs *should* be granted for turning progress into disaster. Maybe you remember that old joke about a mathematician, a statistician and an economist who were asked to give the answer to "2+2". The mathamatician, without hesitation, answered "4". The statistician said, "In all probability it lies somewhere between 3 and 5." The economist pulled down the shades and whispered, "What would you like it to be?" Whether the reputation is deserved or not, the fact remains that even with upright intentions numbers in the hands of different economists show different results—often "whatever you want them to be". Attorneys are paid to do the same thing with facts.

TOMORROW'S CREATIVE SOLUTIONS

Subsidies, even vouchers, interfere with the workings of a free market and inhibit new creative solutions to problems. Even now technology is in the wings which will allow housing in the future to solve problems in other fields, notably crime and health care. The so-called "smart-house" replaces ordinary wiring with a single cable capable of handling control and data signals as well as audio-video signals.

About 150 tiny computers will serve the controllers which receive power and signal information. Anything that uses electricity can be programmed to function according to the wishes of smart-house owners. Smart-house wiring standards are written into the 1987 National Electrical Code and may initially cost $5,000 to $7,000 above ordinary wiring but the benefits are phenomenal—especially in high crime areas or in homes providing shelter for handicapped or elderly persons who depend on special equipment and supervision.

We need to develop more efficient cost effective building techniques and innovative financing. According to one reckoning the nation needs 7,600,000 three bedroom, three bath homes costing under $30,000. Can we do it? We are doing it. These houses are coming to market with the new hi-tech manufactured homes. We did it with the automobile and by George we'll do it again, but this time with homes!

Not long ago the Washington Post quoted Congressman Henry Gonzales of Texas on the subject of providing adequate housing in the United States. "The Japanese can do it, and they are not necessarily geniuses and we dullards." Perhaps the Congressman was unaware how inept the reference to Japanese housing really was. Comparing the ratio of Japanese homeowners to American homeowners is as laughable as a comparison of the space each country considers adequate for it renters to inhabit. "More than one person to a room" is *not* considered overcrowding in Japan!

The American dream of home ownership can continue to be a reality—all we need is to keep government at all levels out of the way.

HIGHWAYS

OUR DISINTEGRATING INFRASTRUCTURE

It has been said that nobody cuts a ribbon over a pothole that's been fixed or a bridge that's been shorn up. Lobbying for repairs doesn't result in showy political gains for politicians. It's little wonder then, that the 41,369-mile federal Interstate Highway System fell into disrepair.

According to the Congressional Budget Office, in 1982 two-thirds of this system was in only poor or fair condition. States, in their eagerness to accept federal money (90% of the cost) to build new interstate highways, gave little thought to maintenance costs. It wasn't until 1976 that Congress voted to chip in any federal funds for maintenance and by then the roads were already twenty years old.

In 1982 the estimated cost of repairing or replacing 23% of the 574,000 bridges in the United States considered safe only for cars and light trucks was $47.6 billion. The week following the April 5, 1987 collapse of the New York Thruway bridge it was widely reported that a federal inventory had classified more than a fourth of California's bridges as either structurally deficient or obsolete. How can this be reconciled with an Associated Press report, date line Sacramento April 10, 1987 that claimed the inventory ". . . found that 16,472 of the 22,270 bridges in California are in fine shape, but that 1,669 are structurally deficient."? Looks more like 7 percent than 25 percent doesn't it? Federal funding for bridge projects was supposed to have been $225 million in each of the next five years but the demonstration projects included in the 1987 highway bill will eat up $40 million in 1987 and $25 million in each of the next four years.

But the problem doesn't end with roads and bridges. The Army Corps of Engineers classified 8,794 of the nation's 65,000 nonfederal dams as unsafe and the Environmental Protection Agency estimated that in the neighborhood of $120 billion must be spent by the year 2000 to adequately handle the burgeoning sewage problems caused by changes in population and ordinary growth.

The Surface Transportation Assistance Act was legislated in 1982, authorizing more than $70 billion in outlays over a four year period and adding five cents a gallon to the federal gasoline tax.

Outlays for public construction started rising rapidly by late 1983. These funds led to a 43% increase in highway, bridge and mass transportation spending. Lower interest rates allowed municipalities to borrow cheaply. Almost two-thirds of the funds they borrowed over the last three years was used for construction. Nationwide the take from property taxes is increasing at better than a 7% annual rate. Spending on public works projects increased at a breathtaking pace from 1983 to 1986. All this unbeknown to Hodding Carter III who reminded us of all the horror stories the press uncovered a few years ago. In the April 2, 1987 edition of the Wall Street Journal he said: "The stories are gone, but the conditions remain virtually unchanged where they are not worse." Oh well.

THAT INFAMOUS HIGHWAY BILL

Motorists pay at the nation's gas pumps to fund the Federal Highway Trust Fund making it hard, therefore, to understand how Congress could refuse to authorize the release of these user-fee revenues. But when the 99th Congress adjourned in October, 1986, it left unpassed the 5-year reauthorization bill for federal highway and mass-transit projects. A portion of that bill authorized funds for no frills works on the nation's highways that most voters would approve. However, the bill was so loaded down with extraneous items, in the end the baby was thrown out with the bath water. Some of the bath water included a proposal to expand "Buy American" provisions to cover cement and related products used in highway construction. An attempt was even made to permit states to reject lowest bids for highway contracts from companies that have connections in South Africa.

The 100th Congress in its first three months, passed two budget-busting bills; HR 1, the Water Bill, and HR 2, the Highway Bill, over President Reagan's vetoes. Out of a possible 535 votes, a grand total of only 34 votes were registered against the Highway Bill.

The administration had no problems with the $70 billion authorized for the federal highway program ("the baby" in the 99th Congress' bill). These funds, used for building or repairing highways and bridges, are apportioned to the states by a set formula and were running dangerously low in many states. This made HR 2 a "must pass" bill, always an ideal vehicle for the transportation of pork.

In the President's words (vetoing the bill March 27, 1987):

> "The bill authorizes funding levels of $87.5 billion over five years, $10.1 billion more than my original request and more than is brought in by highway-user taxes. . . . It represents a failure to constrain federal spending, especially pork barrel spending.
>
> "(Provisions) . . . include add-on funding for 152 special interest projects. The five-year federal cost of the 152 highway projects is estimated to be $1.4 billion, and nearly $900 million of this amount is not subject to any spending controls. The total cost to complete these projects is estimated to be $5.5 billion, and they have not even been selected through the established mechanism that relies on the expertise of state and local officials."

Massachusetts will benefit unfairly by a revision of the formula used to distribute funds. The new bill will allow Massachusetts to build a third Boston harbor tunnel and to reconstruct the central artery of I-90 as an underground highway instead of an elevated highway. Both projects are outlandishly expensive and unlikely to have been considered "worth it" by local taxpayers without help from the rest of us (federal dollars).

Was the Administration's proposal that such projects be brought under the annual spending ceiling and any federal funds be at least matched by state or local funds so outrageous? Some think so.

Senator Moynihan referred to the President's veto as a "mindless act".[13] Hodding Carter III accused the President in his second term of having ". . . no more understanding of the government's paramount responsibility to keep the nation's framework healthy than he did in his first. As in the interstate-highway fight, he is more concerned with old slogans than pressing national needs."[14]

JOB PROGRAMS

All job programs almost guarantee inefficiencies. Local governments anticipate that they'll receive federal funds for public projects and hold their own money back from these particular projects. A few years ago an analysis of the Local Public Works program suggested that local governments, awaiting federal money, postponed $22 billion of spending, thus lowering the GNP by perhaps $30 billion.[15] Also there is a real tendency to exaggerate needs if someone else is footing the bill. Communities may not need storm sewers capable of handling the heaviest downpour on record, and what's wrong with closing some bridges to ultra-heavy trucks? A big part of the gap between resources and needs will be closed, not by increasing funding but by finding more realistic ways of dealing with situations—unless of course we're willing to pay for gold-paved streets with tax dollars.

TOLL ROADS IN CALIFORNIA?

Legislation has been proposed in California, pioneer of the modern freeway, to allow counties to build toll roads as an alternative to overcrowded freeways. The bill, proposed by State Assemblyman Nolan Frizzelle (R-Orange County), would require that any toll road be built parallel to an existing freeway, giving motorists a choice; pay to use the less crowded toll road or use the congested freeway (now less congested thanks to the new toll road).

DEMONSTRATION PROJECTS

On September 25, 1986, Jack Anderson, in his column, discussed the so-called "demonstration projects" supposed to test new ideas or new technology to make the nation's highways safer and cheaper to build. According to Mr. Anderson, most demonstration money goes to districts represented by senior House members under false pretenses.

> One example: Building a $1.5 million bridge next to an existing bridge in order to demonstrate "methods of reducing traffic on an existing bridge".

If a third or fourth grader came up with such nonsense when asked for ways to reduce traffic on a bridge, a teacher might not be out of line for considering him/her insolent and glib. And yet that is the kind of creativity we are getting from United States Senators!

> Another example: $90 million to build a 12 mile highway in order to demonstrate "new methods of painting lines on roads". (Too bad those lines couldn't have been tried out on existing roads!)

Why in the blazes don't *they* tackle something truly creative like automated highways which could double the capacity of current highways and may even be the solution for traffic jams in the future. Such highways would use a power conductor under the roadway that would transmit an electromagnetic field to a power coupling which would allow the command sensor to steer, control speed and brake the car. General Motors said that the technology is here today and modifications for today's cars would cost about $2,400 to enable them to use the electronic highway. The problem is in finding funds for research and development of such a project.

I'm not suggesting this idea presently be funded, you understand, especially in light of the need to cut our deficit, but surely this is the new technology "demonstration projects" should be targeted to rather than the pork-barreling described above.

According to the Federal Highway Administration, "Bridge Repairs" is one of four discretionary programs which are being drained by demonstration projects to the tune of $534 million. But even bureaucrats get creative if things get desperate enough and columnist Jack Anderson told of five bridge projects which were "reincarnated as demonstration projects by the House Public Works Committee: in order to get a share of the funding."[15]

AN UNPOPULAR MORAL STAND

People rarely consider the "rightness" or "wrongness" of an act, believing mistakenly, if the law allows it it must be "right". I hope you are beginning to realize that many laws are "wrong"—or at least debatable from the point of view of justice. I realize defining justice would take a whole other book and indeed as many books as there are people in this country. Our Constitution attempted to define justice in terms of individual rights and liberty but that attempt has been twisted, turned and distorted over the last 200 years so that an individual must look to his own conscience for an understanding of what America stands for.

A terrible tragedy occured near a small school in our county. Two youngsters were killed as they attempted to turn onto a busy highway. A reflex-response from the majority of shocked and grief-stricken parents at the school was to demand a traffic light. The intersection did not meet the state authorities priorities for funding but they agreed to the permit if alternate funding could be found. Tireless dedicated parents convinced the city and the county that funds could be had from two developers who, as a condition of their building permits, were required to post money for the eventual improvement of the highway. Something not in enough demand to merit taxpayer expenditures was laid off on individuals (companies, partnerships, businessmen, profit mongers—whatever you wish to call them) and whatever you wish to call the act—it's a socially accepted and well established form of black mail—and it was wrong! We are uncomfortable with "right" and "wrong" and pretend that there is no such thing as moral truth forgetting that reason and morality are the only weapons that determine the course of history. There can be no compromise when it comes to basic principles, moral issues, matter of knowledge and truth—matters of rational conviction. Relativism has all but made public discussion unintelligible. Undefined amorphous terms are used to replace once legitimate concepts in people's minds. The Bolsheviks purposefully called themselves a name which means "majority" even when they were only a small minority. (Illusion!) Similarly *Pravda* the communist party's official newspaper means "truth". (More illusion!) The main issue in our society today is not rich v. poor but the individual v. the state.

MASS TRANSIT—WHO WANTS IT?

Lyndon Johnson signed the Urban Mass Transit Assistance Act (UMTA) in 1964 in an effort to change the preferred behavior of American citizens. Public transit ridership had been declining nationwide from 24 billion rides a year in 1947 to only 9 billion in 1963. That should have told the government that citizens prefer their own cars but, as is so often the case, elected officials marched to their own drummer.

Over the past 23 years, the UMTA has cost taxpayers some $45 billion. During that period, ridership continued to decline, mass transit operating deficits soared and subsidies per passenger skyrocketed 1,250%! Large capital improvement grants went into projects that no city administration would have seriously contemplated building with local tax money. Examples are plentiful: The 63rd Street Tunnel in New York City was supposed to cost $145 million but so far it is ten years overdue with a $800 million tab and will probably require an additional $300 million for completion.

Miami's Metro Rail system was over budget by $210 million and opened two years late. For the cost of $1 billion someone figured each of the systems 16,500 passengers who on the average rode the system during its first year of operation (ridership had been projected at 100,000 daily for the first year) could have been given over $60,000 each for cab fare instead. In a 1985 speech President Reagan quipped that taxpayers would have been better off if they had simply purchased a limousine for each Miami rail rider. Not to be outdone, the nation's capital has a glaring example of its own. The Metro in Washington DC was seven years behind schedule and $4 billion over budget. It loses about $300 million a year and carries fewer passengers than the local bus system.

Senator Lloyd Bentsen of Texas supported the construction of a mass transit system in Houston even though local voters refused to OK a $2.3 billion bond issue for it. Bentsen saw it as a way for Texans to get billions of federal dollars. That's what I call parochial short-range thinking unworthy of a Senator. But those who live in glass houses . . . Californians, such as myself, must point to our junior Senator Pete Wilson who worked to replace a perfectly fine bus line with a new light-rail system in San Diego. Even though it is doing better than most, able to provide 80% of operating expenses from rider revenues, the bus system it replaced covered the same route, carried the same number of passengers *and* showed a profit! Even closer to home is the San Francisco bay area fiasco where buses would have cost one-fortieth of what BART (Bay Area Rapid Transit) cost. The system in March 1987 was reportedly carrying 60,000 less riders per day than a year earlier!

When Ronald Reagan tried to cut spending by the Urban Mass Transit Administration (UMTA) Congress simply scoffed and approved a large number of new starts. Congressmen like Senator Mark Andrew of North Dakota need to be taken to task. With typical double-talk he calls projects, which everyone agrees will not be able to pay for themselves if and when completed, "investments in the future."

Of course public mass transit has its supporters mainly unions and construction businesses. The UMTA states that any city assuming responsibility for a transit system must honor all existing transportation union contracts, taking care to preserve all the workers' "rights, privileges, and benefits (including continuation of pension rights and benefits) under existing collective bargaining agreements . . ." Public agencies under this stipulation not only can't reduce work forces, but are forced to rehire laid-off workers at the first opportunity or offer them free retraining. Such meddling by our ever present and all pervasive law makers means that efficiency considerations take a back seat to union benefits and privileges. Since Uncle Sam began employing transit workers, their wages have risen 25 percent to 40 percent more rapidly than the average American wage. Declining labor productivity and high pay account for 50 to 75 percent of the operating deficits in American transit systems.

Between 1964 and 1974 construction expenditures for transit projects rose dramatically. The federal government went from providing 25 percent of construction cost to 80 percent by 1974 when it also began picking up 50 percent of the tab for operating expenses as well. It was really like having a rich uncle! Of course this meant that these new systems were virtually cost free for the cities because state governments usually picked up the remaining construction and operating costs.

In a blatantly shortsighted move, Congress decided to finance only new systems even though rehabilitating existing systems would have cost less in many instances. Cities that did not come up with new all encompassing systems saw subsidies slashed. In the 1987 highway bill eleven cities divide 80 percent of the mass transit funds, including $870 million for Los Angeles' metrorail.

Professor Jonathan Weiner of the University of California at Irvine likes to lay the blame for over neglected mass transit systems on the oil industry and the vested interest he claims they have in promoting the automobile. (As if travel by automobile needed to be promoted!)

The truth is most Americans do not like to use mass transit; they have a love affair with their automobiles. Inexpensive gasoline, good highways and affordable cars all foster that love. Even the very poor own automobiles, with car payments taking up an estimated 20 to 40 percent of their household budgets, and those that don't own cars still prefer to ride in them. A study showed low income people in the 1970s accounted for 27 percent of all taxi rides but only 12 percent of all transit riders.[16] The fact is new systems haven't increased development, reduced traffic or helped the poor; new systems have merely cost taxpayers a huge amount of money. Yet Denver, Colorado has succeeded in convincing UMTA to cough up federal funds ($1 million startup costs) for a spanking new 17 mile mass-transit link between Denver's downtown and the southeast corridor. The system is estimated to cost $800 million with the federal government expected to foot approximately 40 percent of the bill, the other 60 percent to be financed via revenue bonds which are to be paid off by a tax on commercial property on either side of the route. Denver expects to have the system operating in three years with fares expected to carry 50 percent of operating costs, this despite the example of Washington D.C.'s Metro, which if you remember, was 7 years late and posts a $300 million annual operating loss. "Wallyrail's" (the Denver transit, named for promoter George Wallace) most attractive promise? To ease air pollution. It's biggest obstacle? To pry Denverites from their automobiles.

SO WHY DO YOU STAND FOR IT?

Policy makers all too often substitute their will for the will of the citizens. It is well to remember that government is not divine but a group of sometimes less than competent humans and what we mean by government interference is the imposition of the will of this small group over the will of others.

EDUCATION

DEMAGOGUERY

Listen to the demagoguery that met the Reagan administration's FY1988 budget in the area of education:

"The economic battles of tomorrow are being fought really in the classrooms of today and too many of our children are being disarmed unilateraly by educational policy and budget dogma that are both anti-student and anti-opportunity and anti-future. The prospects are bleakest for children most neglected in recent years."

Senator Ted Kennedy, Jan. 14, 1987
Labor & Human Resources Cmte.

"The fiscal 1988 federal-budget proposal for education would reduce access to college for millions of students, and should be rejected by all who care about the future of our nation and its economy."

Richard Rosser
President, Natnl Assn. of Independent
Colleges & Universities in a letter
to the Wall Street Journal 2/4/87

"This columnist finds it beyond understanding that a president who pledged to dam up 'a rising tide of mediocrity in American education, and who gives lip service to making America competitive again, would in a time of crippling trade and budget deficits try to cut federal funding for education by almost 30 percent."

Columnist Carl Rowan, Feb. 1987

Now what do you suppose brought on such a rash of eloquent outcrys? Over and over representatives of the Reagan administration reiterated that the federal contribution accounts for only 7 percent of the entire education budget in this country; 93 percent is funded by states and local governments. A document accompanying Secretary of Education William Bennett's 1986 annual report on the nation's schools showed "states with relatively high proportions of federal funding tend to have the poorest test results and graduation rates." So the outcry was over a reduction in federal funds. The $19.5 billion earmarked for education in the FY1987 budget was to be reduced in FY1988 to $14 billion mainly by substituting student loans for grants (gifts).

INCOME CONTINGENCY LOAN PROGRAM

Student loans extend, not deny, educational opportunities. The FY1988 budget requested $600 million for the Income Contingency Loan program (ICL) whereby a student repays money borrowed for college according to a repayment schedule based on his after-college income. Money could be borrowed for under-graduate or graduate education at an interest rate three percentage points above the Treasury bill rate. In order to give the new graduate time to get established, required payments would not exceed $30 per month for the first two years after graduation. The maximum anyone would ever have to repay under the new proposal is 15%.

In 1987 the ceiling on guaranteed student loans was raised to $17,000, to be increased to $50,000 if the Congress, by some miracle, decides to go along with the Department of Education's proposals for the FY1988 budget.

"Sure", said the critics, "more opportunity but at what cost and to whom? Gifts (grants) were free you know." ("Free" to whom from whom?) But the proponents had already thought a great deal about this fairness issue and were well prepared to do battle.

Borrowing for college expenses has tripled in the past decade from $3.5 billion in 1975–76 to $9.8 billion in the 1985–86 school year. A 1986 report from the College Board, concluded that data aren't available either to confirm or reject the contention that students are being overburdened by debt—in fact "overburdened" has yet to be defined.

The study found the total number of grants and loans remained at about $21 billion with the new emphasis on loans instead of grants. According to the National Association of Student Financial Aid Administrators Chronicle of Higher Education, the average student repaying a college loan in 1985 was 28 years old, owed approximately $6,500, earned a B average and made $1,000 per year in payments from his annual income of approximately $20,000. The cry of unfairness stems from findings that disparities continue between the salaries white males can expect upon graduation and those anticipated by women and minorities. The latter will not only find loans harder to repay but will end up paying more in stretched out interest payments.

Columnist Carl Rowan has been preoccupied with the income of the parents of black college students somehow inferring the parents' economic status would affect the student's ability to pay-off loans. He quoted Richard Rosser, president of the National Institute of Independent Colleges and Universities as saying: "These students, absolutely the truly neediest, are being hurt by a federal aid policy that asks many to take out college loans bigger than their families' incomes."[17] The size of their families' incomes should have little to do with paying-off a student's personal loan because if the family could afford to do the "paying" the loan would not have been made in the first place. It is hard to understand Mr. Rowan's contention that ". . . when the Reagan administration reduced grants and emphasized loans, it dealt a real blow to blacks who aspire to become scientists, physicians and mathematicians'."[18] In some cases this may be true as where the desire to help poor parents conflicts with the obligation to repay a loan as agreed. But personal desires and "outside" obligations are bound to conflict in everyone's life and this seems a spurious reason to denigrate the ICL proposals. And before you start calling me "cruel and heartless" you might as well know all five of our sons are expected "to work their way through" college so as to experience a sense of independence, self-worth, accomplishment and to achieve the status of "manhood" much sooner than their dependent peers. Some people are dependent all their lives and never begin to know what they are really capable of achieving.

Senator Claiborne Pell suggested to William Bennett, Secretary of Education who was testifying before the Senate Labor Committee on January 14, 1987,[19] that having to pay back college loans would limit the choice of jobs open to these college graduates. He pointed out that the lower paying social service jobs would go begging. When Secretary Bennett recalled that he had owed the equivalent of $30,000 in todays dollars when he graduated from law school and was not deterred from choosing a career in the much lower paid educational field as opposed to law, Senator Pell would not concede but scoffingly complimented the Secretary also pointing out that "not everyone has your drive and ambition."

In a similar vein, Senator Paul Simon told the Coalition for Higher Education Assistance Organizations[20] about a medical school graduate in his district (Greenfield, IL) who was $80,000 in debt and although he would have liked to serve in an inner city area, he couldn't according to Senator Simon, because he needed money to repay loans.

On January 19, 1987 Bruce Carnes from the Department of Education, argued with Senator Simon that the new proposal for income contingent loans offered more access and flexibility than student aid in the past and was also fairer to the taxpayers.

Many Senators have voiced various criticisms of the ICL (Income Contingent Loan) proposal. The program is not progressive. How is a graduate's income determined? Obtaining IRS data is difficult and it is not desirable to have the IRS collect debts owed to the federal government. A graduate could end up paying 21% for the life of the loan depending on the T-bill rate at the moment the loan was made if no adjustments are allowed. (Loans could be refinanced at anytime so the last is not a valid criticism.)

BACKWARD INCENTIVES

In response the Reagan Administration has pointed to the need-based student aid (Pell Grants, 1972) as being in part responsible for skyrocketing college costs which took off in the mid 1970s. In the past student aid has penalized savers (couldn't qualify) and provided no incentives for colleges to keep their costs down. Mark Tucher of the Carnegie Forum, spoke of our backward incentives and offered the "learning disabled" label as one example. Schools receive more money for "learning disabled" kids and therefore there is a certain reluctance to improve these kids and lose the additional monies the handicapped bring from the federal government.

Furthermore Mr. Carnes pointed out that the drop-out rate for kids on loans was lower than for those on grants. Apparently it is easier to walk away from someone else's investment. In 1985 the Department of Education reported that former undergraduate and graduate students defaulted on $3 billion in low-interest loans subsidized by the federal government under the Guaranteed Student Loan Program. An additional $1.1 billion had been defaulted in the National Direct Student Loan program of low-interest loans to students through their schools. Most graduates were earning money and simply making economic decisions not to repay the low-interest loans.

In the summer of 1985 the Department of Education asked the IRS to withhold taxrefunds from one million defaulters on federal student loans unless they started paying their debts. $229 million was collected in student loans in 1986 which shows the get-tough-policy paid off!

FAIRNESS

Mr. Carnes, in an effort to show fairness, talked about borrowing from the taxi driver (the new symbolic average man) rather than making him provide as a gift, a college education which would almost assuredly net the recipient-student more than the donor-taxi driver could hope to make in his working career. William Kristol[21] has pointed out that studies have shown the average college graduate makes $640,000 more than the average high school graduate over a lifetime. According to *American Demographics* magazine, households headed by college graduates had median incomes in 1985 which were 54 percent higher than incomes of high-school graduates. Senator Simon and other critics are quick to point out that the taxi driver should subsidize the college student because his job and his future depend to a large extent on the college educated. The Reagan administration, as far as I can tell, agrees with this analysis, the only question being how much should the taxi driver be expected to pay? Don't forget he's being asked to chip in for child-care so those with children can work, for farm subsidies so small farmers can keep their treasured way of life, for mass transit so people will have alternatives to his cab service, for parks, for highways, for schools he will never personally use—all for his own good. Perhaps the ultimate show of concern for his wallet was expressed by a Ms. Reynolds[22] of the California Board of Education who argued college educations should be more fully financed because college costs, on average, $5,000 per year and to keep a person in prison costs closer to $20,000 per year. The point being that the college educated are less likely to end up in prison. Violà; a $15,000 per year saving (or so she implied)! With the number of conscientious officials and bureaucrats looking for ways to save him money "in the long run", our taxi drivers won't have to worry about his own priorities—he won't have any income for them anyway!

SENATORS REFUSE TO CUT

It is hard to believe members of Congress have any inclination whatsoever to curtail spending. I offer the following quotes from a Senate Committee on Labor and Human Resources which aired on C-Span Jan. 14, 1987. You be the judge.

> "There is no legal obligation put upon you to cut your budget."
>
> Senator Lowell Weicker of Ct. to
> Secty of Education William Bennett

> "Gramm-Rudman didn't dictate these priorities—only the bottom line. . . . Ted Bell (Bennett's predecessor as Secretary of Education) was in there fighting for every dollar from OMB (Office of Management & Budget)—I just don't hear that fight from the Secretary of Education today."
>
> Senator Paul Simon of IL to
> Secty of Education, William Bennett

Senator Simon went on to state that it is the function of the Department of Education to *demand* more funds.

My own angry notation: "My G-d, these Senators aren't trying to cut spending; they're trying to expand and scurry around intent on ferreting every possible dollar."

MORE DOLLARS?

Over the past six years Congress has allocated $18.8 billion more to education than the Reagan Administration has requested. The fact is we spend more on education than the Japanese do; our system is simply inefficient and must be reformed. We can't go on viewing education as another target for the money slingers.

According to Secretary Bennett: "We have increased education spending by 300 percent in real dollars in 27 years and we have not increased the results in that proportion. . . The basic problem with American education is not that it is underfunded. It is underproductive and it is underaccountable. It is overregulated."[23]

Man is a combination of mind and body and the man who does no more than physical labor and let's his mind vegetate will probably end up providing necessities of life but no more. The man who studies, thinks and expands his mind may discover new knowledge and benefit himself while making society richer at the same time. But this will not occur because money was thrown at education. A mind is under an individual's control and society, via government mandates and dollars, can neither dictate nor prevent its use. Many of America's greatest success stories began with a human being in abject poverty, often not knowing the English language and forced to support a myriad of relations. Man's indomnitable spirit and determination can overcome any and everything if it is only given the freedom to express itself. The freedom and the need. All the hand-holding in the form of grants and subsidies will never make up for the force of will.

"The man at the top of the intellectual pyramid contributes the most to all those below him, but gets nothing except his material payment, receiving no intellectual bonus from others to add to the value of his time. The man at the bottom who, left to himself, would starve in his hopeless ineptitude, contributes nothing to those above him, but receives the bonus of all of their brains."[24]

SAY WHAT?

Perhaps it's time to set the record straight.

Hodding Carter III on April 2, 1987 referred to ". . . repeated studies of education that suggest that we need more, not less, investment in this basic element of national infrastructure (education)."[25] Such studies (they were not identified by Mr. Carter) would seem to refute Mr. Bennett's document mentioned on page 72 reportedly showing federal funding had an inverse affect.

How relevant is the recent finding by the Carnegie Task Force on Teaching that black teachers have dropped from 12 percent of the teaching force in 1970 to 8 percent in 1980 and are projected to make up only 5 percent of that group by 1990? Is it significant that over the past 15 years the percentage of minorities enrolled in the nation's prep schools has doubled? The National Association of Independent Schools included both private-boarding and day-college preparatory schools in the report it issued May 24, 1987. What are we to make of the May 21, 1987 passage of The School Improvement Act by the House on a 401–1 vote? (Phil Crane of Illinois was the only man brave enough to face probable denounciation as a foe of both education and children for voting against the legislation.) What can we believe about the New York system which excused itself for failing to close its schools in recognition of Passover because it would lose too much state aid? What do we do with the information offered by Secretary of Labor William Brock in his testimony before the House Education & Labor Committee On Welfare Reform (May 5, 1987) that in the seventies 48 percent of the education budget went to teachers; in the eighties that number fell to 38 percent. Are we satisfied with the Milpitas, California system which yanked a small young man, obviously hungering for an education, from its system when it discovered he was 23 years old and attending an 8th grade class? What is the proper response to the dismal test scores of the majority of American children in math and science? Does the answer lie with the teachers and their inability to motivate and instruct? Will the 25 grants given out on May 24, 1987 by Secretary Bennett have their intended effect—i.e "to boost teachers' understanding of math and science."? Should the August 1986 proposal of John Silver, President of Boston University, to grant tax incentives to companies allowing early retirement benefits to those qualified in science who will go into teaching be taken seriously? Will the National Science Foundation be given the funds it seeks in order to raise the number of University-based science, technology and engineering centers in the nation from the present 11 (1987) to 100 by 1992?

LOOK WHO FAVORS SUBSIDIZING!

Have you ever wondered why so many people in academia and journalism are biased towards and seem to empathize with subsidized institutions and industries? Could it be because the market value of the intellectual's output is not commensurate with input, since in the intellectual domain excellence is only recognized by a few? Businessmen are rewarded handsomely for filling established desires but the intellectual's goal is to change public opinion and the rewards for that are of a spiritual rather than a material nature.

SPIRITUAL REWARDS

People who recognize spiritual rewards will make the difference and turn around our educational system. That is the conclusion reached by a Department of Education report released in the spring of 1987 which highlighted men and women who by dedication, perseverance and hard work as principals of troubled elementary and secondary schools *were* able to turn poor schools into success stories. Of course they had help from parents and community but their own determination and optimism were the prime ingredients.

In his new book, *The Closing Of The American Mind,* University of Chicago philosophy professor, Allan Bloom laments the recent emphasis our colleges and universities have put on learning a skill at the expense of learning how to think; that's *how* to think, not *what* to think. He denounces academia's egalitarian idea of openess as ". . . not a means to exploring different answers to the great questions, but an excuse not to try to answer them at all."

Unfortunately Professor Bloom is not alone in his criticism of undergraduate education in America in the 1980s. The Department of Education, the National Endowment for the Humanities and the Carnegie Foundation have all come up with similar conclusions. Traditionally higher education gave us leaders, philosophers and statesmen—all sorely lacking in today's society but needed more than ever as science and technology open up possibilities that may best be left unopened or at least controlled.

As the late Frank H. Knight, founder of the "Chicago School" of economics once said, "The only hope for democracy is the intelligence and public spirit of the citizenship as a whole, for in the nature of democracy, whatever teachers and leaders it pays heed to must be chosen by itself."[26]

HEALTH

PRIORITIES

The first question to ask when there are limited resources and unlimited health-care needs is where can these limited dollars do the most good?

In the best of all possible worlds there would be no disease and in the runner-up world there would be adequate funding for research as well as funds for therapy and transplants. But that is a dream world; the reality is when one cause is undertaken another must be set aside. What do we do with the fact that cystic fibrosis affects 30,000 young people? Choices are a fact of life. Unforunately it has become standard practice to give taxpayer dollars to the squeakiest wheels; that is the whole purpose of lobbying.

More than 150,000 infants are at high risk for conjunctivitis (a serious eye infection) during birth and another 50,000 may not even get a chance at life as that many potential mothers are made infertile each year due to chlamydia. Chlamydia is a sexually transmitted disease which infects approximately 4.5 million people each year. Over the next five years 22.5 million people will be infected with chlamydia, almost one in every ten Americans. A nationwide control program would cost $50 to $60 million the first year according to Meredith Burke, writing for the Wall Street Journal early in 1987, and yet no (zero) federal funds are being set aside in the Administration's FY1988 budget because of limited resources.

In California Medi-Cal, the state and federally funded health-care program for the poor, has jumped beyond budgeted levels and the result has been an end to the surpluses. The billion-dollar reserve touted during Governor Deukmejian's reelection bid pretty much evaporated after the election. Only the windfall to the state, thanks to the 1986 federal tax reform legislation, could brighten the picture. Surpluses were an illusion manufactured by underestimating costs. Yet on March 24, 1987 state Health Services Director Kenneth Kiser announced AZT, the drug which is not a cure but prolongs the life of those with acquired immune deficency syndrome (AIDS) and has an estimated per patient annual cost of between $7,000 and $10,000, would be available to Medi-Cal patients at no cost to them or with an optional $1 per perscription fee. That brief announcement could cost California taxpayers an estimated additional $7.5 million in 1988 and chances are many who would not otherwise have the incentive to do so will find ways to qualify for Medi-Cal.

Dr. John J. Coury Jr. of Monterey told a Rotary Club audience recently that the financial cost of AIDS is enormous, estimating an expense of $40,000 to $150,000 per case. If the Center for Disease Control in Atlanta is correct we can expect 270,000 cases of AIDS over the next five years which means, according to these figures, that AIDS could conceivably cost the nation over $40 billion by 1991 without even considering the productivity drain on the country due to loss of citizens in prime working years and the emotional impact such a tragedy would have. Dr. Coury went on to state matter of factly that the cost has to be borne because AIDS victims ". . . are human beings and they must receive compassionate care and treatment." "Must"? It is a choice that many Americans, if given a choice, would freely make. But "must"?

TOUGH QUESTIONS

How much protection do we want from government and what are we willing to pay in terms of freedom as well as dollars?

The Baby Doe case, in the news a few years ago, is a good example. The issue was whether the government could force the Does into an operation which might prolong the life of their badly handicapped child. The courts decided the government had no rights here. Yet isn't it one of government's roles to protect the lives of its citizens? Isn't a baby born in America a citizen of the United States? Legally—yes. Then doesn't government have to interfere?

The majority of Americans who were polled concerning the Doe case felt strongly that the government should not meddle in private family affairs. Then who, if anyone or any entity, should decide who is to live or who is to die and on what basis?

How does one determine the "quality" of life—especially for someone else? Would the DeBolt's[27] adopted daughter, Karen, born without arms and legs, have been judged to have such a low quality of life ahead of her that the government should look the other way if no one were to help her survive her first few days of life? What about Helen Keller? Should she have been put out of the supposed misery of living in a no-man's-land with neither sight nor hearing? Yet any who are familiar with the lives of either Karen DeBolt or Helen Keller would agree that these are two of the happiest and most inspirational persons to have lived.

Should one be allowed to live out his own destiny or be eased out of life by a benevolent society? Isn't failure to act, i.e. not to feed, operate or hook up to an available life support system, as culpabale as the overt act of taking life? The law indeed says "yes", but only if there was in fact a *duty* to act.

We're back to the original problem—what is government's duty in this regard? Does age make a difference? Does the government have a duty to a fetus? A newborn? A two year old? Anyone between the ages of 12–18 or just those over age 21?

Should one be allowed to practice euthanasia—to disconnect a person from a machine so they might die (here comes one of those buzz words) "in dignity"?

Again, who decides? The family who must foot the bill for keeping a commotose loved one alive on a machine? The doctor? The competent but suffering patient himself? Should government have anything to say about genetic engineering? Sperm banks? Cybornetics? Artificial insemination? Test-tube babies?

Is it inevitable that society be controlled in the final analysis, by science and technology? Genetic engineers are closing in on the BRAVE NEW WORLD scenario. Cloning is possible on some levels; many defects can be detected before birth and aborted. Sperm banks and test-tube babies are realities in the eighties. Technology is, as usual, far ahead of the philosophers and statesmen. It may soon be possible to genetically plan society to be harmonious, content and productive. Perhaps mankind is evolving to the higher order of the honey bee. An elite agressive, ambitious few supported by content working drones (Please—that's "tongue-in-cheek").

TRYING TO ACHIEVE EQUALITY

Those who worship the concept of equality are deluding themselves if they think equality can be purchased with tax dollars. There is no such thing on this earth as true equality. Even at birth some babies are born healthy and others with deformities, some are born into financially secure families and others to families living in poverty, some have loving productive parents who will read to them and encourage them and others are born to parents with emotional problems who will beat and otherwise abuse them.

What's fair? What's equal? Better to ask what is the proper function of government!

NOT DOWN BUT UP

The renowned economist, John Galbraith, has been quoted as saying: "We have been slow in accepting that a more equal society means levelling down." I for one refuse to ever accept such a notion! As Americans our mission is to inspire and pull others up. Our ideology is based on opportunity and upward mobility.

It has been said that socialists view a man in a fine grand house, driving a fancy car and enjoying all manner of luxuries and think

"No one should have so much." A capitalist looks at the same man and says, "Everyone should have as much."

How often have you heard that one of the tests of a civilized society is how well it cares for the weak, for the elderly, for the poor, for the young? How often have you heard it said that one of the tests of a civilized society is how much freedom and opportunity it allows its people?

According to some estimates 35 million persons are without health insurance in this country. Who is to be responsible for them? Should we *make* them self-insure? Should we *make* employers provide insurance for them? Should we *make* those who have made sacrifices in order to provide for their own families also take these people under their wing?

The Associated Press on December 29, 1986 released an article by Mary Helen Gillespie in which she reported the plight of a 40 year old man who had such severe allergies he was forced to live in a "shiny cocoon" of tinfoil. He required all sorts of special care with clothing, food, masks for breathing, medication and tin foil covering his room and most everything in it. The family, headed by a far from wealthy retired railroad worker, paid for everything themselves and sought no outside help. Of course it was a struggle to do it "on their own". Should this family then be taxed to help another family down the street who has different priorities; to whom self-reliance means little? PRIORITIES—let people make their own and don't penalize some at the expense of others.

Each person has his own life to live and it is not the business of government to tell its citizens where the starting line is. My namesake, Helen Keller, worked for years just to communicate but found her blindness was nothing compared to the ignorance in which so many sighted people were entrapped. She once said: "My darkness has been filled with the light of intelligence, and behold, the outer day-lit world was stumbling and groping in social blindness."

A similiar idea has been attributed to John Kennedy: "I do not say that all men are equal in their ability, character and motivation, I do say that every American should be given a fair chance to develop all the talents he may have." Who could disagree? Almost everyone when it comes to interpretation.

FAIR CHANCE?

Questions are infinite. Is it fair for a walking man to be able to use public transportation which is not accessible to a man in a wheelchair?

Is it fair for a child whose family provides a higher education for him to have advantages like extra time for studies and so forth that is denied to a student who must work his way through college?

Is it fair for some elderly people to be well cared for while others languish in poverty and neglect?

These are loaded questions. Who would oppose the poor, sick, elderly, or very young? Who can afford to ignore cost?

WHAT ABOUT COST?

Poor people often wait for an ailment to worsen and then use hospital emergency services; the most expensive form of medical care; twice what it would cost in a clinic.

Laws to provide emergency treatment exist but the definition of emergency is varied and often vague. A common definition is prevention of death and serious illness. The emergency is generally considered to end with the treatment given in an emergency room. What then?

I recall a discussion of this topic on a popular San Francisco radio talk-show which took place on February 16, 1986. The hostess responded to an irate caller who asked, "At what point in our history did medical care become a right?" with the usual "richest country in the world" rhetoric. A spokesperson from a local county hospital (taxpayer supported) called to relate his experience with an illegal alien who had escaped from official custody and was being pursued by the police at the time of his admittance to the hospital. Open heart surgery was performed and Alameda county picked up the tab for $20,000 to $30,000. The comments of the talk-show hostess revealed an attitude which is common in our society and which needs to be examined. The fact that someone else had to do without because scarce dollars were used in behalf of a non-citizen who happened to also be a fugitive from our laws, to this radio personality was a signal that the county simply did not get enough money. She was proud that indigents in this country get ("and are *entitled* to") the same care as President Reagan. (Perhaps you've noticed whenever people talk of entitlements and rights they seldom explain "how entitled" or by what logic or justice and at whose expense.)

An incensed listener called saying that anyone who had two cars had no right to publicly provided medical care—they should be obligated to spend money on medical insurance like other prudent people do. The hostess adroitly turned the statement to provide an entree into insurance-company-bashing by *agreeing* that it is a tragedy that many people are denied insurance.

ECONOMICALLY JUSTIFIABLE? NO WAY!

She would no doubt find herself in agreement with Robert Kuttner, who sometimes writes for the *New Republic*. In the June 30, 1986 issue of *Business Week* magazine he says: "What is perfectly rational for the profit-maximizing insurer—to deny coverage to people in high-risk groups—is irrational for society."

Steve Kelman, professor of public policy at the John Kennedy School of Government at Harvard, shares Mr. Kuttner's concern that cost-benefit analysis might be applied to social problems in order to justify giving aid. Both gentlemen think as collectivists in terms of obligation and duty supposedly imposed on society. ("*We* have an obligation" "*We* have failed to help") Professor Kelman fails to realize that the end of such thinking leads to the opposite of what he supposes and is instead the very cause of the problem he purports to solve. He suggests that a cost-benefit analysis might well show ". . . that the discounted present value of the benefits society gains in the future from helping people is less than the cost to society of helping them right now, that doesn't mean we shouldn't help." He finds an economic approach ". . . oddly out of step with the American tradition of cherishing individuals, for it takes our attention away from individual human beings. It is too ready to sacrifice an unfortunate minority on the altar of the maximum collective benefits."[28]

COLLECTIVE THINKING

That is the logical end of collective thinking. In the American tradition in which individuals are cherished, collectives (substitute government entities) do not help groups or individuals but individuals relate to one another as free agents according to the priorities dictated, not by majority rule, but by their own non-legislated individual ethical and moral code or lack thereof. Churches and other volunteer social organizations are a large part of the American tradition. Coercive government has too long usurped the role of charitable organizations and in the process given amunition to those who would point to a selfish immoral America.

Free (uncontrolled) enterprise means if one person does not satisfy our desires we can turn to another. We determine what is to be produced by directing our dollars. Socialists cannot tolerate the fact that dollars rather than needs should determine how a nation's resources are used. But that is the only way a minority can have a say. Under the philosophy of the highest good for the most a minority's wishes would be disregarded. In view of that fact it is truly amazing that when Russell Long retired from the Senate at the end of 1986 after 38 years in Congress he summed up his philosophy: "To adjust ourselves to what we think is the best for the most."

Professor Kelman concludes his article by saying "There's one thing worse than a bleeding heart, and that's a cold one." Some people have a tendency to label anyone who disagrees with them as selfish, insensitive and devoid of compassion all the while seeing themselves as big-hearted, generous, selfless and beneficent.

Northwestern Insurance Company stated recently (early 1987) that it was paying an average of $147,000 per AIDS patient and had already paid out close to $6 million. If insurance companies are not permitted to screen out possible AIDS victims who's going to pay? Naturally it will have to come from increased premiums on *everyone's* insurance policies. I realize Mr. Kuttner and the radio hostess I alluded to are not alone in their sincere belief that *everyone should* pay for the unfortunate. However, there are others who believe that those who do not want to help, or are themselves financially unable to help, should not be forced to do so. In a free country one person or group should not be permitted to tell others what they should or *must* do with their dollars. If organizations like the United Way, Salvation Army, Red Cross, Alcoholics Aynonomous, Goodwill Industries, St. Vincent de Paul and so on and so forth, presented the case of the needy to the American people, and, as in the best of all possible worlds, they responded, freedom for all would be preserved. But, as James Madison once said, if men were angels no government would be needed.

PROBLEMS INHERENT IN A FREE-MARKET

What about the free loaders?

In the Harvard Law Review (April 1972) Guido Calabresi and A. Douglas Melamed discuss pareto optimality, the idea that individuals know best what is best for them as opposed to paternalism. Pareto optimality, they say, can be approached more closely by systems which involve some coercion than by a system of totally free bargains. "All societies have wealth distribution preferences. . . Difficult as wealth distribution preferences are to analyze, it should be obvious that they play a crucial role in the setting of entitlements."

The authors refer to three types of entitlements:

1) Entitlements protected by property rules (trade voluntarily—least amount of government intervention)

2) Entitlements protected by liability rules (government sets value—eminent domain)

3) Inalienable entitlements (transfer not permitted by society)

They say on page 1107 "There is no reason to believe that a market, a decentralized system of valuing, will cause people to express their true valuations and hence yield results which all would in fact agree are desirable." Therefore since this is true the authors think the justification is given to allow deviation from the market and permission is given to decide the value collectively and impose it by force. This, they say, would eliminate potential hold-out and free-loader problems. It is, they believe, too difficult and too expensive to use market methods to exclude free-loaders and avoid hold-outs. Further "Liability rules represent only an approximation of the value of the object to its original owner and willingness to pay such an approximate value is no indication that it is worth more to the thief than to the owner. . . no guarantee of the economic efficiency of the transfer."

But in favor of liability rules is the fact that "distributive goals" are served by them rather than by property rules. Of course that leaves the questions of *whose* goals and one wonders if paternalism might not creep in here.

The authors use the following illustration to back up their earlier contention that systems which involve some coercion approach pareto optimality more closely than systems dependent on completely free bargains:

They speak of Factory A which employs poor workers but creates pollution as a by-product which harms B's homes. Choices given are:

1) Enjoin Factory A (Possible good economic efficiency effects if it is found pollution hurt B more than A saved by using cheap coal but poor distributive effects.)

2) Nusiance damage (Poor distributive effects as both A and workers are hurt, but good economic effect for B.)

3) No Nusiance (Good distributive and poor economic.)

4) Compel A to use better more expensive coal and pay A to do so. (Good distributive and good economic effects.)

Although Mr. Calabresi and Mr. Melamed favor alternate #4 I would still advocate only property rights and am willing to suffer with the hold-out and free-loader problems until someone comes up with a better solution than suffering just a smidgin of coercion. That is too high a price to pay.

Just to tie up loose ends regarding the "inalienable entitlements"—the authors believe it is cheaper to disallow their transfer. Simple! They go on to state that the external costs may justify inalienability when those costs "do not lend themselves to collective measurement which is acceptably objective and nonarbitrary. . . . Such external costs are often called moralisms." Selling organs or children would make others unhappy so it isn't allowed. However reading certain books, seeing certain movies may make some people unhappy but these acts are nevertheless permitted. Why? The simplest answer is the unhappiness they cause is not as widespread.

DISCRIMINATION AND DISTRIBUTIVE JUSTICE

In a collectivist society allocation of resources is a real problem. That was vividly brought home to me by a letter to the editor of the Wall Street Journal in late October, 1986. The writer used ambiguous terminology. He spoke of "distributive justice" which I found meant something different to the writer than to me and probably no two people who read those words would agree on the meaning.

"Discrimination" has been identified so closely with civil rights and racism that its normal meaning has been forgotten. However it is impossible to live a rational life indiscriminatingly. We discriminate when we choose a Ford over a Ferrari or peas over broccoli. The physician writer dismissed as nothing more than an evil temptation the very thought of making decisions about how to allocate scarce resources on the apparently wicked basis of ability to pay, ability to contribute to society, and "individual merit."

The reason I remember the letter so vividly is that it was written by an educated adult American who thought enough about the issue to write a letter to a newspaper and yet his conclusion was like that of the Senators whose only suggestion to eliminate bridge traffic was to build another bridge. The writer concluded that the best way to ensure "fairness" (whatever that is) is to have a lottery for prospective transplant recipients. Apparently he felt mankind had not progressed beyond the reading-entrails-and-casting-lots stage.

Here we are on the brink of the 21st century being advised to leave life and death decisions to chance.

THE BOWEN PLAN

President Reagan has endorsed the plan of Otis Bowen, Secretary of Health and Human Services, to provide coverage against catastrophic illness to the approximately 30 million elderly Americans eligible for Medicare. For an additional fee of only $4.92 per month on the Part B premium, the federal government would pick up all hospital and doctor expenses over an initial outlay of $2,000 (deductible) per year. Many conservative Congressman think the Bowen plan is too vague and also does nothing that cannot be provided as effectively by private insurance.

According to James Moorefield, President of Health Insurance Association of America, only one in a thousand of those eligible for Medicare stays in the hospital over 60 days each year. The real need is for long term custodial care as the growth of the 85 plus segment of the population picks up momentum. Only about 130,000 people had private nursing home coverage as 1987 began because, says Mr. Moorefield, "Myths about Medicare's coverage of long-term care have hampered the growth of such insurance products, simply because most people think that they don't need the protection of long-term care coverage."[29] In 1986, of the $39 billion spent on nursing home care, private insurance and Medicare each paid under 2 percent, approximately 50 percent was paid by patients and their families and the rest was picked up by Medicaid which kicks in only after a patient has been impoverished.

Liberal Congressmen, like Henry Waxman of California are convinced the Bowen plan does not go far enough; it does not cover long-term nursing home care, prescription drugs or eye or dental care. Senator David Durenberger of Minnesota echoes the "far too little" cry as did Claude Pepper of Florida who plans to introduce a bill in the 100th Congress to include coverage of Alzheimer's disease, Parkinson's disease and hearing aids. Private insurance and government health care programs generally will pay for treatment in hospitals more readily than similar care at home even though home care is cheaper. Congressman Pepper's bill would change this kind of nonsense. It would also make it possible to purchase additional insurance through Medicare. For $60 per month or 20 percent of a person's income the elderly could gain protection against, among other things, the cost of long term custodial nursing home care. It's not often that I find myself in agreement with the distinguished Senator from Florida but in this case I totally agree the need is for long term care which should be funded by increased premiums and higher deductibles and could be done by the private sector if the government didn't preclude it.

Secretary Bowen favors tax incentives to encourage people to fund their own plans for long-term care. The 1986 tax reform discouraged IRAs somewhat but did not do away with them completely. Without IRAs private retirement savings in general would be seriously weakened. Since IRA funds immediately belong to workers, vesting problems are done away with and workers experience the freedom and self-reliance that comes from not being tied to any one company. With private pensions often a worker is forced to rely on others (see "portable pensions" discussed elsewhere) and is even more helpless when it comes to Social Security where retirement benefits can be reduced or even lost for a variety of reasons.

LET'S SIMPLY REQUIRE . . .

Senator Edward Kennedy, new chairman of the Senate Labor and Resources Committee, an old pro at mandating benefits to foster social goals, has done it again with proposed legislation to require businesses with 20 or more employees to provide minimum health insurance for those that work more than 17½ hours per week.

Former Secretary of Health and Human Services, Joseph Califano testified before the Committee on Labor and Human Resources on January 19, 1987: "What we need is a minimum health-care law just as we have a minimum wage law. Let's simply require that each employer assure its employees of a minimum level of health care—physician treatment, hospitalization, preventive service for the employee and his or her family."

In 1986 the nation's health care cost amounted to almost $450 billion or 11 percent of GNP. In 1986 employers contributed $90 billion towards employees health care or 20 percent of the total but it is NEVER ENOUGH!

Senator Kennedy came up with a plan no one could be against—if it were free. To solve this *one and only objection* the costs are dumped on the private sector, which then redistributes them by reducing wages, lowering dividends, raising prices and delaying capital improvements—Senator Kennedy's idea of *free!*

The House has an alternate plan with no more thought given to preserving freedom than the Senator's proposal: ". . . legislation is being drafted that would use revenues raised by a new tax on insurance companies to pay the costs of free hospital care."[30] When will our officials acknowledge that nothing is free—costs are only transferred from one segment of society to another.

ANOTHER RIGHT?

In opening the Committee hearing on January 12, 1987, Senator Kennedy declared "Already a new consensus is emerging to assure that every citizen has access to the essential health care that constitutes simple justice." (more gobbledygook) On access, Mr. Califano said that "good health is not a right but access to good health care is." Rights, Shmites—somewhere on the left a new "right" is born every day. He went on to admonish listeners that no society can deny the right of its citizens to necessary health care. Nice sounding words with no meaning. "Society" (a group of individuals) can do anything they choose to do in a free country as long as they do it within the limits prescribed, in America's case, by the Constitution. Nevertheless Mr. Califano pontificated that we have denied citizens the *right* to health care for too long and joined a long list of the righteous who like to point out that "We are the only industrial society that does not . . ."

THOSE "OTHER COUNTRY" EXAMPLES

Always there are those who point in admiration to the free health care provided by socialist and communist countries. How often we have heard that America is "the only industrialized society that does not . . ." Don't these people ever wonder why it is people from all over the world are trying to get into this supposedly heartless, uncaring country which provides citizens, aliens and visitors with the best of everything?

According to Kenneth Prager, a physician who in 1987 wrote about his experiences with the Soviet health care system, that system is far from "free"—that is if a patient desires clean linen and delivery of medications. Forget about meals—those must be brought to patients from home—an idea which many hospital patients would no doubt love to see emulated in this country. Cash or other goods must change hands if a really competent physician is to be secured and the same goes for many medications. What is not "allowed" on the surface goes on underground. Human nature does not change when a political system does. There is a hierarchy of medical facilities, technology and care in the Soviet Union with the best in all cases being imported from abroad. Modern medicine, as we have found in this country, is very expensive and the Soviets have chosen to allocate their limited resources to military and space technology. As a consequence there are shortages of everything from wheelchairs to needles and scapels which, as they become dull through overuse, cause more pain than an American would put up with. Syringes, catheter and intravenous tubing are reused with increased risk of infection and, according to Dr. Prager, "The aged are afraid of being hospitalized. In a medical system that is chronically short of the most basic supplies, the elderly are considered expendable and will be the first to feel the brunt of such shortages."[31]

WHO PAYS?

According to Mr. Califano, the total annual cost of uncompensated care is over $8 billion which is borne by providers who shift costs to employers who do provide health benefits. We have seen this over and over; the healthy and prudent paying for the weak or imprudent—the ant paying for the grasshopper—the little red hen being forced to be a cool chick and share her bread. Is this what you want? It is not happening by divine right—it is not even written in stone that hard working prudent Americans should be forced to play the chump—it is government policy, that's all and those elected men and women can be changed. I'm not even suggesting it's bad—I'm just asking you to recognize the situation for what it is and intelligently and willfully choose to reject it. This is probably the only country in the world where you can still determine policy, only unhappily a great many citizens no longer believe this is the case. Just realize that making it easy for people to be dependent encourages dependence and this has been the fear of thoughtful policy-makers for 200 years. Also be aware that helping and sharing with others is universally one of the greatest feelings a human being can experience and when it is taken over by government and you are forced to "share" by proxy something wonderful has been taken from you. People who want the freedom to say "yes" or "no" are not selfish—far from it. They are often compassionate human beings who are trying to preserve something that is precious to everyone; something that has been unique to our system of government and that the founders realized was fragile.

SENATE COMMITTEE ON AGING JANUARY 26, 1987

I took notes on a hearing that occured on January 26, 1987 before the Senate Committee on Aging which I wish to share with you, not because anything very newsworthy took place there but because of the mood that dominated.

Senator John Heinz said: "We stand at a crossroads, either we expand or cave in to compulsive budgeteers." Words with no relation to reality. If there is a compulsive budgeteer he is definitely not strong enough to pose a threat of the sort that Senator Heinz seems to be gathering forces to face, and if he were he would be a shoo-in for President in 1988. As Senator Heinz continued he made it clear he did not want to stop with the limited catastrophic coverage proposed by Secretary Bowen (which the President not long after this hearing endorsed) but was going to fight for a more comprehensive coverage for all Americans regardless of age or ability to pay.

Mrs. X,[32] a 68 year old lady from Beaver Dam, Wisconsin, testified about the illness of her 73 year old husband, a former civil service employee once with the weather bureau and the IRS and then 21 years as a self-employed tax consultant. Unfortunately Mr. X contracted heart disease in 1980 and the couple were forced to sell their home and move into a small apartment. Thirty percent of their income was earmarked for the portion of health care not reimbursed by Medicare or private insurance. (Average is 15%) Over the past seven years bills had stacked up. Mrs. X expressed a fear that she might have to turn for financial help to her 75 year old brother who was apparently healthy and lived on a boat.

Senator Melcher asked Mrs. X: "You will be able to pay these bills with the help of your brother?" She answered: "Yes—No—I shouldn't have said that. That would be asking him to sacrifice and I don't want to do that." Mrs. X had not looked into the possibility of receiving Medicaid.

Mrs. Y of Alma, Oklahoma, a 68 year old lady making $600 a month working as a cook, and whose 83 year old husband was in a nursing home, testified next. Because of the way Medicare is set up she really could not afford to quit working, according to her testimony. People help her, voluntarily, not because they are forced to do so, but because she is a pleasant, likeable, jolly lady. She told the Senators that her insurance agent had sent in the insurance coverage for her car knowing she'd pay him, although she doesn't know how or when. She doesn't like "people" to do favors for her.

Throughout the hearing Senators continually put words in the mouths of those who testified. In a court room it would be called "leading the witness" but in the committee hearing no one was there to object.

Senator Heinz asked: "Should families be doing more, should people themselves be doing more or should government be doing more here?" What would Mrs. Y answer? Senator Heinz knew what he hoped she would answer but she said she didn't know. Undaunted Senator Heinz tried another tactic: "Would you have paid $100 a month starting at age 45 for *real* security? (What *else* could she have answered?)

Senator Pressler began by pointing out that what we had here was the typical white middle class in trouble. He asked Mrs. Y what kind of insurance she should have bought? She answered that 20 years ago she didn't think of insurance. Senator Pressler reassured her "There's no way you could have managed better."

In response to a question from Senator Pete Wilson she answered that she refused to pay $60 a month to keep up her husband's supplemental insurance (got to be too expensive) and she never looked into Medicaid. She felt bad about taking money for her utility bills from her one daughter and son-in-law; just as badly as Mrs. Y would have felt taking help from her brother.

It is not uncommon to feel terrible about taking help from family and friends, it's so much easier to look to government to fill the void. People seem to forget the government means young families with new babies, other older people struggling, middle aged folks caring for aging parents while putting the kids through college.

The following exchange displays real artistry in leading the witness.

Senator Melcher to Mrs. Y: "Shouldn't somebody step in here and take care of this?" Mrs. Y: "Well, I think they should." Senator: "Who?" Mrs. Y: "I think the government." Senator (in his best patronizing manner): "I kinda thought that's what you wanted to say . . . There ought to be someone picking up this tab." Senator Melcher went on to say that "our question" (presumably the Senate Committee's) "is how high a priority is it?" Mrs. Y's parting sentiment: "I just like to pay my honest debts so I can face people."

Mrs. Z of Newpost, Michigan appeared on behalf of her 97 year old mother. Mrs. Z reminded me of Ms. Reynolds, whom you may recall, tried to save our representative taxpayer, the taxi driver, $15,000 by getting him to put up $5,000 for college expenses to avoid the $20,000 he might otherwise be forced to pay to keep a potential delinquent in prison. Mrs. Z exhibited the same tendency to "blackmail" when she spoke of home care assistance as far more "profitable for the government . . . they have to pay less."

Do you find it the least bit strange that *everyone* is *entitled* to care? Throughout this hearing the real question has not been "should government pay?" but only "how much?".

Senator Pressler to Mrs. Z: (leading the witness again) "Are the people in you situation those who have worked hard, had small savings and owned a house?" Obviously the Senator is appealing to the large middle class voters, sensing perhaps, a certain intolerance for the overworked appeal to befriend the "poor, the sick, the elderly"? Of course Mrs. Z answered yes to the Senator's question, admitting that the middle class is in trouble. Senator Pressler: "Was there any way you could have planned?" (He obviously wants her to say no.) Mrs. Z: "Yes." She says that people could have planned better, people don't think; people have to be educated. Although this is not what Senator Pressler wanted to hear he plunges ahead spouting the words he wants to have in the record: "Even if you had bought insurance, you'd find no way to escape your situation without government providing some kind of catastrophic insurance." Remember, the Senator drew this conclusion, not Mrs. Z.

All three ladies thought they could have done better, but the Senators excused them and patronized them until they began to see themselves as heroines and the Senators as Gods.

WELFARE

AID TO FAMILIES WITH DEPENDENT CHILDREN (AFDC)

The Reagan Administration has compiled a list of 59 federally assisted programs that it considers welfare. Medicaid, which provides health care assistance to the elderly, is the biggest spender. However, AFDC (Aid to Families with Dependent Children) which began modestly as a minor part of the 1935 Social Security Act as a program to tide widows and children over until survivors claims were available, in 1986 "rang up $2 billion in federal, state and local administrative costs and dispensed an estimated $15.8 billion in benefits. . . . The federal government pays, on the average, 54% of the costs."[33]

Over the years, rightly or wrongly, AFDC has been blamed for encouraging young women to have babies they can't support; babies who will end up supporting them by serving as a meager, but steady, meal ticket. Since in the past AFDC has presented an attractive alternative—a step up the ladder for many—current reformers propose to add one more rung. Help with education, job training, work placement, child-care and health insurance should make workfare even more attractive than passively receiving AFDC benefits. Unhappily the biggest problem is not attracting recipients to workfare, it is attracting taxpayers. Time magazine (2/16/87) reported that a New York task force estimated extending three parts of its workfare program, child-care, education and training and administering the guaranteed jobs program nationwide, would cost $5.9 billion annually. Proponents ask us to view the additional $5.9 billion as an investment which over time will decrease the current outlay of almost $18 billion as former recipients become taxpayers, (an argument which would no doubt infuriate Professor Kelman—see p. 84). But the disillusionment with AFDC, whether administered as a traditional welfare program or as some form of workfare, goes deeper than cost. A program formulated to pay mothers to stay home with their children is bound to encounter difficulty when it has to be financed by working mothers.

WORKFARE

When Ronald Reagan was governor of California, he was unsuccessful in his attempt to tie welfare to work. As President, however, in his 1981 Budget Act he convinced Congress to allow states to test new employment approaches to welfare reform, including workfare.

Workfare more often means job-search-help rather than actual government jobs. According to Douglas Besharov of the American Enterprise Institute,[34] about half of new entrants to AFDC will use the program as a temporary crutch for an average of 4 years whereas the other half will average almost 7 years on the program with a quarter of those receiving aid for 10 years or more.

In the 1960s and 70s it was considered cruel to require unfortunate people to work (slave) in order to receive help, but in the 1980s the consensus seems to be that a combination of education and work are essential to encourage sound habits of self-reliance and bolster the morality of the country.

Our federal welfare system encompasses at least 59 programs incorporating more than 6,000 pages of regulations. One of the Reagan administration's goals is to turn more of the administration back to the states. Most governors are wary of plans offering increased flexibility as they have come to recognize that as an attempt by the administration to put more expenses onto the states in return.

The Work Incentive (WIN) program required recipients to register but not necessarily participate in work programs if their children were at least six years old. The Department of Health and Human Services has proposed a program for FY1988, GROW (Greater Opportunities Through Work—cute, eh?) which requires participation by parents of children over six months of age.

The Governors, at their meeting in February 1987, proposed a $1 billion program (85 percent to be funded by the federal government) calling for a national standard of need and minimum level of benefits to be adjusted for geographic differences and tied to a percentage of the poverty standard, meaning more COLAS. (Yeeeek!)

"There will, of course, be a certain number of relief cases where work will not furnish the answer but it is my thought that in these cases all of the relief expenditures should once more be borne by the States and localities as they used to be."[35] A free book to anyone who writes to me correctly identifying who said the above and when. (On you honor, of course, not to consult the footnotes.)

Books have been and are yet to be written on the subject of welfare reform. My intention here is to question if the money spent is a legitimate and judicious use of taxpayers dollars (oh yes and in 25 words or less . . .)

Perhaps my point can be made best by referring to Massachusetts' voluntary and highly publicized workfare program, ET (Employment & Training Choices). ET provides job training, a year's free child care, a back-to-work clothing allowance, a travel allowance and four months of free Medicaid to participants. According to Massachusetts' governor, Michael Dukakis, ET *saved* the Massachusetts' taxi driver over a $100 million in 1986. Since ET's inception in 1983, Massachusetts had placed 30,000 welfare recipients in jobs, with an average starting salary of $12,000. Each placement reportedly saved the state almost $8,000 through reduced AFDC, Medicaid and food stamp outlays.

Not surprisingly the senior Senator from Massachusetts, Edward Kennedy, is enthusiastic about using ET as a model for a national program. Before we start tallying up the *savings,* let's give an ear to the critics of ET.

Warren Brookes, in the January 19, 1987 edition of the Wall Street Journal, cast his vote for New Hampshire's workfare program over ET. Brookes claimed FIP (Family Incentive Plan—New Hampshire's workfare) is less elaborate and more than six times cheaper than ET. Under FIP the New Hampshire caseload for AFDC fell 30 percent whereas the Massachusetts' caseload fell 4.4 percent, according to Governor Dukakis, over the same period of time.[36] (Brookes claimed an increase.)[37] New Hampshire's Governor Sununu attributes FIP's success to a booming economy with only 2.2 percent unemployment rate (Massachusetts' rate is 4.2 percent; both states enjoy rates substantially below the national average) and caseworker incentives based on the number of AFDC recipients placed in jobs. New Hampshire also made an important commitment not to reduce staff as caseloads fell. Massachusetts may not have to cope with that problem. According to the U.S. Department of Health and Human Services over the slightly more than three years of ET's existence, new applications for welfare have increased 9 percent. Under federal regulations an increase in benefits expands the number of eligible families.[38]

LEGISLATING COMPASSION

Despite the increase in benefits afforded by ET, a welfare-rights advocate group called the Coalition For Basic Human Needs sued Massachusetts to force it to just about double its cash grants to welfare recipients. On January 5, 1987, Superior Court Judge Charles M. Grabau of Boston, interpreted a 1913 Massachusetts' statue, ensuring adequate shelter, to mean that the state must provide benefits sufficient to enable healthy circumstances for raising children. Judge Grabau has enlisted this broad interpretation of the statute to justify his ruling that monthly benefits to a family of three on Massachusetts' welfare roles be increased from $491 to $845. Massachusetts, represented by Judge Charles Grabau, is a state that would never think of legislating morality but it (he) is attempting to legislate compassion.

If you live in Massachusetts don't you think it's time to speak out? If you live in any of the other 49 states (federal government provides half of all AFDC grants) how long are you going to take it? If you keep quiet, reassuring yourself these cases are merely occasional deviations from the norm—headline grabbers that pose no real threat, then it may be too late for all of us.

I have no quarrel with those who would idealistically prefer action to rhetoric. Who would not prefer to see Mrs. Y, the 68 year old lady cooking in a supper club in Alma, Oklahoma, reading a book on her porch, lying in the sun or knitting sweaters for her grandchildren? I want to see a cure for AIDS and cystic fibrosis and cancer and —*you* could fill a book with similar words. Wanting good things for others is a normal human feeling; such wants make us social beings. But in Massachusetts "wants" have been given the force of law.

IS THIS A JOB FOR THE FEDS?

The January 1987 edition of the American Bar Association Journal assured its readers that "Lawyers are litigating on behalf of the homeless, promoting the passage of federal assistance and sponsoring legal outreach programs at shelters across the nation." That's all well and good for those who agree with David Crossland, co-chairman of the Washington D.C. Bar's Ad Hoc Committee on the Homeless, that "Only the federal government can adequately respond to the huge problem of homelessness."[39]

In Coker v Bowen, plaintiffs, including the National Coalition for the Homeless, are suing the U.S. Department of Health and Human Services to make it force the 25 states participating in the Emergency Assistance to Families (EAF) program to provide either shelter, the dollars to obtain shelter, or assistance in securing shelter to homeless families which they claim participation in EAF requires.

SO WHO'S BLAMING THE DEMOCRATS FOR THE DEFICIT?

I followed closely the House debate in early March 1987 which ended by authorizing $500 million (on top of the $6 billion already available to ease the plight of the poor) for emergency aid to the Homeless—an amount which everyone who participated in the debate knew perfectly well wasn't available and would have to be sought via a supplemental appropriation at a later date. If you are reluctant to blame the Democrats for our deficit (as I was before listening to so many House debates) then I recommend you witness some floor debates via C-SPAN.

House Republican leader Robert Michel of Illinois tried his darndest! "If we believe that a billion dollars is the cure to this social ill, then let's not exacerbate the fiscal ill by making it new money. We should transfer the funds from existing accounts." But the House was not about to repeat the December fiasco whereby emergency aid to the Phillipines mandated no "new monies" be used. (see page 00) The Michel amendment was defeated after it was first sabotaged by Barney Frank (D-MA) to require that money come, not only from existing programs but specifically already underfinanced foreign aid programs. Robert Walker (R-PA) introduced a "deficit-aware" amendment, similar to Michel's, which was also flatly defeated. The attitude of the democratically controlled House was summed up in a stunning performance by Henry Gonzales (D-TX) who epitomized the collectivist mentality, with these words: ". . . the federal government has a legal and moral obligation to feed, clothe, and house the homeless of this country."

The Republicans tried once again to insert some semblance of reality into the debate by pointing to the $6 billion already allocated to feed and house the poor. Said Clyde Holloway (R-LA), "We just have to put the money where it is needed. . . . This is a ridiculous bill. We have to stop somewhere and have the backbone to stand up and say 'No.' We have to go back to the work ethic. There is going to be the rich, the poor and the middle class. If we don't have that, we're going to be a socialistic country." Ah, but does anyone care?

RIGHTS, RIGHTS AND MORE RIGHTS

Liberals like the courts to protect rights not specified in the Constitution but are only too happy to have them overturn certain enumerated rights. Article I of the Constitution protecting contracts is an explicit expression of economic rights. Prior to the New Deal contracts between two parties as to wages and conditions of employment were upheld time and again despite efforts to impose regulations. "The employee may desire to earn the extra money which would arise from working more than the prescribed time." said Supreme Court Justice Rufus Peckham in the case overturning a New York state law which prohibited bakery workers from working over 10 hours a day or 60 hours a week.[40] The law was determined to be an infringement on freedom and the right to contract.

The courts warned FDR that individual rights, according to the Constitution, took precedence over any attempt to regulate the economy by Congress. Minimum wage and compulsory retirement laws were invalidated as violating the due-process clause and beyond the scope of the commerce clause. But as Judge Stephen Williams of the U.S. Court of Appeals (DC) said in his early 1987 address before the Federalist Society: ". . . before a determined judge it doesn't make a great deal of sense what the Constitution said."

Over the past 50 years the courts have continued to overrule attempts to uphold the due process and commerce clauses in cases where the ability to contract or exercise private property rights are involved.

Harvard professor Stephen Macedo argues that property rights, which were supposedly protected by the framers of the Constitution with the insertion of the Fifth Amendment and its taking clause, were among the rights considered by our inspirational ancestor John Locke as natural unalienable rights.[41]

In 1979 a trial court judge ruled that language in the New York state Constitution justified the finding of a brand new right—the "right to shelter". Civil rights lawyers spend months combing through state constitutions, statutes and city ordinances looking for ways to make governments provide housing or extend other benefits to select groups of citizens. Legislators give birth to new law but these practitioners seek to deliver entitlements by twisting and turning the old laws, hoping a judge will be able, through their contortions, to make out what was formerly invisible—a brand new right!

Twist as they will, so far no one has been able to set a nationwide precedent by finding a "right to housing" in the U.S. Constitution. But it's not from lack of trying. In 1983, federal court Judge Leo Glasser of Brooklyn, ruled that if "a state promises to provide emergency shelter to eligible families as part of its agreement with the federal government to administer Social Security benefits, it is illegal to fail to provide housing".

The idea is familiar. There may not originally be an obligation to do something but once you, or in this instance, a government entity decided to do it voluntarily, a duty arises to do it well and completely. To put it in down-home vernacular, "If you can't do a job right then don't do it at all." Many of us have heard that admonishment from our parents and grandparents and may have passed it along to our own children. As it happens, it is good legal advice. In the educational field ex-students have been known to sue school districts because of the poor results that were achieved in their educations. In order to get passer-by physicians to help accident victims, Good Samaritan laws were instituted holding a doctor blameless from the results of such emergency administrations.

NEVER ENOUGH

I had the proverbial rich uncle when I was young. I remember the feeling I got from the adults in the family; my uncle could never do enough for anyone no matter how generous he was. "With all those millions he could have . . . or he should have . . ."; it's human nature. You may think it's trite and refuse to believe it but one of the indisputable truths in the world is NO ONE APPRECIATES ANYTHING UNLESS THEY GET IT OR DO IT FOR THEMSELVES. Believe it or not!

THE HOMELESS

In 1986 alone, homelessness nationwide increased by an average of 20–25 percent. Some observers claim that families with children account for more than 30 percent of the homeless. Others claim the homeless are not your typical average American at all, but are drug addicts, alcoholics and the mentally ill.

As with so many policies born of good intentions the phase-out of approximately 500,000 beds in mental hospitals across the nation and the enactment of stricter laws for involuntary confinement which took place in the late sixties didn't have the anticipated results. The idea was to provide more effective community based voluntary care which, however, many people with serious mental disorders refused to accept. On top of that, the organizations and expense involved in providing services was underestimated. Out of the 2,000 planned federally funded community mental health facilities, only 800 were ever established. Untreated illness, more often than not, led to alienation and life on the streets and once on the streets the new laws protected the rights of persons to continue to refuse help.

The American Psychiatric Association (APA) has recommended involuntary confinement as a solution to the homeless problem provided the following guidelines are observed: the patient must be obviously mentally ill so that he is incompetent to make medical decisions (a judgment call), exhibit mental deterioration involving hallucinations or delusions (judgment call), show obvious suffering (judgment call). Furthermore, there must be evidence that the disorder is treatable (judgment call) and facilities available to do an adequate job (judgment call).

Civil libertarians, on the other hand, remain dead set against paternalistic social intervention and are adamant that the law must prohibit involuntary treatment of any sort, no matter how effective it might claim to be. The only exception would be if the person is deemed dangerous to himself or others (a judgment call).

The APA insists that adherence to its proposal would result in only the most ill and most likely to be helped ever being confined. According to Professor Stone, ". . . paternalistic intervention, with appropriate legal safeguards is not only justified but is the obligation of a humane society."[42] (Where have we heard that before?)

California currently has a law which states that an individual must be so "gravely disabled" that he/she cannot provide for his/her own food, clothing or shelter, before the state can step in.[43] Under such policies society must be prepared to witness an ever increasing number of non-dangerous mentally ill people inhabiting doorways and parks.

There are people who work with the homeless who claim that most of them are average Americans; normal people who've led normal lives and held normal jobs until WHAMO—they found themselves and their families out on the streets.

The truth is the homeless are made up of some of both groups. Perhaps you saw the Donahue Show's airing of the homeless issue on December 8, 1986. Mr. Joseph Mowry, a gentleman who went to the Soviet Union to obtain publicity for the homeless (and was subsequently used for Soviet propaganda) was a guest, along with Soviet newsman Iona Andronov. Mr. Andronov found it hard to understand how "the richest and greatest country in the world" (sound familiar?) allows poverty. "It's a shame", he said to audience applause, "In the USSR you have not homeless people on the street." I only wish Mr. Donahue had retorted something like, "In USSR you have not free will." In America still, to a certain extent, we allow free will. Freedom to fail goes hand in hand with freedom to succeed.

WHO SPEAKS FOR AMERICA?

The voices we most often hear expressing American views are not the voices of what I call the backbone of America—the entrepreneurs, the working people who have no time to make speeches, write books—appear on talk shows—and most revealing of all—they are not the ones who run for office. These folks are pursuing the American dream, not talking about it or promising to get it for voters. They aren't busy asking what you can do for them but simply ask you to either join in the endeavour to produce or step aside and see what their ingenuity and hard work can yield.

The GNP of the Soviet Union is 55 percent of the USA GNP, but purchasing power for Soviet citizens is well below that of even some third world citizens. In rural areas women still draw water from wells and there is no electricity. Yet they are far advanced in military weapons and space technology. Incredulous! Author David Aikman says that in China, "Economic changes are forcing political changes they are not ready to take." In the USSR, on the other hand, economic changes have not been strong enough to get anyone interested in political change. (Gorbachev is a new phenomenon—and a whole other book!)

NOT *MY* FAMILY—YOU DON'T!

Getting back to the Donahue Show, a representative homeless person admitted that through his own mismanagement he ended up on the streets. Sure the City provides shelters, he said, but people get killed in those shelters. He told us that he had once been a cook in the navy but he used to drink. He didn't want charity or welfare, he wanted a place he could afford. ("Want" was his word.) He had nine children but wouldn't go to his family in "this shape". (Shadows of Mrs. X who didn't want to burden her brother and Mrs. Y who felt awful taking help from her daughter. See pp 90–93.) A young woman in the audience asked the question others were wondering about: "When the homeless have family, why not go to family?" Why, in other words, should taxpayers come to the rescue and let family members off the hook because a father is too embarrassed to let his daughter see him in a degraded condition? It's not his reluctance I'm questioning, that's natural and only too easy to understand, but where is the justice (one of those sticky words again) when taxpayers are asked to juggle their priorities and pay for someone else's mistake? Perhaps swallowing one's pride is a contribution owed to society—if you are a person who goes along with "owing" things to society, that is!

NO MORE BOOT-STRAP STORIES

One lady in Mr. Donahue's audience didn't see any opportunities in this country for today's youth. She gave the impression that children of immigrants were raised in luxury and surrounded by wealth. I wanted to tell her to read Herman Wouk's latest novel "Inside, Outside" which would give her a more realistic impression of what motivated immigrants in the early years of this century. In that novel a character comes to America not knowing the language and spends two years (ages 18–20) working as a sorter and marker in a laundry 16 hours a day, "in a damp cellar lit by one electric bulb" for the unbelievably meager salary, even in those tough days, of $2 a week. His friends do the same job on the street floor for $5 a week and are envied by the hero because they have access to a toilet! His choice was to beg or eat at a charity kitchen. He ended up owning a laundry. Fiction, you say, and rightly so, but you talk to older people in this country and you will find many successful men and women who have such stories to tell—non-fiction. It is well to remember that Americans come from a pioneering tradition and the one thing we share is the psyche of immigrants to a promised land. Many people believe the safety-net has already become so comfortable that opportunity does not beckon the way it once did. Opportunity and the American Dream, they say, was embraced more enthusiastically by those with empty bellies.

Vic Snyder, representative of a Washington D.C. organization that serves the homeless, vehemently expressed his opinion: "I'm tired of the white middle class talking about lifting themselves up by their boot straps." It appeared that a great many of Mr. Donahue's guests and members of the audience felt the same way. Only stupid, tiresome and uncaring people ever refer to hardship, discipline and work.

"SPOIL" THE UNFORTUNATE?

On the other side of the issue are groups such as the Heritage Foundation which reported that efforts to feed and house the homeless have been growing in recent years. Some "conservatives" (whatever that term is supposed to mean nowadays) believe that making "homelessness" a successful activity will only increase it. The very idea infuriates liberals; who loftily scoff: "as if we can "spoil" the unfortunate by making things "too easy"!

EVERYONE HAS A SOLUTION

Mr. Sigel, a civil rights advocate and guest on Mr. Donahue's Show, expressed his solutions to the homeless problem: 1) expand job training, 2) provide foster care, 3) build low-income housing, 4) get lawyers to keep people from being evicted.

Lawyers, governors, Congressmen, all have solutions as does Benjamin Page, Associate Professor of Political Science at the University of Chicago and author of yet another collectivist manifesto, *Who Gets What From Government*. On page 17 Professor Page says, "If we view inequality as harmful to society and destructive of human welfare, it is natural to conclude that the state ought to redistribute income so as to achieve more equality."

Marcus Raskin, author of *The Common Good* and fellow of the Policy Institute for Policy Studies and Co-Chair of SANE, a peace organization, would surely agree. On a C-SPAN interview in December 1986, Mr. Raskin told viewers a humane society would mandate an equitable share of the goods off society. (You don't suppose . . .?)

According to Mr. Raskin, President Reagan's policies have been disastrous with emphasis on a two class society with no chance for the poor and working poor. He was appalled that corporations are permitted (by whom?) to renounce responsibility (to whom?) by leaving the country to set up shop elsewhere.

Mr. Raskin says that equity must be seen in terms of inequity. The class system is OK if there are guarantees for health-care, day-care and education. Guaranteed minimums by government are absolutely necessary according to Mr. Raskin. He claims that the poor are the ones that built this country. "We have the socialization of risk and the privatization of gain, when a corporation appears to be losing money we want to privatize the gain."

A C-SPAN caller who used to live in England talked about how ruthless American society is: "If you're poor it's your own fault." He claimed that socialism in Europe has been conducive to a more humane society. I could only suppose the caller was a visitor. How sad for him, I remember thinking at the time, if he opted to live in such a ruthless country as America.

I can hardly recommend Mr. Raskin's book to you but I do recommend a review of it by Philip Gold which appeared sometime after the C-SPAN interview. The following is an excerpt from that review found in the February 2, 1987 edition of *Insight* magazine: "Indeed, if Marcus Raskin excels at anything, it is at devising schemes for 'redistributing' the 'social product'—read here wealth he did not and could not produce—at the expense of those who did produce it and, ultimately, at the expense of those struggling for the opportunity to do so."

The more I hear, the more convinced I become that there will eventually be at least two classes of people in this nation; those who have solutions and those for whom those solutions are devised.

The hero in Herman Wouk's novel would have been prevented from working 16 hours a day in a damp cellar without a toilet for "unjust" wages by people with solutions. Their solutions would have taken away his opportunity to get ahead as surely as the regulations proposed by do-gooders today. Poverty is a by-product of oppression. It has been said that the "haves" are those who have freedom and the "have-nots" have not freedom.

As a lady in Mr. Donahue's audience said, "Let the people, not the government solve the problems." Amen.

AGRICULTURE

FARMERS WOULD HAVE ADJUSTED "ON THEIR OWN"

In 1870 most working Americans were farmers. Farming was the American way of life and the family farm was handed down from one generation to the next. Thanks to the first world war Western Europe became dependent on U.S. farm products and the sudden demand encouraged American farmers to borrow in order to obtain more land to put into production. With the end of the war farmland prices fell in this country as Europe's demand for U.S. farm imports dwindled. Consequently many American farmers went bankrupt during the 1920s. In 1929 President Herbert Hoover established the Federal Farm Board and the parade of contradictory government interventions began. There were production inducements such as price subsidies and crop insurance and production deterrents like marketing agreements and acreage allowances. The inducements were more powerful and so the stockpiling of farm surpluses began in earnest in the 1930s only to be alleviated by more government meddling, this time in the form of food distribution to the numerous unemployed. Government meddling is like splitting a piece of wood by using the wrong size nail and then trying to put it back together again with the help of many smaller nails. Try as you may the wood will never be as strong as it was before the hammering began.

FROM 21% TO 2.9% OF THE EMPLOYABLE POPULATION

As the second world war broke out about 21 percent of the total U.S. employable population was connected with agriculture. As for the American farmer, the Second World War was a repeat of the first, with a shrinkage of demand for American agricultural products once the European farmer exchanged his sword for plowshare. New labor saving equipment, innovations and entrepreneurial vigor made farm productivity soar and caused a steady decline in the number of Americans finding employment on the nation's farms: 9.8 percent in 1956, 5.5 percent in 1966, 3.8 percent in 1976 down to 2.9 percent in 1986. William H. Peterson of the University of Tennessee cited the following example of gains in farm productivity in an article for the Wall Street Journal: In the fifties it took 2.4 man-hours to produce each 100 pounds of chicken-broilers and 6.5 man-hours to produce each 100 pounds of turkey. Today only .1 of a man-hour is required for the chickens and .3 for the turkeys. "In each case we see about 95% reduction in man-hour requirements."[44]

PROTECTING FARMLAND FROM DEVELOPERS

According to the American Farmland Trust, 58 percent of America's most important farming counties ". . . are inside of or next to metropolitan areas. Together, these 372 urban fringe counties account for 30 percent of the nation's agricultural production . . ."[45] The Trust suggests that these lands be kept in farming by using tax incentives, paying farmers the difference between the land's agricultural use and what he could get for the land if sold for development and by making it "attractive for farmers to donate their easements, or land use rights, to a local land trust."[46]

FARM SUBSIDIES AND CONTRADICTORY POLICY

The cost of farm programs has increased six fold since Ronald Reagan took office, from $4 billion in 1981 to $25.8 billion in FY1986. The subsidies to farmers in various forms took 15 percent of the FY1986 budget. The increase in farm support costs was between 500–600 percent in five years. Ronald Reagan has tried, perhaps half-heartedly and certainly without success to cut back on the number and size of farm subsidies. Pete DuPont campaigned for the 1988 Republican Presidential nomination pledging to phase-out the federal farm program over a five year period and won support from some farm organizations.[47]

Deficiency payments in FY1986 were double the payments in FY1985 and consequently participation in the program shot up to include 85 percent of all farmers. "The skyrocketing subsidies explain why . . . real per capita income in the nine Grainbelt states has risen nearly 10 percent faster than in the nation as a whole. . . In Nebraska . . . corn farmers will receive more than $750 million in deficiency payments."[48] According to Warren Brookes, writing for the July 14, 1986 issue of INSIGHT magazine per capita income in Iowa was on a par with the rest of the nation in 1986 and yet that state consumed agricultural subsidies averaging nearly $18,000 per farm and worth close to $2 billion. But that was nothing compared to the give away to dairy farmers documented by Mr. Brookes, who gave as an example one farmer who received $9.9 million ". . . in the tax-financed slaughter of his entire dairy herd in a program paying 12,000 dairy farms an average of nearly $105,000 each to get out of the business." Our agriculture policy is a perfect example of the dangers inherent in leaving your business to the policymakers. While some dairymen were paid to kill their cows and get out of the business other provisions of the farm bill would make milk production more profitable and thereby encourage the expansion of herds. Oh yes, under pressure from cattlemen the federal government agreed to purchase the slaughtered dairy cows to prevent a glut in the meat market.

While on the subject of contradictions the farm bill on the one hand tries to recapture markets lost to third world countries such as Brazil and Argentina while the Treasury Department opposes any policy that might cut into those countries exports and threaten payments to our overextended commercial banks.

PLAYING THE SYSTEM

Farmers have learned how to "play" the federal government and can reap a record crop while receiving subsidies for idling land at the same time. All they have to do is idle the rocky or wet spots they never would have planted in a free-market economy. Taxpayers foot the bill for billions of dollars for water programs to allow farmers to grow surplus crops where normally only catcus would have grown. Centralized planning is always a fiasco yet some members of Congress are eyeing the possibility of expanding export credit and subsidy programs and paying farmers to idle up to 50 percent of all land set aside for certain crops. Farmers certainly aren't stupid, and although they can hardly help taking advantage of such stupid programs, they don't enjoy taking taxpayer money for being non-productive. Some Congressmen have proposed direct money payments to farmers without all the hoopla—let them plant or not and introduce the element of a free-market with a gradual scaling back of "welfare" payments over time. Many believe it would be cheaper than the present charade we are playing with agriculture. The 1985 Farm Bill spends billions of dollars undoing what other government programs have done and ends up giving the most dollars to those who need them the least. The acreage reduction program served as a signal to competitors to increase their own production. There is no doubt subsidies are self-perpetuating as well as self-defeating. If a program guarantees $3 a bushel on every bushel of corn grown it is inevitable that the biggest growers will reap the most benefits.

The number of rice growers in Yolo County, California increased from 50 to 72 in 1986, not due to an increased demand for rice but because people figured out how to take advantage of the rice-subsidy system. In 1986 50 rice producers received government checks for more than $1 million each (All the action is not on Wall Street even though the Ivan Boeskies get all the headlines.) The scam goes something like this; the maximum government subsidy is $50,000 a year so the key is in knowing the exact number of acres to plant in order to qualify for that subsidy. The government presumes by having such a cutoff only smaller growers will benefit. "O ye who underestimate the ingenuity of your fellowman!" All a large grower has to do is plant the right number of acres and then rent similar parcels to "new growers" (knaves, as Shakespeare might say), each for a handsome sum because after all each parcel is automatically worth $50,000 to each and every new rice grower. Overabundance, as Lenin predicted, is turning out to be the nation's curse.

OUTRAGEOUS

Somehow or other in the summer of 1986 the United States managed to import more agricultural products than it exported. On top of that, the "Do as I say, not as I do" President, in an attempt to capture the farm vote and keep the Senate under Republican control, bragged that his administration spent, in 1986 alone, more than any other administration had spent in its entire term! (Gosh! Golly! Gee Whiz!)

People who have analyzed the breakdown of the subsidy payments have found large amounts of taxpayer dollars going to foreign investors, executives with part-time farms and to the farmers with net worths exceeding a million dollars who have the financial clout necessary to make it on their own.

It's hard to understand how twice as much could be spent on farm programs than was authorized ($15 billion over budget in FY1986) but that was what happened the first year the new farm program was in effect, and without tackling the real problem of farm debt and overproduction. Only about 17 cents of every dollar went to the desperate full-time farmers; 7 percent of the farmers took 70 percent of the government payments.

SURPLUS BUT AT WHAT COST?

Elmer Learn, an agricultural economist at the University of California at Davis, divides farms into three categories; the part-time for fun farms with annual sales under $20,000; the middle-sized full-time family farms and the large commercial farms which have always benefited from federal programs to an excessive degree. He suggests (going along with the time-honored advice Joseph gave Pharoah) that surplus food stocks may not be all that bad and in fact may well be a prudent practice for a society if not done as a consequence of poorly planned farm programs.

On July 14, 1986 Tom Barlow of Kentucky agreed with this assessment in an article for the Wall Street Journal in which he compared surplus capacity in electricity with agriculture. Both make the population more comfortable but the public is not willing to pay for food security with the same grace with which it subsidizes utility surplus. According to Mr. Barlow, consumers are paying almost $15 billion a year in their utility bills in order to enjoy a plant surplus valued at $75 billion. Insurance for electricity and food is something that society is better off for having and not necessarily the disaster it is made out to be.

FARM DEBT

Most farm debt, including the most shaky, is held or guaranteed by the federal government. Examples are plentiful of farmers who have the federal government write off their loans but are then able to use fat federal payments to plant crops that when harvested they will get paid to store. Rice growers were an example, not an exception. The Farm Credit System, which had its beginnings in 1916 and presently serves farmers through some 2,000 offices nationwide, lost $2.7 billion through mortgage and loan defaults in 1985. That was a historic record for a U.S. financial institution. (Please, no applause.) Congress went back to the drawing boards and came up with the 1985 Farm Credit Corporation of America which it authorized to tap into the $3.2 billion in surplus reserves held by healthy institutions, calling the theft "capital sharing". Understandably these healthy institutions wondered why in the world profits earned via prudent lending practices by one institution should be used to pay for the misfortune or bad judgment of others. As always happens when government gets its foot in the door (this time by backing loans of member farmer cooperatives), it feels justified in extending its demands and is not deterred by even the knowledge that the funds it would like to confiscate represent private ownership. By the end of 1986 five states had issued temporary restraining orders preventing the system from siphoning capital from the strong to shore up the weaker institutions.

Another segment of the 1985 "Farm Fix" involved accounting gimmicks which if ". . . the loan-loss accounting change (had) been in effect in 1985, the system's reported net loss of $2.7 billion could have been trimmed to about $100 million."[49] Although it is sometimes hard to believe, Congressmen, just like farmers, are not stupid and there is little doubt but that they realized such accounting proposals were nothing more than a charade—an attempt to deceive, or as they would prefer to put it, a stall for time to figure out something more substantial to do.

AMERICA MUST CHOOSE—REVISITED

In the spring of 1934 Henry Agard Wallace, Secretary of Agriculture under FDR, produced a visionary pamphlet called *America Must Choose.* In it he explained that the choice was no longer between nationalism and internationalism but that man now had "such control over nature that the doctrine of the struggle for existence is definitely outmoded and replaced by the higher law of cooperation."—something that is very much needed among world leaders today as the old problems repeat.

Our government intends to bring before the 92 country General Agreement on Tariffs and Trade (GATT) a proposal for a phased reduction of all nations' farm-support programs, which according to the World Bank amount to a minimum of $110 billion a year worldwide, and suggest new trade rules to promote peaceful settlement of disputes. The Administration would also like to see health and sanitation requirements standardized so these can't be used as a barrier to free trade. On June 5, 1987 in a presummit television address in Venice, President Reagan referred to our costly "farms race" and appealed to other nations. "Let's jointly defuse this growing farms race by setting a goal of a subsidy-free world for the year 2000," he said.

Between 1981 and 1986 the U.S. share of world trade dropped from 42 percent to 25 percent. Some people direct their anger towards Europe where farmers are heavily subsidized and the United States picks up more than a fair share for Europe's defense. The fact that the European Community can barely afford to pay its current subsidies bodes well for a GATT agreement in the future. In Japan consumer activists are fed up with the government Food Control Laws which are estimated to cost every Japanese resident the equivalent of $600 a year. These activists are beginning to pressure the Japanese government into softening its attitude towards world economic cooperation.

INEPT POLICY MAKERS

Unfortunately strings were attached to the 1985 Export Enhancement Program which ended up making us unpopular with regular customers as well as competitors. We offered more competitive prices to countries that rarely bought from us leaving strong customers like Japan paying the higher unsubsidized prices. You can't have attorneys with their fingers in every pie, trying to do what businessmen, salesmen and natural negotiaters should be doing. But the main problem is the repeated attempt to impose centralized controls. Government has encroached more and more on dealings between citizens, often interfering with the freedom to contract by imposing its own rules and regulations. Government is not divine in this country, nor even, in most cases, divinely inspired. What we mean by government interference is the imposition of the will of one small group (elected officials) over the others (average citizens). The fewer decisions they have to make and the more responsibility individual citizens assume over their own lives the better off the nation will be. Flexibility is the key. Former Secretary of Agriculture, John Block admitted that the 1981 Farm Bill was the result of assuming the world would be clamoring for our grain and that our biggest problem would be meeting the demand. ". . . the bill set high target prices, which were made up by the government if market prices were lower; set floors under which U.S. export prices could not fall; and encouraged production by setting crop requirements for farmers to receive income support." All this from the gentleman who campaigned for president as a proponent of free markets. ("Do as I say . . . Ok Ok!) The inevitable result of such a program is that farmers can no longer compete in world markets but still overproduce. The hunger and famine in the world can no longer be blamed on global underproduction but is a result of political decisions. In 1984 Western Europe produced more wheat than the United States and nations such as India and Saudi Arabia became exporters instead of importers of food.

ONE FOR LENIN

In 1983 the Williamsburg Summit produced a ban on Western subsidies to the Soviets which was restated in a NATO Ministerial Communique in June, 1983. The Communique stated that subsidizing trade with the Soviets frees their resources for other efforts and helps to further their alleged goal of world domination. It also validates one of Lenin's most famous predictions—that capitalists would one day be compelled to unload their surpluses on Mother Russia at bargain basement prices.

Insight magazine, on September 8, 1986 ran an article titled "The Grain Glut: Perils of Plenty" by Richard Martin which alluded to Senator Moynihan's observation that our wooing of the Russians with our grain was a fulfillment of Lenin's prophecy. The Senator pointed out that Lenin felt certain that as we ran out of markets for our goods we would be forced to approach even the communist world. So, as Richard Martin pointed out in his article, the following would have to have made Lenin extremely happy: "FOR SALE: 4 million metric tons of American wheat, at a price $11 to $13 a ton cheaper than domestic customers are paying. The prospective customer: the SOVIET UNION."[50]

But in 1986 the Soviets snubbed even the $15 a ton discount we offered them and bought wheat at a better price from France. In 1987 the discount was doubled and we got hooked in a reverse play of the 'ol Tom Sawyer and the whitewashed fence episode. They may have gotten the best of us, but they weren't the only ones. The sale to the Soviets followed a less publicized sale of 1 million tons of wheat to China, subsidized about $30 to $34 a ton.

The Soviets have seen how China, by rewarding farm workers, has been able to increase agricultural output in a mainly socialist environment. They too have a program to offer bonuses to the most productive teams on Russian farms. But as Gale Johnson and Karen McConnell relate in their book "Prospects for Soviet Agriculture in the 1980s" the Soviets have ideas but those ideas usually don't survive the bureaucracy. The obstacle course for a typical farm program might include a run through the Union-Republic Council of Ministers, the U.S.S.R. Ministry of Agriculture, the U.S.S.R. Ministry of Fruit and Vegetable Farming, the U.S.S.R. State Committee on Labor and Social Questions, the U.S.S.R. Ministry of Procurements, the All-Union Central Council of Trade Unions and the U.S.S.R. State Committee for the Supply of Production Equipment to Agriculture.

But then there is really little need for either China or the U.S.S.R. to increase their productivity as long as a capitalist country like the United States has farmers that over produce and taxpayers that are willing to subsidize the sale of that bounty to the less productive communist nations. So what about the promise not to subsidize the Russian economy? What about the argument that using subsidy programs to prop up the Russian economy mitigates our own costly defense program? This is one more blatant example of the "Do As I say, Not As I Do" President in action. But it is not a new or sudden breach. Henry Kissinger wrote the following in 1982 for the *New Republic:* "Lenin's legendary dictum that capitalists would compete to sell the rope with which they would be hanged has come true with a vengence—for Lenin never guessed that Western governments would provide the money to buy the rope and subsidize the price and facilitate the purchase."

PROPOSALS

Ideas got us into the present agricultural mess and ideas are being bandied about in an attempt to get us out. One such idea is the "marketing loan" program. Loans would be used to reimburse farmers who would permit prices to drop to the world level. Opponents of the plan suggest such loans would encourage bad planting decision and more overproduction.

"Save the Family Farm" was a brainchild of both Senator Harkin of Iowa and Congressman Gephardt of Missouri. It would force cutbacks in production with more subsidies—subsidies which preserve the inefficient at the expense of the efficient and price U.S. farm commodities right out of the world market. Remember the only reason we made those sales to China and Russia is the taxpayer subsidy our leaders decided we would go for. Isn't it interesting that, "In the face of the mass migration off the American farm, Agriculture Department employment charged ahead fourfold, from 26,050 in 1930 to 105,569 (in June, 1986)".[51] Proof that bureaucracy feeds upon itself and multiplies. (As if there weren't enough proof all around us already!)

It's not as if American agriculture would suffer in open world competition. We have the best land, climate, developed infrastructure and most advanced technology. Perhaps the best idea is being advocated by Republican presidential hopeful Pete DuPont who says we should gradually end *all* subsidies. (I thought we had a president who said that already.) If left to the free-market eventually only the most competitive land would be utilized, as was the case before the government decided to control things. Marginal land would be idled for the proper reason, and not because some Washington-type in a three piece suit decided which acres should and should not be planted.

Oh well, at least, said Richard Martin writing for *Insight,* Lenin would be please to know "The breadbasket of the world, after a decade of misguided policies, goes on sowing the seeds of its own decline."

THE ENVIRONMENT

SUPERFUND

Environmental lobbyists are considered important and no one wants to risk offending this vocal activist group any more than they wish to offend the elderly. We should not then be surprised that the 99th Congress approved the Superfund legislation expected to raise funding by 465 percent over a five year period.

Some observers feel the $9 billion pushed through the 99th Congress at the last moment, may have been long on show and short on wisdom. The EPA (Environmental Protection Agency) after all, had only asked for $3.7 billion. There is doubt that enough is known about toxic clean-up to spend the money efficiently over the next five years. According to Congress's own Office of Technology Assessment, there is a shortage of trained technical personnel in this area.

Since "getting big business" is always politically attractive, it's doubly nice that the funding for Superfund will fall on business and not add to the deficit. $2.4 billion in new revenue is anticipated from a tax of $12 billion on each $10,000 of corporate income over $2 million a year. Additionally, a tax of 8.2 cents per barrel on domestic oil and 11.2 cents on imported and a tax on 42 industrial chemicals. Only those earning less than $2 million in taxable income would be exempt from the levy. Not surprisingly the chemical industry was the only industry in favor of backing the Superfund bill because, even though the Chemical Manufacturers Association estimates member companies will contribute at least $2.2 billion to the Superfund over the next five years, the minimum corporate tax spreads the clean-up burden to other industries. Naturally food processing, electronics and consumer products industries insist that the minimum corporate tax is unfair to companies that don't directly cause toxic-waste pollution.

The worst aspect of the bill is the uncertainty it creates regarding a company's liability. The old statue of limitations for damage suits stemming from toxic-waste ran from the date the injury was suffered; under the new bill the statute runs from the time the injury is discovered. Some problems may incubate for years and companies will have to plan under that shadow.

ACID RAIN

The Hudson Institute, a New York based research organization, conducted a study in 1983 for the Hoosiers for Economic Development Committee of Indiana which showed the likelihood that a program to control acid rain might make a barely noticeable change in the measured amount of acid rain in upstate New York even after 10 years and a commitment of $100 billion. Furthermore the study said there was, in the past, insufficient technical understanding of the sources and impact of acid precipitation. Since 1978 reliable data has shown that the amount of acidity has remained stable.

A few years ago *Science* reported the conclusions of scientists that acid rain antedates the industrial revolution. Scientists discovered that volcanoes in Italy, Greece and even the equatorial Pacific contributed to elevated acidity in Greenland between 1500 B.C. and A.D. 1500. If acid rain dates back almost 3,500 years spending a few more years on research won't hurt the environment that much and may keep us from plunging into a regulatory program costing upwards of $100 billion without being certain of its effectiveness.

President Reagan for years has insisted the acid rain problem needs further study before regulation is begun. He and Canadian Prime Minister Brian Mulroney requested more information back in March, 1985. They wanted to see a report on the methods that could be developed to reduce the sulfur and nitrogen oxide emissions from coal burning plants.

The simplest and most cost efficient way to reduce emissions is to switch from high-sulfur to low-sulfur coal. The Minneapolis based Northern States Power Company has spent $1 billion on pollution control, reduced sulfur dioxide emissions by 53 percent over the last 14 years and doubled profits in the last ten. One reason is its switch 15 years ago from high-sulfur mid-western or eastern fuels to the cleaner low-sulfur coal. The early switch gave the foresighted Northern States Power Company a price-edge over its competitors.

Low-sulfur coal is found in a couple far-western states with only three votes in the House of Representatives, as opposed to the 105 votes held by Representatives of the eight high-sulfur coal producing mid-western states. These Representatives know where their bread is buttered and will see that any pollution-control measures do not destroy the value of high-sulfur coal. To that end, billions of dollars may be poured into expensive technology which will meet tough standards no matter the type of coal burned. Requiring univeral installation of this technology will ensure the lower priced high-sulfur coal favored status.

Once again, regulations block the way to cost efficient free-market adaptation. But all is not lost according to a piece in the February 16, 1987 edition of *Time* magazine. Apparently a research organization has figured that there would be "a net gain of up to 195,000 American jobs and $13 billion in annual sales for U.S. companies" thanks to the large purchases of capital equipment and supporting goods and services such legislation would mandate. An example of making lemonade from lemons.

But in March 1987, both the Hudson Institute and NSA studies were vindicated when the data collected by the scientists advising the EPA suggested that little or no lake acidification is occurring in the Northeast from acid rain. The conclusions of these scientists which were presented in March, 1987, back up the claims made by the coal and electric utility industries that there is no proof that lakes and streams will suffer substantial and increasing damage if sulfur dioxide emissions from coal-fired power plants continue at current levels.

Unfortunately the finding comes just after President Reagan reaffirmed a commitment to a $2.5 billion program to subsidize power plants that demonstrate ways of cutting acid emissions from coal boilers. "A little here and . . ." At any rate the commitment didn't begin to satisfy Sierra Club director Michael McClosky who claimed it was just ". . . a smokescreen to obscure the administration's opposition to acid rain control". How could *anyone* be opposed to cleaning the environment *if* we knew what we were doing!

On March 25, 1987, EPA Administrator Lee Thomas told a group of House Republicans there may not be a need to bring emissions down at all because acid rain is being neutralized by the exchange of hydrogen ions for calcium and magnesium ions in the soil and the Northeast appears to be in a steady state.

CENTRALIZED PLANNING

Productivity is one of the buzz words for 1988. There are many that argue that in order to compete in our global market place we must become lean and efficient and that the way to achieve this is through centralized planning. Centralized planning can be seen in a closed-minded Congress that is determined to push through a program to clean-up acid rain, perhaps wasting billions of dollars for a problem that has been neutralizing itself for thousands of years and may well continue to do so if left to its own devices. It would appear the meaningfulness of the program may be in the enhancement of a particular politician's standing with environmentalists.

The state controls by penalties not profits. Losses are the only penalty in a free market. The individual is forced by competition to seek his own success in serving the market as exemplified by the consumer. Obedience to the market ruled by uncontrolled prices is rewarded by profit whereas disobedience is punished by loss and bankruptcy. Collectivist economies try to replace this guidance by planning which is ever so much more dangerous for us all. If a businessman miscalculates the worst that awaits him is financial ruin, but if a planning commissioner miscalculates, or in the case of acid rain, the Congress or the President himself, we all suffer in countless ways. Who will deny that a million ordinary citizens or business men making calculations have a far greater chance that good and bad judgments will offset one another than if a handful of experts were doing the same thing?

No single man or group of men is capable of deciding the correct relationship between the multitude of events which are changing moment by moment in our complex society. It is absolutely mind boggling to realize that without any human direction—with no person deciding who shall perform what task and prescribing what goods and how much of each shall be produced and brought to market, the economy functions. Not only functions, but in a relatively short time this free-market has produced the highest living standard the world has ever known. Admittedly people today are subject to a great more regulation than they were a few decades ago, but pure capitalism (which admittedly exists nowhere!) is the system of government which leaves to the people decisions about production, consumption, saving, buying and selling and even acid rain.

THE FREE-MARKET

Capitalism has been referred to as a system of ordered anarchy, amazing in the precise synchronization of all its parts. In any large city today millions of citizens are dependent for their basic necessities on the efforts of others. The fact is modern man is less self-sufficient than ever before. Some urban dwellers would have absolutely no idea how to obtain a loaf of bread if all supermarkets and bakeries were eliminated. Yet, unbelievably accurate quantities of goods are available on a continuing basis to serve a population of over 240 million people with little shortage and little surplus. What genius is in charge of such a vast and complex operation? NOBODY! The free-market juggles the supply and the demand as no government official could begin to do. The millions of consumers have previously been in the market place as producers and adjusted their output both in quantity and quality to demand so that no great loss has to be endured. Where there are pockets of unemployment and surplus agricultural products that is due to government policy. The more regulations, subsidies, incentives, penalties—the more interference by government the harder it is for *NOBODY* to do his job ensuring that the economic gears of society mesh properly.

Included in the President's Economic Report to Congress on February 6, 1986 was a creative approach to regulation in general: "The Environmental Protection Agency has approved arrangements that enable firms to earn credits for reducing emissions below the required limit, which they can sell to other firms facing higher costs of emission control. In this way, environmental quality is maintained and improved while the costs of compliance decline." Market forces *can* work even when controls are deemed necessary.

THE CLEAN AIR ACT

Congress amended the Clean Air Act in 1977 to require the EPA to set new, more stringent standards for four types of pollutants; nitrogen oxides, ozone, carbon monoxide and lead. The idea was to prevent deterioration of air quality in areas such as federal parks, forests and unpopulated stretches of the Rockies and Sierra Nevadas that already met the standards that applied to urban areas. The stricter standards were originally to have been set by August, 1979 but the EPA, on its own initiative, cancelled the program in October, 1981 before the task of drawing up regulations was completed. Suit was brought by four environmental groups in March, 1986 to enforce the EPA's compliance with the law. Despite arguments that the air quality in question poses no human health hazards and that there are many, many more important things to do, the District Judge, William Schwarzer, ruled in San Francisco April 9, 1987 that the EPA must come up with new more-stringent air quality standards by October, 1988.

A law is to be enforced which may not only prove to be unnecessary but may muddle the situation and prove costly in more ways than can now be imagined. However, it is refreshing to know some entity other than the ordinary citizen is being made to adhere to the law of the land, at least until those who are responsible for these absurdities are replaced.

THE WATER BILL

In his radio address January 3, 1987 President Reagan warned that although no one would dispute the desirability of clean usable water in this country, the Clean Water Bill calls for more spending than is necessary. He reasoned that the states would be more conservative with their own dollars and that the federal government, with its gargantuan deficit, should not continue to give dollars it doesn't have to help pay the cost of constructing expensive new sewage and waste water treatment facilities in individual states. But there were few politicians in either House that had the guts to vote against the Bill; after all, every state had money on the line and the measure was backed by an effectual coalition of construction companies, municipalities and environmentalists.

It was no surprise then that in February, 1987 the House voted 401–26 and the Senate 86–14 to override the President's veto and adopt the $20 billion legislation. The Bill authorizes $9.6 billion in grants and $8.4 billion in revolving loan funds for sewer-construction projects as well as $2 billion for clean-up programs. It would provide for construction of about 180 projects and require that half the cost of inland navigation projects be financed by eventual doubling of the tax on barge fuel to 20 cents a gallon by 1997. It would also impose a federal user fee at coastal and Great Lakes ports of 0.04 percent on the value of cargo going in or out. For flood-control programs, a local contribution of 25 to 30 percent of the cost would be required with 5 percent due during construction.

WHAT LEVEL OF FUNDING IS PRUDENT?

Senator James Exon of Nebraska was the only Democrat in Congress to vote to sustain the President's veto of the Water Bill claiming, "the issue is what level of funding is prudent." Senate Minority Leader Bob Dole of Kansas declared that a vote to sustain the President's veto was a vote, not against clean water, but for cutting back on the deficit. HEAR! HEAR! Senator Steven Symms of Idaho also tried eloquently but in vain, to persuade the Senate that pollution exists in our money supply, our fiscal policy and in the ". . . integrity of the credit of the United States." House GOP Leader Robert Michel of Illinois claimed, along with his colleagues, that clean water was not the issue but ". . . wise and prudent use of tax dollars . . ." was. In the end even the President's offer of a $12 billion compromise was rejected.

President Reagan's main objection to the Water Bill was based upon the principle of federalism which holds that certain responsibilities are the legitimate business of the federal government whereas others are the business of state and local governments. For our first 200 years the construction of a local dam or sewage line naturally belonged to the latter as did the cleaning up of a harbor. (Boston got $100 million for harbor clean-up via the Bill.)

The EPA attempted to appeal to those swayed by the cost-efficiency-argument, so abhorrent to Mr. Kuttner and Professor Kelman, by claiming if water supplies were brought to a higher standard by reducing the lead content, $800 million could be saved in costs related to health and public-works maintenance.

GETTING THE WRONG RESULT—*AGAIN!*

But here again we have an example of policy-makers striving for one result and ending up with the opposite. According to David A. Todd, an environmental consultant in Houston, Texas, "Strong evidence exists that stricter environmental standards for water quality have actually led to increases in the amount of lead that is dispersed in the environment. Short-term, small-scale gains are likely to lead to long-term, large-scale problems that will not easily go away."[52] Mr. Todd refers to the numerous agencies and regulations that dominate the lead-recycling industry and which together with the drop in the market price of lead are making recycling unprofitable. Lead/acid batteries were purchased for as much as $5 each in 1979 but a recycler can only afford to pay about 30 cents today. Consequently in 1987 about 28 million batteries may not be recycled and a total of 260,000 tons of lead will simply be scattered in the environment. The choice comes down to removing about 500 tons of lead from drinking water and thereby driving out the recyclers who prevent about 500 THOUSAND tons of lead from possibly reaching *future* water supplies every year. Mr. Todd has compared the lead-recycling industry to the complexities inherent in nature, i.e. predators, scavengers, a food chain and a decay cycle. Both nature and the lead industry, if left unregulated, are capable of taking care of their own waste.

GET GOVERNMENT OUT OF THE WAY

The Arizona Groundwater Act, passed in 1980 under the protective eye of former Governor Bruce Babbitt, has been referred to as landmark legislation by its admirers and as toying with socialism by its detractors.

CITIZENS CONCERNED ABOUT THE PROJECT claim that if subsidies from the federal government were eliminated, Arizona could solve her water problems and that Arizona's water shortage is a myth. Farmers, who use most of any state's water, find it cheaper to pump water from the ground than to purchase water from the project. Taxpayers are subsidizing cheap water supplies (they are charged prices far below what it costs to deliver the water) for farmers to grow unwanted crops which are also subsidized. According to Richard Martin who wrote a cover story for *Insight* April 13, 1987, the Central Arizona Project, known as CAP, would actually have ". . . adverse environmental effects . . . (and) severe inequities in the allocation and price of water." as side effects.

As Henry David Thoreau once said, "No government ever furthered an enterprise but by the alacrity by which it got out of the way."

A 1986 study by the World Resources Institute found that the Bureau of Reclamation, created in 1902, recovered only 17 percent of what irrigation projects cost and that contrary to expectations, such systems invariably lead to poor use of water as well as investment capital. Farmers who have benefited from the Bureau's projects over the last 50 or 60 years are only required to pay off capital in 1980s dollars with no regard to inflation and interest. This amounts to a powerful subsidy and uneconomic use of taxpayer dollars. The benefits are designed for the "little guy," but large growers find the regulations easy to circumvent by paper divisions of their property into several tracts—like the rice farmers, they become "little guys"![53]

As Mr. Martin points out, "America has chosen to go on building super-expensive federal water projects with no forseeable economic return."[54]

WHAT'S THIS ABOUT A DEFICIT? WHAT DEFICIT?

COURTS AND PRISONS

HIKING COURT FEES

The 99th Congress quietly hiked the civil filing fee from $60 to $120 (100%), the bankruptcy filing fee for Chapter 7 & 13 went from $60 to $90, for Chapter 11, from $200 to $500 (on business naturally) and a new Chapter 12 for farm filing bankruptcy with a $200 filing fee, was created. All in hopes of raising an additional $21 million in FY1987.

Providing a fair, adequate, efficient and affordable court system is one of the few legitimate tasks of federal government. What happened?

The U.S. Courts Administration office has a FY1987 budget of $1.19 billion, $161 million more than the FY1986 budget and $35 million less than requested. The problem—Congress created 52 new bankruptcy judgeships without appropriating funds for their salaries. Oh well, we can't all be perfect. Just be glad none of these Congresspersons are running *your* business.

FRAUD AGAINST THE FEDERAL GOVERNMENT

Unfortunately some people haven't been running the business at the Justice Department all that well either. Between 1976–79 there were 77,000 alleged cases of small scale fraud against the federal government. Nearly 12,900 cases were referred to the Justice Department for action, but because only about 40 percent were ever prosecuted the government lost an estimated $150 to $220 million.

For example one company billed NASA for $27,000 in overhead expenses which went towards a Mercedes and a Cadillac for the company president and his wife. A government audit disallowed the payment, (somebody was on the job), but the government declined to prosecute since the taxpayers suffered no actual financial loss. How is it the government "loses money" when you get a tax-credit or get an exemption, or somehow don't pay enough taxes, but when someone else overcharges a government entity "no actual financial loss" is suffered? If that attitude doesn't tell potential crooks to sock it to the taxpayers I don't know what does! It says loud and clearly that the coast is clear. If the government should happen to catch you, it is too busy to take you to court anyway.

THE LEGAL FEES EQUITY ACT

But you are aware by now that we have a lot of laws that encourage what we mean to discourage and vice versa. For instance, under our court system, unless otherwise agreed, it is customary for each party to a litigation to pay his own attorneys, no matter who wins. Congress was persuaded by certain interest groups (read here civil rights activists-attorneys) to pass a law reversing this "pay your own way" policy in civil rights actions. The definitions of civil rights is crucial. Fee shifting laws allow an attorney to work on a case even though damage may be small and still collect fees from the defendant. The problem is most defendants are government entities and that means taxpayers end up footing the bill for what often amounts to little more than a lawyers' exercise. This seems particularly outrageous when the plaintiffs' award is a nominal dollar and the attorneys' fees are $100,000!

The Legal Fees Equity Act seeks to correct this foolishness and should have taxpayer support. Activists argue that issues involving principle, as opposed to dollars, will be ignored if lawyers are not paid for their services. This unexplicably ignores the pro-bono work traditionally undertaken by many firms. It also betrays the idealism initially underlying public funding of legal aid societies.

On the other hand, the "private attorney general" statute in California permits a court to award fees to private attorneys whose legal action "results in the enforcement of an important public right affecting the public interest." News agencies who collect material, spending time and money in a successful challenge to show certain actions of government are wrong are also awarded fees to compensate them on behalf of the public.

"PAY-YOUR-OWN-WAY" HURTS INNOCENT DEFENDANTS

In his March 25, 1987 column, Jack Anderson reminded us what we already know; that there are many (too many?) practicing attorneys in this country. Of course he may have gotten a little carried away when he attempted to lay all the problems that have occurred since Adam and Eve at their feet. "Entrepreneurs have been driven out of business, doctors have abandoned their practices, journalists have stopped exposing wrongdoing, manufacturers have shut down plants, local governments have cut off services—all because they can no longer afford the high cost of defending lawsuits."

However it is certainly true that under our present judicial system the defendant loses if he loses the suit (so what else is new?) and even if he wins the suit because of the aggravation, time and legal fees spent on his defense. Because of contingency fees (a plaintiff doesn't pay a penny unless the case is won and then the lawyer gets a fixed percentage of the award) an innocent citizen can be sued—harassed—picked on—with immunity by anyone with a concealed grudge. If it hasn't happened to you yet then I wonder where you've been. Reform and alternatives have to be explored. One idea might be to give the defendant the option of having the case tried by Judicate rather that through the traditional court system where, as we have seen, he is certain to be trounced.

"JUDICATE"

Judicate is the nation's only private court system (civil, not criminal) and it employs over 300 retired judges. The idea (which came about through disillusionment with the nation's backlogged court system) was the 1984 brainchild of Philadelphia lawyer Alan Epstein who raised $4.5 million through a stock offering to get it off the ground. Judicate offers speed and efficiency in cases involving the rights of individual litigants which could otherwise take as much as four years just to get on a civil trial docket. Although it offers no jury trials Judicate adheres to many of the formalities of traditional courts including publishing its internal procedures. Insurance companies have been Judicate's best customers to date, paying $125 for a one-hour settlement conference and $375 for a 3 hour conference after first paying a $75 filing fee. All fees are obtained from both plaintiff and defendant. Although it only processed 400 cases in 1986 it is prepared to handle thousands and feels there is more than enough business from frustrated citizens to satisfy both its own need for business and that of its only rival, the non-profit 50 year old American Arbitration Association which uses arbitrators instead of former judges to settle disputes and in 1986 processed 47,000 cases.

JUSTICE IS ONE THING BUT THIS IS RIDICULOUS!!

I will reiterate my stand that providing an impartial efficient court system is one of the few legitimate obligations of the federal government. Sadly, in recent years, the judiciary has gone overboard exercising, in many cases, less judgment than a typical six year old.

Jacob Schlesinger, writing for the Wall Street Journal, told of an Indiana Judge who had a legal assistant spend half his time for three months working on a case for which the judge then spent six weeks writing an opinion before dismissing the case without prejudice so the obviously less than normal plaintiff could start the process all over again; of course at taxpayer expense! "Obviously less than normal" is, I realize, a judgment call, but you should have read the pleadings.

Mr. Schlesinger told of inmates bringing suit against a television station in New Orleans because they were "embarrassed" by a last minute cancellation. A Wisconsin radio station was sued for emotional distress suffered because prison inmates timed 57 minutes of music when 58 minutes had been promised in an hour program. It is little wonder that 90 percent of the suits filed by prisoners are dismissed as frivolous—I mean what better way to use "time" than to attempt to sabotage the system responsible for putting them in prison in the first place.

Hyperlexis means a tendency to sue over grievances previously ignored. Hyperlexis is sweeping America. One result has been the doubling of the number of civil suits filed in U.S. district courts in recent years. Unfortunately it is not always easy to distinguish between legitimate and frivolous. Your legitimate suit of the 1980s would often have been a frivolous suit if brought in the 1950s.

THE COMPREHENSIVE CRIME CONTROL ACT OF 1984

The Comprehensive Crime Control Act of 1984 set up the U.S. Sentencing Commission composed of three federal judges, four private citizens and two non-voting administrative members. Under its draft proposals federal judges would no longer have total discretion in sentencing criminals. Instead each crime would be assigned a number of points and the points would determine the sentence. If a judge felt strongly that a different punishment was warranted then the point system could be set aside in specific cases and with strict safeguards. The procedure would not be absolutely cut and dried but parole would be abolished and plea bargaining would all but disappear as attorneys could no longer benefit from the characteristics of either a "soft" or a "hard" judge.

The first guidelines released in September 1986 by the Sentencing Commission and immediately denounced by the American Bar Association (ABA) gave judges virtually no discretion in sentencing and provided harsher sentences for many crimes. The more recent guidelines (1987) increased judicial power, advocated more lenient sentences and once again opened the way for plea bargaining, to the delight of defense lawyers everywhere.

Attorney General Edwin Meese III has urged the Commission to add death penalty guidelines to its drafts since the federal criminal code already provides for death sentences in a few cases. However, they refused, by a 4 to 3 vote, to issue death penalty guidelines.

CHEAPER TO IMPRISON THAN TO EXECUTE

Since it costs about $20,000 per year (varies from state to state) to keep a person in prison, most people would suppose a savings to the taxpayer by imposing the death sentence rather than life imprisonment. In October, 1986 C-SPAN featured a discussion between liberal civil rights lawyer, Joseph Rauh and the more conservative judicial reformer, Patrick McGuigan. I bring this up in order to illustrate the extent of the misconceptions surrounding the prison vs death penalty issue. Mr. Rauh said "It's true it's cheaper to keep than execute." This is the reality:

The Supreme court ruled in Furman v Georgia (1972) special substantive and procedural protections are required before a state court can impose the death penalty. Largely due to this 1972 ruling, it is cheaper to keep a person in prison, even for life.

Two professors at Mt. Holyoke College, Profs. Ellis and Moran, estimate it costs about $4.5 million to sentence one person to death in California and $7.3 million in New York because more time must be spent on cases seeking the death penalty. More investigation of facts, more pre-trial motions, more expert testimony all add up to longer more complex and more costly trials. In the first place, only 10 percent of the cases tried actually result in the imposition of the death penalty, but the other 90 percent are tried at just as great expense making that one death sentence bear the cost of all. The so-called "super due process laws" took effect in August 1977 and from then to December 1985 1,847 capital cases were tried with only 190 actually resulting in the death sentence. And that is cost to sentence, not execute; the 55 persons sentenced in California have since had their cases overturned.

The dollars reflect societies' doubts. Costly and cumbersome constitutional protections are the outgrowth of the American people's desire to assure fairness in capital cases. In the previously mentioned C-SPAN program, Mr. McGuigan said, "Economic consequences should have no bearing." That sentiment, multiplied many times over the years, has played a large part in the formation of our present deficit.

In California alone there are about 250 trials seeking the death penalty each year. It has been estimated that abolishing the death penalty would save taxpayers about $125 million a year. If these figures are to be given any weight at all, it is readily apparent the death penalty uses a disproportionate share of our criminal justice dollars.

Some observers believe the death penalty law in California distorts the criminal justice system. They contend the death penalty would be missed only until society adjusted to a different set of maximum legal punishments. Execution for murder is a one in a thousand long shot which frustrates many who suffer from violent crimes because it marks their loss with less than the law's maximum punishment. Presently a long prison sentence tells victims their loss was not as notable a loss as those where the death penalty was achieved.

A SOCIETY OUT OF CONTROL

Why are there so many criminals? Largely because our society depends on individual control. Mob psychology, not individual control can be found in the college students who were found to be throwing dog feces in children's Halloween bags and setting them on fire. Others out of control have taken to putting razor blades in Halloween candy making it necessary to set up x-ray stations around the country where children can get their treats tested.

On April 24, 1986 "No Self Control By Americans" (my title) was the subject of a Phil Donahue Show which discussed the issue of priests and women sleeping together. How can we expect self control from teenagers and lay persons in general if spiritual-moral leaders have none? One lady in the audience pointed out that the job description for a priest demanded celibacy. If a man doesn't want to uphold that part of the bargain he should get out of the priest business—change jobs. There are plenty of worthwhile things to do with such training, she declared. A year later The Reverend Jerry Falwell was telling the same thing to Jim and Tammy Bakker.

Are we a nation of jelly-fish where discipline is seen as troublesome and old fashioned? No one can deny the lack of accountability and little sense of obligation at all levels in America today. Restraint and character are no longer fashionable; excesses and excuses are the rule. We are without doubt, an undisciplined nation; strangers to morality. The priests that were discussed on Mr. Donahue's show were morally wrong according to their professed religion. A very angry lady called and said: "I made a commitment (marriage) 30 years ago and I have to live with it. There are times when I'd like to walk out." Someone in the studio audience responded simply, "It sounds like she's not happy." That person assumed the caller should do whatever it takes to be happy—i.e. "walk out". That would be the path of least resistance. But happiness and satisfaction can be achieved by pursuing ideals and ideals can be achieved by overcoming temptation and weakness. I know, I know—it sounds corny. Overcoming anything is archaic and rarely considered worthwhile anymore.

Younger Americans seem unaware that ideals are not instantly achieved and discarded but rather demand time, work and discipline to achieve. As the late Chaplain of the Senate, Peter Marshall was fond of saying, "Unless we stand for something we shall fall for anything."

OVERCROWDED PRISONS

A lot of young people in this country have fallen into crime. Over two-thirds of the states are presently under court order to end overcrowding in prisons. The Bureau of Justice Statistics reported 546,659 prisoners in federal and state correctional facilities as 1987 began. Federal prisons are currently operating at between 27 percent and 59 percent above capacity with the worst offenders being Hawaii at 188 percent above capacity, Massachusetts at 167 percent, California at 165 percent and Connecticut at 163 percent. In 1983 Texas passed a law restricting its inmate prison population to 95 percent of prison capacity.

HUMILIATION AS AN ALTERNATIVE

Public humiliation is swift, inexpensive and effective, at least for those convicted of non-violent crimes and living in smaller communities. Having their names and picture followed by an apology for their behavior printed in the local paper could modify the actions of small town inhabitants more effectively than a prison sentence. Already some communities print the names of "Johns" caught visiting prostitutes or have judges who force drunk drivers to display bumper stickers which tell the world of their crime. We thought we had left the world of Nathaniel Hawthorne's *Scarlet Letter* far behind, only to discover our advanced system of justice now throws non-violent, often merely misguided offenders, into a system where they are likely to be raped, introduced to drugs (Introduced? I admit that's naive), and more advanced criminal acts by hardened felons. Weekends spent in the local jail, community-work projects and home detention all have the triple "economic benefit" (forgive me Professor Kelman) of allowing the criminal to work to make restitution to the victim, provide for his family and keep them off welfare and save taxpayers the expense of his room, board and supervision in a prison facility.

HOUSE ARREST

A 1987 study for the Correctional Association of New York figured the state could save $468 million in prison construction costs and $121.7 million each year in confinement costs if they stopped incarcerating the approximately 12 percent of their prison population that "had never posed physical harm to another person."[55]

Florida is experimenting with house arrest. A prisoner can leave his home only to go to work and is allowed two hours each week to shop for groceries. Probation officers make surprise visits to prisoners' homes and places of work while a computer makes robot-phone calls. One gimmick is a device that must stay on a prisoner's wrist and is placed in a box when the phone rings so that a substitute can't answer. Another device triggers an alarm if a prisoner walks beyond pre-set boundaries. It costs approximately $3 a day to check up on these people whereas jail in Florida costs $18,000 per year which is almost $50 per day. Convicts in Florida are often given a choice of one year in jail or two years under house arrest.

In Georgia, house arrest convicts can't drink or use drugs and have to work for the community.

Reduction of crime is the main logic for jail but 30 percent of jail prisoners are rearrested. On the other hand, fewer than 15 percent of prisoners commit new crimes while on the street under house arrest rules. Favoring the concept of house arrest is the idea that if a criminal works he can pay retribution to the victim. Generally a victim is more interested in being paid back than in revenge.

PRIVATELY OPERATED PRISONS

As of early 1987, only four states had passed laws allowing privately operated state prisons (TX, MN, TN & MA) although 40 states contract-out to the private sector for medical services, vocational training and other services. This may be the wave of the future as the alternative is to have taxpayers cough up a lot more dollars for a lot more prisons.

Some people object to privatizing the prison system because entrepreneurs would provide the service for profit rather than for humanitarian reasons. The idea that running a prison facility is more than providing a service; that it is somehow "the doing of justice" is nonsense. Justice is the province of the courts, not the prison facility.

A less frivolous objection is that states who contract-out prison facilities may be waving the defense of soverign immunity and thereby increase liability under the Civil Rights Act under which the majority of prison-conditions litigation is brought.

But the main challenge would appear to rest on constitutional grounds, claiming not all government functions can be delegated (as Gramm-Rudman proved) and the challenge would seek to prove that incarceration is one such government function.

In 1986 the ABA urged those areas considering privatization to wait until certain legal issues surrounding privatization were resolved. In February 1987, the Criminal Justice Division of the ABA launched a nine month study to determine its recommendation as to whether the government can delegate normally government functions to the private sector. If so they were to determine how and to what degree.

SOMETHING TO BELIEVE IN

The need to have something to believe in is greater today than ever before in our history. Nature abhors a vacuum, so if this basic need in man is not filled by things positive and uplifting it will be filled by things negative and destructive and our courts and prisons will continue to overflow.

DEFENSE

WHICH IS MORE IMPORTANT?

"Without an adequate defense there is nothing else to consider." I was happy with the foregoing assertion until I came across the following statement made in 1933 by FDR's Budget Director, Lewis Douglas (Arizona Congressman 1927–33): "I say, which is more important? A national defense which is perfectly futile, if the credit of the government collapses, or an unimpaired credit of your government? For myself, I say 'An unimpaired government.' For it is upon that that all human values of our people ultimately rest."[56] I say "Bravo" to Mr. Lewis, but unfortunately we have no choice as taxpayers but to go along with the gargantuan defense budget submitted year in and year out, trusting blindly in the judgment of our elected officials. Exaggeration on both sides of the aisle may have left the public with the sense that there has been some massive build-up in defense whereas real defense spending in 1986 was 19.8 billion below the amount projected in President Reagan's 1981 budget and just $2.2 billion above the projections made in President Carter's 1980 budget. President Carter had planned to ask for $1.28 trillion for FY1982–86 while President Reagan actually managed to get $1.45 trillion.

DEFINING DEFENSE SPENDING

One of the problems inherent in tracing defense spending is finding a generally accepted definition. Defense spending used to be measured by program (Conventional, Nuclear or Strategic Forces for example) or by mission (NATO, or Nuclear Deterence). Today it is more often broken down into military components which, according to the annual report of the Secretary of Defense, for FY1986 showed in billions of dollars $96.1 allocated to Navy and Marines, $94.9 to Air Force, $73.1 to Army and $17.3 to Defense Agencies and miscellaneous. When defense spending is measured by appropriation the same report shows the following breakdown, also in billions of dollars: Procurement=$92.5, Operation & Maintenance=$74.9., Personnel=$67.8, Research & Development=$33.6 and miscellaneous=$12.6. The total in both cases amounted to budget authority of $281.4 billion in FY1986.

But even if there is agreement on the definition of defense spending, chances are the so-called "black budgets" or secret classified spending (from $4.6 billion in 1980 to $22.5 billion in 1986) is not included nor are the portions of the budgets of various government agencies allocated to defense included.

If we could have unbiased facts presented to us we might be able to help the decision making process. Wouldn't "they" love that? "This weapon makes more sense than that, this base is superfluous, that system is more cost effective" and so forth. As it is, we are subjected to clearly distorted rhetoric designed to persuade not enlighten us.

GETTING THE DOLLARS

A Washington Post-ABC News poll taken early in 1987 showed 31 percent of those polled supported more defense spending over the 22 percent who supported more in 1986. Up, but far under the 72 percent who supported more defense spending in 1981 at the beginning of the Reagan administration. The outcome of the misconception just mentioned that there has been a massive defense build-up since 1981.

The military brass, along with all other government agency heads, learned long ago that the only way to obtain funds anywhere near what they want is to pad the bill in anticipation of cuts. This is a game where to tell the truth can be fatal and it has been played so long and so well that most players no longer really know the truth.

A variety of studys, reports and just plain observations point to the unpleasant, but indisputable fact, that more dollars buy higher overhead and prices rather than more defense.

Dr. Gordon Adams,[57] head of a non-partisan defense-budget project, claims that since the Russians get so much more than we do for their money it doesn't make sense to compare the dollar amounts spent in an effort to determine parity. We spend much more on personnel and maintenance and less on procurement and research. The research and development budget is the fastest growing in the defense department because it has the most to grow!

Chart IV

Distribution Of Defense Budget According To FY1986 Appropriations

Personnel	$67.8 billion
Operating & Maintenance	74.9 billion
Procurement	42.5 billion
Research & Development	33.6 billion

A Congressional Budget Office report showed that although more money was spent 1982–85 vs 1977–80, there was not a significant increase in the number of weapons purchased. Allowing for inflation, the Army is spending the same amount of money (42 billion in 1983 dollars) on new tanks as it did toward the end of the Korean War, but the number of tanks produced has declined 90%. In 1951, the military bought 6,800 fighter planes at a cost in 1983 dollars of $7 billion whereas in 1983 $11 billion purchased only 322 planes, 95% fewer than in 1951. Remember, that's allowing for inflation.

One reason? The Reagan administration prefers the more expensive sophisticated weapons. Other reasons were cited by the very down-to-earth and colorful representative of the Congressional Research Division, Colonel John Collins in his testimony to the Senate Armed Services Committee on January 20, 1987:

1) Our objectives are too fuzy. ("help friends help themselves")
2) Our perception of threats is skewed. The Department of Defense (DOD) defines "intensity of peril" in terms of enemy capabilities. Although there is a low probability of nuclear war it is given a high priority by DOD. There is a higher probability of conventional conflict but it had no priority until Congress stepped in, according to Colonel Collins.
3) The Colonel believes we have no real strategy ("Match ends with means while minimizing waste" he referred to as a mere game of intellectual judo) DOD assumes arms control depends on superiority but we got taken in Salt I although we were "superior", according to Colonel Collins. He bemoans the fact that there are very few military strategists at the top.

Former Assistant Secretary of Defense, Lawrence Kolb, who testified at the same hearing, agreed that there is no relation between strategy and programs and that in fact each service follows it own separate strategy.

IT GREW AND IT GREW AND IT . . .

Many experts agree the system is spectacularly overmanaged and overcommanded with too many officers adding their two cents. There are almost as many 3-star military officials today with 2.2 million active duty military as in 1945 when we had 12 million men under arms.

In 1947 the Office of the Secretary of Defense was created with 50 persons attached to it. By the mid-eighties the Office had 2,000 employees. Today there are eleven separate defense agencies with staffs of a thousand or more, yet Secretary Weinberger's FY1986 budget requested an additional 18,500 civilians for the Pentagon (referred to by critics as a "Republican jobs program"). Everyone is responsible; therefore no one is responsible.

A couple years ago Senator Warren Rudman (NH) proposed a 10% cut in Pentagon's overall work force, claiming this would save $12.5 billion over a three year period. Unfortunately his plan was defeated in committee.

NO COORDINATION

Former Secretary of the Navy, John Lehman reported to 32 committees in 1986 instead of only four reported to by his predecessors as recently as 1975, yet he was one of the most ardent foes of centralized planning at the Pentagon. He believed giving greater authority to the Chairman of the Joint Chiefs of Staff would limit the unusual independence the Navy has traditionally enjoyed. Unhappily the invasion of Grenada showcased the dangerous lack of coordination by the various services. Army helicopters carrying wounded soldiers couldn't land on Navy ships standing off Grenada because the pilots lacked the proper training.

Centralized planning was recommended in the report issued by the Packard Commission in early March 1986. The Packard Commission was President Reagan's Blue Ribbon Commission on Defense Management, chaired by David Packard of Hewlett-Packard Company. It recommended strenghthening the Secretary of Defense, the Chairman of the Joint Chiefs of Staff and field commanders at the expense of top brass within individual services, slashing Pentagon bureaucracy and streamlining procurement procedures.

PROCUREMENT

The question most often asked in recent procurement discussions has not been "what can do the job?" but rather "what service gets what?". Central management needs real authority so someone can be held accountable. The problem up until now has been that no one is in charge—the "buck" never stops anywhere but is continually passed.

We have often attributed our past successes to "American Ingenuity" which I interpret to mean our ability as a people to innovate, adjust quickly and think creatively—something we cannot do when hundreds of thousands of us are buried under a mountain of paper and sunk in a sea of numbers and specifications. The defense establishment has been described as a "huge socialistic enterprise badly in need of deregulation."[58] How else could the incredible waste have developed; waste which has both amused and angered us from headlines across the nation over the past few years? Heros and villains get all mixed up in one-liners. We remember the common allen-wrench worth less than $1 modified by General Dynamics to maintain the radar antenna on the F-16 fighter air-craft priced at $9,600; but we forget that the Pentagon never bought the darn thing but should be congratulated for discovering the excessive charges and putting a stop to the transaction. Sure, the Pentagon actually paid $435 for a hammer but received a refund for the over charges and subsequently bought 87,000 hammers for $6 to $8 each. But unfortunately the story doesn't end there. The Pentagon reacted by adding 7,000 people to solve its spare-parts problems and those people will still be on the government's payroll long after the hammers are worn out.

According to computer records the Army paid more than $565,900 for 46 shipment from Frankfurt, West Germany to Washington, DC between May 1984 and June 1985. The shipments of household goods of soldiers could have cost $51,300 if they had been made though less expensive companies. More than 11 times less!

On a more personal basis, the following is an excerpt from a letter from my son who was on active duty with the Air Force, stationed in Italy at the time of the incident described:

> "Altogether the Air Force spent $7,000 in AFFF foam concentrate which was used to help control the fire. AN OUTRAGEOUS AMOUNT! I saw so much waste. Any city department would never have done that; maybe a couple hundred dollars but no way $7,000! Somehow the tank got premixed with water and ruined 100's of gallons of it and it had to be dumped. I can now understand the federal deficit. This was just one minor incident that occurred at one small base overseas in one day. I can imagine the expense and waste if it happens every day somewhere at some base."

Lest we forget the Navy, perhaps you recall the episode on the "60 Minutes" television show in April 1983 that highlighted three warships whose standard furnishings were ripped out and replaced to satisfy the interior decorating demands of high-ranking naval officers. Or maybe you remember the following extravagence reported by the Associated Press in June 1985:

1) A dining set was rented for $1,500 whereas the Navy could have purchased a similar dining set for $450.
2) $99.50 was spent for a silk plant instead of paying $10 for a live plant.
3) $140.25 was paid for each of four plastic brown trash cans and $171.82 each for four standard galvanized steel liners. (We have four plastic brown trash cans at home which I bought for $4.95 each at a K-Mart sale. (You don't suppose . . .?)

Two of the most humorous and unbelievable illustrations of a bureaucracy gone wild were reported by Columnist Jack Anderson and the Wall Street Journal respectively.

The first is a recital of specifications for army procurement officers for things one would never imagine would be covered. Specifications which, according to columnist Jack Anderson, "simply hamstring procurement officers who might otherwise use their common sense to find better buys on the open market."

Doughnuts must only be *so* greasy and must retain a certain amount of glaze when transported. There are twenty pages describing the standards for cocoa and nine pages for the marshmallows a soldier might want to float on top. Chewing gum and olives each get seventeen pages.[59]

The second article takes the reader step by step through the bureaucratic process whereby two diodes costing only a few cents at any Radio Shack emerge as Pentagon spare parts worth $110. Just the right amount was allowed at every level by watch dog bureaucrats for a contractor's labor, overhead, administrative expense and profit. The Wall Street Journal editorialized "We need to make contractors provide their products at fixed prices, and let them worry about what to spend on expense accounts and what profit margin they need. We need to give managers the authority to make decisions, and if they make too many wrong ones, fire them and find someone else."[60] BRAVO!!

Some people believe improvements in the procurement process is impossible unless it is taken from the military and put under civilian control where there is less self-interest and more protection against reprisals. Pentagon whistleblower A. Ernest Fitzgerald claims that defense contractors frequently charge the military much more than they do private buyers for the same type of work. Contractors often must factor in the cost of expensive warranties, inflating the cost of one piece of equipment compared with a non-warranted counterpart. Overhead for storing a $1 bolt and an exotic $1 billion piece of equipment may be equally apportioned between the two, resulting in hair-raising numbers but yielding little insight into budgeting problems.

THE DEFENSE CONTRACT AUDIT AGENCY

The DCAA (Defense Contract Audit Agency) was formed in 1965 in response to an earlier wave of congressional concern about Pentagon procurement problems; further proof that there is "nothing new under the sun". In 1968 the DCAA reviewed 582 contracts worth less than $4 billion to determine whether the contractor accurately estimated labor, material and other costs. Seventeen years later it reviewed over 100,000 contracts worth approximately $300 billion. Over a seventeen year period the agency grew from 166 employees to 4,600 employees; from a budget of $20 million to a budget of $180 million. Does this sound like bureaucracy on the move?

On the one hand the DCAA has been referred to as a toothless tiger. Auditor's rulings are often overturned by contracting officers. I came across something as innocuous as a refusal by an auditor to pay a company's parking tickets amounting to $105, which was overturned by a contracting officer. I have heard about the denial to DCAA of legal access to contractor documents and the antagonism between DCAA auditors and the more powerful Pentagon procurement officers.

On the other hand I read the DCAA "may be the most feared (agency)." It is easy to point to savings generated by detecting fraud and inefficiency but that must be balanced by the much harder to detect but even larger costs of overregulation.

A bill proposed by Representative Jim Courter of New Jersey, to eliminate the DCAA failed to make it through the 99th Congress and it is uncertain whether it will be reintroduced in the 100th Congress.

3.5 TONS

The instruction book on procurement runs 32 volumes and takes up six feet of shelf space according to Gregory Fossedal, a media fellow at the Hoover Institution at Stanford, who wrote on this subject. Mr. Fossedal told of 240,000 pages comprising bids of five competitors for the C-5A cargo plane. He claimed the relevant material weighed 3.5 tons and took several trucks to deliver. Since withholding information on a contract is now a potential felony, companies are often forced to err on the side of over-documentation.

Studies have shown that one third of procurement costs can be traced to regulation. Mr. Fossedal gives a striking example of this in relating certain facts surrounding the UC-15, an experimental plane built several years ago by McDonnell Douglas Corporation: "The company bid $164 million and estimated the project would take 2½ years. When the government offered special immunity from most oversight bureaucracy the prototypes were rolled out ten months early and cost $84 million."[61]

The Defense Department should rely to a much greater extent on "off the shelf" components and services available in regular commercial channels instead of insisting on rigid military specifications which raise prices.

Congress is expected to pass legislation requiring defense program managers to obtain a waiver in order to write specifications for anything that is already produced and available commercially.

1984 COMPETITION IN CONTRACTING ACT

The 1984 Competition in Contracting Act requires the Defense Department to set up open competitions for most procurements. That, and other such laws created a legion of 7,000 price cutters, employees known as "competition advocates", to search for new suppliers by working with procurement officers in the 200 major military buying offices. Some 60 percent of the Pentagon's total procurement dollars go to contracts that are competitively negotiated with so-called qualified companies; 5 percent are awarded on a formal, closed-bid basis and the remaining 35 percent go either to fund programs where only one defense supplier has been found or to extend previously awarded contracts.

WHAT DO YOU MEAN UNCLE SAM DOESN'T "BUY AMERICAN"?

No one would seriously question the prerogative of American citizens to have access to products from around the world, however most Americans would be not only amazed but infuriated to know that their taxpayer dollars often go to purchase products made by foreign firms even though comparable American-made products are available. Most citizens assume their government "Buys American".[62] If in some rare instance something is required by a U.S. government entity—federal, state, or local—that is produced only by foreigners, that agency need only put the word out that there is a market for such and such and entrepreneurial Americans will rush to fill that need. 100 million Americans wanting to get ahead will provide all the competition that is necessary if the need is publicized.

Until Congressman Leon Panetta presented a restrictive amendment to the FY1987 defense authorization bill, the Department of Defense was stocking commissaries with products which used foreign grown commodities. This practice hurt not only American farmers and American food processing companies that purchase strictly American grown commodities but according to the Congressman also exposed members of the military and their families to unknown risks of pesticides.

ViON, the American distributor for Hitachi of Japan, is an outrageous example of using taxpayer dollars to purchase "Made in Japan" goods, even if it hurts! Jack Anderson devoted a couple columns, in May and June of 1987, to ViON's escapades. After a two year investigation, on April 7, 1987 ViON decided to plead guilty to the U.S. Army's charges that it had not provided the computer equipment it had agreed to, and which the Army had paid for. As part of the settlement, ViON was required to inform the Army of any subsequent contracts it obtained from federal agencies. How then, citizens are entitled to wonder, could the U.S. Customs Service award a $19 million contract to ViON the day after it had pleaded guilty to 50 counts of fraud and been fined $579,407? Perhaps Customs didn't know about the fraud which had occured at the Defense Department? No, Customs *knew* but no one said they *couldn't* buy from ViON so—? Maybe Customs needed the computer system in a hurry and it wasn't made by American companies? No, IBM had appealed the Customs' contract for the Hitachi system, claiming its own system was more capable of fulfilling Custom's needs than the one ViON was peddling. Maybe this is an isolated case—surely other government entities wouldn't "Buy Japanese" when comparable American products are available—not with all the "talk" on Capital Hill and hand-wringing over our trade deficit? Think again—on the very day that President Reagan announced sanctions against Japan (April 17, 1987), the Agriculture Department let Storage Tek, an American firm, know that it had lost a $48 million computer contract to ViON. According to Jack Anderson's account of the ViON fiasco, Storage Tek and IBM had both come in with bids lower than ViON's Hitachi price.

Next time some celebrity appears on your television set advising *you* to "Buy American" you'll know where to send them.

COMPETITIVE BIDDING

Senator Phil Gramm of Texas tried in vain awhile back to get military contracts exempted from the costly Davis-Bacon Act and other regulations which preclude true competition. And speaking of true competition, what about the idea of allowing local communities to bid competitively for the right to have military installations located within their boundaries as opposed to the "pork" give away staged by congressmen on the basis of seniority for the benefit of their constituents? The administration has tried time and again to close unnecessary bases but the pork-barreling continues.

Getting back to the realm of possibility, it is particularly important to select wisely the systems open to price competition—those characterized by relative technical simplicity and large production quantities are especially desirable.

In the past, the Senate has urged the Pentagon to have two or more companies compete on contracts for major weapons but would let it make exemptions. The House, on the other hand, would greatly limit exemptions and would force the military to recompete single-producer contracts instead of simply rubber-stamping them. There have been eleven Pentagon and congressional studies since 1964 that have concluded that competitive bidding saves as much as 52 percent in dollar costs compared with sole-source procurement and improves product quality besides. The Air Force is doing something about it. During FY1985 the Air Force received $9.4 million in voluntary refunds due to overcharges and suspended or barred over 60 contracters. The Air Force had made reliability and maintainability an important evaluation item and given it equal status with cost, schedule and performance.

Some observers believe competitive practices will only increase current defense expenditures. They claim that having two sources for every program is false economy because of the increased production and tooling expenses. In 1985, 39 percent of the dollars committed in Air Force contracts involved competitive bidding. Of course it's difficult to have bids without written specifications. Bidders quite naturally prefer detailed information as to the Pentagon's needs. Nevertheless the Air Force has launched a war on unnecessarily rigid and costly specifications, convinced that giving industry broad performance goals for new weapons, rather than detailed design specifications, is a wise practice. In the June 17, 1985 issue of Forbes magazine, a Mr. Luttwak was interviewed on this subject and offered the Army's success with the Multiple Launch Rocket as an example of what should be done: "Far from specifying every last thing, the Army told the contractors, 'I want a rocket that can go a certain range and deliver this kind of payload or one that will give more payload at a somewhat lower range.' It specified the performance required, and even that was done in a flexible way. The result was contractors could develop the prototype and offer a fixed price." It's great to be able to point to something that was done correctly. So often high-tech state-of-the-art weapons are produced at extremely high unit costs because too small a production run has been ordered. According to a colonel at the Pentagon, "In World War II we never bought the best system. We bought the second-or-third best, because it was affordable and then ran the factories like crazy. And it worked."[63]

WATCH DOGS

There are more than thirty House and Senate Committees that oversee weapons; as if waste and fraud could be curtailed by sheer number of watch dogs. In fact, the law of diminishing returns is obvious here as checkers duplicate, frustrate and unintentionally sabotage each other's efforts.

The Wall Street Journal discussed a study for the Central Intelligence Agency prepared by Robert Magnan in which Mr. Magnan spoke of the reaction of one American general to the autonomy and efficiency of France's 25 member independent service. He quoted the general: "You people (French) do the work of tens of thousands of us bureaucrats in Washington."[64]

The French, Israelis, Germans and even the Russians, work with fixed priced contracts, or close to it. If the product is delivered on time, according to specifications, the manufacturer is paid. Simple—well not exactly, as any home-owner who has contracted for anything will tell you, but it sure beats the not so good 'ol American way where weapons too often fail to function properly and are seldom delivered on time.

The Packard Commission called for extensive prototype testing during the early stages of development as a cost cutting measure. To this end, Congressman Denny Smith of Oregon, in 1984 sponsored H.R. 3106 to create an independent Office of Testing and Evaluation at the Pentagon. The suggestion that testing of expensive weapon systems be carried on, not by the companies that want to sell them nor the branch of service that wants to purchase them, but by a disinterested entity, made sense even to members of Congress and it was enacted into law as part of the Department of Defense Authorization Act of 1984.

HILL AIR FORCE BASE

Maybe it's time for a "good guy" story to show successes in the area of competition. The Wall Street Journal reported such a story on page 17 of its March 6, 1986 edition. It concerned Hill Air Force Base in Ogden, Utah. It started with a not uncommon horror story of procurement officers paying three times the old price for an item which was already in abundant supply in its own warehouses after being donated by the old supplier when he shut down production. Unfortunately newer procurement officers didn't know about the donation and older officers had forgotten about it. Such problems were solved at Hill with the installation of a computerized buying system.

Shopping around saved Hill in another instance when it purchased an off-the-shelf item for $575.40 each instead of ordering from the original supplier at $1,256 each. "Should Cost" estimates also worked for Hill, according to the Wall Street Journal article which discussed a situation where approximately 25 percent was saved by telling a manufacturer what the Air Force thought the item "should cost". Hill spent 41 percent less on competitive contracts and ". . . the base saved $100 million of its $1.6 billion procurement budget in fiscal 1985. . . . Expenses for the competition advocates office, which has 246 employees, were about $7 million." They netted $93 million—not bad. In fact one might say the taxpayers finally got a good deal.

If there is any truth to the folk wisdom that says the press only reports on the unusual then one might be led to believe "good deals" were the norm; they are so little mentioned. On the other hand, stories predominate about shopping sprees by the various services which result in duplications and other inefficiencies. I found one that suggested that the military's system of ordering goods solely on the basis of their federal stock number caused the buyer to never question the price because he had no idea what he was actually ordering!

Although computers solved some of Hill's procurement problems, Dr. Gordon Adams blamed computers for many others.[65] Sometimes supplies get sold at one end and repurchased on another computer. Often one hand has no idea what the other is doing. With 15 million orders processed a year, waste is inevitable. When inventory is not known, it is least troublesome to purchase more—just in case.

MULTI-YEAR DEFENSE BUDGETS

Almost everyone agrees the defense effort cannot be run effectively without predictable budgets. Administrators have to have some confidence that spending on defense won't be downgraded in a year or two. Longer military budgets have been endorsed by almost everyone who has witnessed the spectacle of six congressional committees (Budget, Appropriations and Armed Services in *both* Houses) disecting every line in the Pentagon budget.

However multiyear defense budgets may present a constitutional problem. The U.S. Constitution stipulates that appropriations for maintaining armies shall not last longer than two years. Here is where distinction between budget authority and budget outlays may be significant. Congress could vote on long-term authority but reserve the vote on actual outlays to fall within the two year restriction. In fact the Packard Commission suggested the President give Congress five-year plans and ask it to approve two-year budgets on the basis of these plans. (Where there's a will there's a way!)

Another idea is to mandate a fixed-dollar budget instead of preapproving a long shopping list. This would supply the incentive needed to squeeze the most bang out of those fixed bucks. In past attempts to stretch those dollars, the delivery time was extended; an illusory play because, as any businessman will tell you, stretching out production raises unit costs. Definitely a step in the wrong direction.

WORK MEASUREMENT

Another step in the wrong direction by most calculations, was the work measurement law passed by Congress in 1985. That legislation required work measurement studies from all defense contractors working on projects costing $100 thousand and up. Mounds of paper work were demanded reflecting the labor and materials proposed to the government, the amounts negotiated in the contract and the amounts expended doing the actual work. This attempt to compare the efficiency of various companies was a complete failure.

In testimony before the Armed Services Committee early in 1986, representatives of industry and the Defense Department estimated the new law in the first year would cost up to $30 million per company. The total could easily exceed $1 billion. This is an example of a wasteful inefficient system which was thankfully repealed in August 1986.

THE PROJECT ON MILITARY PROCUREMENT

So let's say we cut down on Big Brother's role and allow our business people and military brass the flexability to act creatively. Can they handle it?

Not unless some fundamental changes are made, according to Dina Rasor, founder and director of the Washington D.C. based Project On Military Procurement which seeks to expose fraudulent and wasteful weapon systems of the Department of Defense. She has spoken before numerous groups and in 1986 appeared on several television shows. She pointed to James Beggs who was indicted for fraud while at the helm of General Dynamics. It seems when a prototype costing taxpayers $40 million, overran its cost projections, Mr. Beggs simply charged the cost against another government account.

And what was his punishment? He was made the head of NASA!

To depend solely on the honesty and integrity of those in positions of power without acknowledging the political nature of men, is naive. Should the military budget be used for social objectives; i.e. to create jobs? Congressmen use budgets that way. Dina Rasor spoke of Tip O'Neil's infamous bailout of a Waltham, Massachusetts clock manufacturer which, when all was said and done, brought the *actual* cost of the simplest wind-up clock to over $500! How does that differ, aside from the sheer size of the numbers, from the case where Boeing won a design bid but Lockheed *needed* the job so the contract for the C5A was given to Lockheed? Boeing didn't waste any time lamenting its fate but instead took its design and turned it into the successful 747 which costs half the price and holds more than what the government (you and I and everyone else who trusted those decision makers) got for its money.

What must we do? First we must care. We can't keep turning our backs and saying "that's the way it is". Most Americans put up with a large number of injustices perpetrated by government without so much as a whimper. For instance the unconscionably low, inequitable and even doubtful returns on Social Security contributions; the interest free loans we unwittingly make the government via our payroll withholdings and so on and so forth. When do we say "hold it"?

I've talked to too many people who are no longer angry, just subdued. Those still angry are really more frustrated than angry and instead of trying to change things they are trying to learn to ignore what isn't right—to live with it. That's all well and good for getting along in most countries in the world where to dissent could mean prison and even death. But by golly this is the USA where the people are boss, not some dictator, monarch or evil despot. In this country "We the people" not only *can* do something, it's our duty to do something. If we say all this nonsense that goes on with the taxpayer's dollars is OK then it will be OK. The same is true whether we're talking about padding a bill, skimping on quality, stealing from employers directly or subtly by not giving full effort to the job, excusing poor performance from our kids at school or our politicians in Washington. We, you and I, are the ones who make or break this country by our tolerance, our overindulgence in forgiveness and understanding.

Those advertising executives on Madison Avenue know what Americans want when they sold a jingle to a supermarket chain that goes. "I work an honest day and I want an honest deal". Advertisers talk a lot about "deserving" lately, but even though we may not "deserve" the most expensive hair color or whatever, we do deserve honesty and integrity from those we elected to office, and we are the only ones that can ensure that we get it. Many believe what Miss Rasor expresses: ". . . the whole procurement system is driven by money, and not by military need. Money and jobs. In the districts where the weapons are built, in the revolving-door jobs for officers after they retire, provided they go along while they're on active duty."[66]

A recent example is the successful fight waged by New York Representative D'Amato and Senator Moynihan to force the Air Force to continue to purchase the T-46 jet trainer which is manufactured on Long Island and the Air Force no longer needs or wants.

According to Miss Rasor we must promote those who discover waste and attempt to generate savings and above all we must discontinue providing unlimited funds.

WHISTLE-BLOWERS

Gramm-Rudman was an attempt to "discontinue providing unlimited funds" as is the Reagan administration's refusal to raise taxes in order to lower the deficit. "Whistle-blowers" are one more weapon in an arsenal against waste. A new law gives civilian whistle-blowers the right to sue and if successful to recover up to 30 percent of any judgment won against companies that have defrauded the federal government. If the government joins the civil suit the whistle-blower is limited to 25 percent of the amount recovered.

I wonder how many situations today are similar to the position of Air Force Colonel Bob Dilger which was reported four years ago.[67] In 1975 Colonel Dilger was ordered to Dayton, Ohio to take over the GAU-8 anti-tank cannon program. The Colonel decided to work at getting the price of the armor piercing amunition down. The Air Force was prepared to pay $83 per round, based on accountant's figures. By not imposing product specifications Colonel Dilger was able to get the cost per round down under $15. While further refining the cannon itself, the Colonel managed to return a surplus of $124 million to the Pentagon. What was his reward? An undesirable desk job. He quit.

I know from having a couple sons in the service and listening to the whistle-blowers that accompany Dina Rasor, that rules and regulations make it easier in many instances to throw away new parts than to wait in long lines and fill out forms to return the unused parts to supply. In so many subtle ways, on a daily consistent basis, we find that we are destroying integrity bit by bit, wearing it down via excessive, oppressive regulations. I sincerely believe that the majority of our neighbors, IF LEFT ALONE, are basically honest, well-meaning and good natured. But a basic tenent that our public officials continually fail to consider is that man will always find a way to do what he wants to do and if a myriad of fool regulations and asinine laws are in the way he'll sure as you're reading this line, find a way around them. Examples are the underground economy and the 70 mph traffic flow in the *slow*lanes out west.

INTEGRITY

Our so-called leaders haven't set much of an example where integrity is concerned. Early in 1981, for instance, the Defense Department forecast a 6.2% inflation rate in fiscal 1984. The actual level turned out to be 3.3% which left a lot of money floating around unaccounted for. The House Armed Services Committee didn't let any moss grow under their feet and quickly came up with an estimate showing by the end of FY1986, the Defense Department could have $51.5 billion in unspent funds. Other studies suggested the Pentagon had reaped $28 billion since 1982 as a result of its inflation projections. In May 1985, Secretary Weinberger conceded that high inflation estimates had produced a nest-egg of about $4 billion. What this really meant was as long as the actual inflation rate was lower than the projected rate, any rhetoric about *no increase after inflation* adjustments was a sham. The excess projected inflation rate already guaranteed hundreds of millions of dollars in "real growth".

Mr. Weinberger's move angered many lawmakers who had fought for a budget increase based on the Defense Department's assurances that the administration's budget plan already had been cut to the bone. A lot of them were disillusioned and no longer believed, or at least could no longer argue persuasively, that cuts hurt. The feeling in the spring of 1985 was that Cap Weinberger had "called wolf" too many times before. But savings on defense don't necessarily translate into savings for the nation as a whole. For example since the armed forces consume about 200 million barrels of petroleum products a year, based on the plunge in crude oil prices the lower fuel costs should have saved the Department of Defense some $2 billion. But any savings in the defense budget from lower oil prices, even if admitted, would have been offset by lower tax receipts from our domestic oil producers.

"KNICK, KNACK, PADDYWACK—GIVE A DOG A BONE"

There has been general agreement that military pay is off-limits for budget cutters. The military received pay increases totaling an average 26 percent in 1980–81. President Reagan attempted to freeze military pay in order to trim back increases in his FY1984 defense budget but Senator John Tower of Texas rode to the rescue of servicemen with rhetoric about even a small raise signifying the country's concern and commitment to our fine young men in the armed forces. I mock the good Senator because he exhibits the type of mentality that got us into this debt and is guaranteed to keep us there. He said the pay boost would cost $552 million in FY1984, a sum he believed "could be absorbed with little difficulty by the Defense Department."[68]

All too long our representatives have figured "it could be absorbed", or "taxpayers will come up with it" and never give any credit to the groups who are directly affected. Some of *them* just might care enough about the deficit to use restraint and may even resent attempts to soothe them as if they were whimpering puppies and required a token raise as a pacifier!

"ABSORBING" DOLLARS

I realize we're into small numbers as Pentagon spending goes, but let's look at a few other places where dollars are "being absorbed."

The Reagan administration proposed in its FY1988 budget that veterans who have no service related disability, have incomes over $20,000 if single and over $25,000 if married and aren't otherwise entitled to free care, have their health care needs attended to outside the VA facilities. The proposal would probably affect only one half of one percent of all veterans applying to VA hospitals for health care, yet it would reduce the number of needed employees by almost 4,000 according to a report prepared by the staff of the House Veterans Affairs Committee.

In 1984 $108 million in disability payments was paid to approximately 35,000 vets. A couple years earlier, Robert Nimmo, former director of Veterans Administration, was reported to have told the press that many veterans were collecting disability benefits they neither needed nor deserved. "Deserved" is an ambiguous word with no merit other than to evoke emotions and I cringe whenever I hear it. The VA was paying for ills unrelated to combat such as diabetes, which is an hereditary disease and has no connection with time served in the armed forces, hemorrhoids and sinus trouble. Mr. Nimmo, President Reagan and everyone even remotely connected with any suggestion for reform would agree, I'm sure, that nothing is too good for our ex-servicemen who were wounded in action in this nation's wars and have lingering health problems as a result. We all owe them an unestimable debt and gratitude and I don't think you'd find a citizen anywhere in this country that would begrudge them the finest care available at taxpayer expense. Please bear in mind that they are not included in the modest reform proposed by the Reagan Administration. But can anyone tell me what in the blazes the House Veterans Affairs Committee means when they report that the Administration's proposal is "inconsistent with congressional intent"? Congressional intent to spend?

The more confrontations I look into between the Reagan administration and Congress the more convinced I've become that any analysis by Congress starts with the premise "We will not cut" and preceeds to find reasons to justify this immovable mind set.

MILITARY HEALTH CARE

The Congressional Budget Office (CBO) estimates that charging military retirees and dependents of active duty personnel a modest fee for visits to military clinics could save $170 million a year by discouraging unnecessary visits and also raise a bit of revenue. Under the Civilian Health and Medical Program of the Uniformed Services (Champus), the Pentagon reimburses retirees and military personal and their dependents for outpatient visits to civilian health facilities. In 1984 the government spent $550 million to reimburse private hospital care for military personnel when military hospitals could have been used to a higher degree. In FY1988 25 percent of the care provided to retirees and dependents was provided by the civilian sector (six million claims) and the cost had skyrocketed to an estimated $1.8 billion.

It is no secret nor wonder the Navy has had difficulty attracting experienced surgeons since their average pay is $70,000 versus nearly $240,000 available in private practice.

An audit of 22 military medical facilities conducted in 1985 showed that two-thirds of the practicing doctors and nurses did not have proper "qualifications and current competence." Throughout the entire system, misdiagnoses are common and waiting lines are so long that people often give up trying to be treated.

In April, 1986 civilian doctors were appointed to monitor the quality of care at military hospitals around the country. On October 1, 1986 the Defense Department began billing private insurance companies for the estimated one million patients who use military hospitals each year. This single charge in billing procedures is estimated to yield about $10 million in new revenue during its first year from the approximately 40 percent of retirees and military dependents eligible for military health care who also have private insurance.

Taking reform one step further, the Pentagon now wants to stop running its own health insurance plan and rely instead on regional contractors who will assume the responsibility for providing health care to retirees and dependents for a set annual fee. The Pentagon hopes to start a test run in six states (CA,HI,NC,SC,GA, & FL) and New Orleans by the spring of 1988.

COMMISSARIES

Originally the commissary and base exchange (BX or PX) were established to provide a subsidy to the grossly underpaid military personnel and their families and to provide goods at stations that were located far from shopping areas. Neither reason is valid anymore and what we have is the government unfairly competing against the private sector. In 1986 President Reagan appointed a special panel of business people who reported that civilian warehouse-type supermarkets were found to be even less expensive than commissaries. If true, there is even less reason to continue subsidizing commissaries.

THE MILITARY RETIREMENT SYSTEM

There is one big-ticket item that concerns military personnel and that's the retirement system. Military retirment costs $20 billion a year. (Now do I have your attention?) The average military retiree is 41 years old. The pension system allows military personnel to work for 20 years, retire in their late 30s or early 40s, and collect half their final year's salary, fully indexed against inflation, for the rest of their lives. Servicemen who put in 30 years retire at three-quarters salary. Military retirees collect six times the total lifetime pension benefits of their counterparts in the private sector. It has been estimated that adapting these retirement plans to the best of those in the private sector would save $58.1 billion over three years and $314 billion over 10 years.

There have been many plans to bring military pensions more in line with civilian pensions. CBO estimated in 1985 that paying current retirees under the age of 62 only half the cost-of-living-adjustment would save $22 billion in defense authority over the next five years.[69] Others have recommended reducing benefits to 20 year retirees and use those reductions to fund a more modest pension for those who served between 10 and 19 years in the service and currently have no vested pension interest. In other words, they now get ZIP when they leave the service. Complimenting these reforms would be the idea that no payment should begin to the retiree reaches age 50 or 62 or even 65. Why not? Remember the average military retiree is 41 and taking the progress of medical technology into account, it is reasonable to assume that more and more of these retirees can be expected to live into their 80s and 90s. It's absolute nonsense to ask the rest of society to provide indexed pensions and health care for them for 40 or even 50 years!

EXPENSIVE WEAPON SYSTEMS

But let's get serious. The safest and sanest way to cut defense spending and improve our security is to cut out useless dangerous and unbelievably expensive weapon systems. I'm talking about the type of programs that stem less from ideology and even error in military analysis than from technological urgings; such idiotic notions that because it's theoretically possible to do, we *should* do it. Let's look at some of the fantasies that have been indulged at one time or another during recent administrations.

The Army's division air defense gun (DIVAD) took eight years and $2.5 billion before someone cried "Uncle". With a radar aiming system that often locked on the wrong target, a power train too weak to keep up with the M-1 Abrams tank it was supposed to protect in battle and a firing range of only 4 miles, no match for the 7 mile range of the Soviet's Hind E helicopters which it was supposed to intercept, the towel was thrown in. The DIVAD was officially not capable of doing the job.

The Bradley vehicle has been described as the $13 billion bungle of all times. It has been the subject of various magazine and newspaper articles as well as television shows. It was designed to replace the old reliable M 113 at more than 24 times the price. It's a good thing we're not at war, and I say that as a concerned mother, because the Bradley vehicle is not an expensive prototype it has already been produced! According to Secretary of Defense Casper Weinberger, as of March 1987 the army owned 4,300 of them and was expecting 6,600 more. If under fire the amunition carried by the vehicle could all to easily endanger the soldiers riding inside, according to media reports. If hit, the automatic fire extinguishers installed inside the Bradley could force soldiers to evacuate while under enemy fire. It can't climb out of a stream—it sinks! It doesn't appear to have been designed with war conditions in mind yet the army continues to stand behind it. (Don't ask!)

How do you suppose *they* tell if a tank that is *proven* 28 percent more effective (M-1) than another (M-60) is worth a price 58 percent higher?

Should *they* go with the more survivable Trident II missiles and risk *saving* $12 billion over a five year period, or support the MX?

Should *they* save $4 billion in outlay, not to mention billions in additional savings on manpower, training and maintenance, by refusing the Air Force the three new wings it has requested by 1991? We're talking about 216 aircraft—I know you knew, but aren't you surprised they're so expensive? I don't want to get into it, but the last time I looked B-1 bombers were going for almost a half billion each and C-5 cargo planes for $150 million a piece and when you consider that the AMRAAM (advanced, medium-range, air-to-air missile) *they* tried to stuff into the F-16 cost $12.7 billion, well you've got to think 216 aircraft for $4 billion is a real deal. Unless of course they're going to need AMRAAM and that'll be extra. (They always get you on the extras!)

John F. Lehman resigned as Secretary of the Navy in the spring of 1987 but because of him it looks like the Navy will reach its 600 ship goal, and this despite the compelling argument of critics that today aircraft carriers are too vulnerable. Secretary Lehman fought hard for those ships and claimed that during his six years as Navy Secretary the number of ship contracts that were awarded competitively rose from 15 percent to 92 percent and navy aircraft had been put on ". . . firm, fixed-price competitive bases." He claimed that a new audit "documented savings of $6.8 billion in buying new airplanes since Reagan assumed office."[70]

CONTRACTING OUT

Between 1980–1983 the Defense Department held approximately 400 bidding competitions to determine if certain services would be cheaper if contracted-out. In 60 percent of the cases that was found to be true and the resultant savings to taxpayers amounted to about $700 million a year. The civilian competition did what competition is supposed to do; make the in-house military services more efficient which added yet another $14 million a year to the savings.

In one instance which was reported in *Nation's Business* magazine, half the support services at Fort Gordon, Georgia were contracted to private firms which cut government expenses more than $600 million and additionally added 200 civilian jobs and about $9 million in extra business to the local community.

GOOD NEWS

The military signs 52,000 contracts every working day; more than 13 million a year. The Air Force alone entered into more than 5 million contracts in 1985. Even a small percentage of mistakes would be good for thousands of horror stories; grist to the reporter's mill. I want to make sure you know the B-1B bomber is ahead of schedule and $1 billion underbudget; the C-5B is on schedule and $500 million under budget. Thanks to a multiyear contract *they* saved $257 on the F-16 fighter and the MX missile passed each of its 12 test shots with better than expected accuracy (1986).

Defense is another legitimate preogative of the federal government but spending must be done wisely. I hope we will see less division of power at the top so the separate services will neither duplicate systems nor strive to outdo one another. The Congress should have the wisdom to give the Pentagon a long-range budget it can depend on—and one the country can afford.

STATE AND LOCAL GOVERNMENT

WHOSE WILL?

What have I been saying about *free* people getting what they want? Where there's a will there's a way is true for the ordinary citizen only when power is diversified and flexible. "Responsive" is the word normally used, but not my choice here because "responsive" can be distorted by the squeaky wheel principle. We are always told that some official is responding to the "will of the people" when he pushes for legislation that you and no one you know "wills"! (They certainly didn't respond to the "will of the people" when it came to their own pay raises early in 1987.)

What is necessary is not for government to *respond,* at least not by stepping in and *doing* something, government's role is to step aside and let people do what needs to be done as long as no one is harmed. But we've come a long way from that principle. Over the years we have bound our citizens hand and foot with restrictive regulations, making certain the only way anything can be accomplished is by appealing (like servants or slaves) to *them.*

LASSEN COUNTY, CALIFORNIA

You judge whether the residents of Lassen County have an alternative to moving to another location.

One of the worst roads in the nation may be California highway 385 located in rural Lassen County (pop. 24,000). California's Caltrans officials say the cost of improving the highway is not cost-effective but the residents, who have witnessed 16 deaths and 218 injuries over the past two years (a lot in such a rural area) want to know the price put on death and injury to their neighbors.

In an article for the Los Angeles Times, Charles Hillinger and Mark Stein discussed the plans the resident of this remote northern California county have for seceding to Nevada as one way to get a safe highway.

The contemplated move would not be without precedent. Hillinger and Stein interviewed Stan Mottaz, a history professor at Humboldt State University who spoke of a split in 1820 by some northern Massachusetts counties to form what is now the state of Maine. He also pointed to the formation of West Virginia in 1863 by the secession of several western counties of Virginia. Professor Mottaz said that in 1850 the area that today makes up Lassen county in California and Washoe county in Nevada was one territory called Nataqua. When the territory of Nevada was formed it included Lassen county and the founder of Susanville (Lassen county seat) was Nevada's first provisional governor.

In 1941 bad roads made residents of southern Oregon and northern California band together to lobby for a new state to be called Jefferson. Nothing came of the effort because by that time it was not a simple thing to secede from one state and join or form another. In the twentieth century a county must obtain the approval of both state legislatures, the U.S. Congress and the President of the United States. A hard enough task without the additional reality that southern California may not be eager to give Lassen county's water to Nevada. However if something could be worked out with the water rights, look at the benefits the residents of Lassen county would reap.

The Las Vegas Review-Journal editorialized: "They (Lassen county residents) would shed a state income tax, corporate tax, inheritance tax, unitary tax and franchise tax. They would pick up clout at the state legislative level, becoming one of the 18 counties rather than one of 58. It would become the fourth-most populous county in Nevada (rather than the 46th most populous in California).

But, would Lassen county get its road fixed? Well, not in exchange for water rights, if they are ever to get the California legislature to agree to the secession.

It's sad to relate, but it would probably come down to the role of the media. If Nevada could reap enough good public relations, repairing Lassen county's roads might be worth it. What else is Nevada going to get from Lassen county's annexation; territory is not in short supply in Nevada but people are and 24,000 new residents may be a sweet enough pot.

I'm not asking you to show an interest in Lassen county, California, but you should pay attention to the principle involved because it sums up America's past, present and questions her future.

Here are the alternatives as I see them:

1) California (symbolizing every other state in the Union) should disregard cost-effectiveness and repair the roads.
2) Residents should go through the secession process as it currently exists after first receiving assurances from Nevada regarding the repair of Lassen's roads. Reason? The boundaries of individual states are a legitimate national concern.
3) Regulations should be erased so that only the two states involved can decide.
4) Residents should be flexible enough to move on and not waste their own time and effort nor that of thousands of people at all levels of government.

SACRIFICE

Planning, whether carried out in the name of a Prince or according to the will of the people, results in the end to minorities being sacrificed to the designs of the plan.

In a society of any size there are bound to be special interests; agriculture, trade, education, business, philanthrophy, manufacturing, old, young, rich, poor and so on and so forth. The danger is that all too often weaker interests are sacrificed to stronger. That is why James Madison found democracy incompatible with secure personal property rights.[71]

Unfortunately 200 years after the Founders have completed their labors, we have a situation where virtually anything at all can be done in the name of the general welfare and the right to regulate commerce among the several states even to the point of negating other parts of the Constitution.

Pressure groups vie with one another for a larger piece of the pie, each fighting for legislation to wrest its own advantages by force from all other groups. This is possible only because the government has claimed virtually unlimited control of the nation's purse strings. (OK—wallets) The results were anticipated and supposedly forestalled by the framers of the Constitution when they limited the levying of any direct tax to "proportion of Census." But ever since the adoption of the income tax amendment in 1913 there has been no constitutional limit on what legislators can do with the people's income.

As Ayn Rand so aptly noted in *Capitalism: The Unknown Ideal* "The degree of statism is a county's political system is the degree to which it breaks up the country into rival gangs and sets men against one another. When individual rights are abrogated, there is no way to determine who is entitled to what; it reverts to the tribal concept of one's wishes are limited only by the power of one's gang."

INCOME TAX WINDFALLS

Many state and local governments must, as we have seen, balance their operating budgets under constitutional or statutory rules. That leads to fast action when shortfalls develop.

Economic stagnation and weakness in agricultural and energy markets have begun to put a crimp in the budget projections of many states. 23 states ended FY1985 with balances totaling 1% or less of yearly expenditures, far less than the 5% cushion administrators normally shoot for.

Since income taxes in many states are based on federal tax law, thanks to the 1986 reform, the revenue of many states will increase unless adjustments are made. But in many cases the increase will not keep up with the demand for services, meaning a windfall does not in all cases preclude a tax hike.

In the spring of 1987, 28 states were contemplating tax increases for FY1988 and 23 had cut their FY1987 agendas to make ends meet. Two years earlier in 1985, the fiscal year-end surplus for all states together amounted to $8 billion—not bad! The fiscal year-end 1987 surplus is estimated at only $1.6 billion. The problem is the same, less funds, but the reasons are different in different localities. The federal government has cut back on grants and other subsidies to cities and they are turning to state capitols in search of funds. The agricultural states and the so-called oil patch and rust belt states have lost revenue and the unemployed require extra help which drives them to the state capitols. Many states are therefore looking at a combination of new taxes; 17 are contemplating an increase in personal income taxes, 16 are considering gasoline tax increases and 13 are toying with sales taxes and 9 are looking at excise taxes on cigarettes.

EXAMPLE OF VARIOUS STATES

Of the 35 states that experienced windfalls, only four (GA,HI,NY & WV) passed the entire amount back to resident taxpayers, seven kept it all and the rest kept some and gave some back to the taxpayers.

California, like 31 other states, has established a "rainy day" fund to weather business cycles. In 1979 California's voters approved a spending limitation (Proposition 4) so although a large faction is attempting to divert some of the windfall to California schools it will probably be returned to the taxpayers.

At the end of 1986 Texas was experiencing a $3.5 billion budget deficit and was having a hard time finding places to cut its $37.2 billion budget. Texans may have an even greater aversion to taxes than do citizens of the other 49 states. Texas has the nation's seventh lowest tax per capita with no income tax and only a 4.5 percent sales tax. However, as 1986 ended Lieutenant Governor Hobby was considering a change in the sales tax, a rise of five cents in the gasoline tax, and a 3 percent tax to be placed on professional services estimated to bring in about $70 million annually from lawyers alone.

Florida will end the practice of exempting professional services from its 5 percent sales tax in July 1987, a move expected to raise $951 million a year, including $156 million from lawyers who are naturally fighting it. New Mexico, Iowa, Hawaii and South Dakota already tax professional services and Mississippi and Tennessee have been successful in fighting the proposal in the past.

More and more states are considering following the lead of the federal government and reducing the number of tax-brackets, the rates and broadening the tax base by eliminating deductions, exclusions and credits. On June 8, 1987 two competing proposals that would do just that were passed by the California State Assembly (AB33 and AB53).

DISTRIBUTIVE JUSTICE

It is comforting to the indolent to think of wealth as the culmination of some undifferentiated, collective activity, that somehow we are all responsible for and therefore some sort of egalitarian distribution is justified. As Ludwig von Mises said in *The Anticapitalist Mentality,* "Men have created all the wealth which the daydreamers consider as a free gift of nature. . . . (Capital) is the outcome of a provident restriction of consumption on the part of man. It is created and increased by saving and maintained by the absention from dissaving."

Unfortunately the majority of Americans follow the example of their government today and refuse to restrict their consumption. Those who do act prudently and with discipline and manage to save enough capital to invest allow themselves to feel guilty for their success and achievement. They are only too willing to subscribe to the "distributive justice" nonsense.

In a collective economy public needs enjoy the same sort of built-in priority that private consumption enjoys in a capitalist economy. In the former all resources are available to the public sector and private consumption is restricted. Just look at the long lines, shortages and number of citizens anxious to escape from communist countries. On the contrary, in a capitalist economy public services are restricted to claims against the private sector, or should be, but as we are all too aware, our annual deficit is a result of spending more than officials are willing to tax (claim).

OFF-BUDGET

For the past 75 years states and local government have used off-budget-entities (OBE) for their borrowing. All these governments had to do is to obtain a corporate charter for the independent entity which can then operate "off-budget"—off the books! Debt of these newly created quasi-public firms is not subject to any constitutional or statutory limits (most state constitutions specify debt limits) nor does borrowing require voter approval. Nevertheless taxpayers are liable for the repayment of principle and interest on the bonds floated by OBEs—if not *legally* liable at least *morally* liable.

Prior to 1820 government at all levels was modest; limited not only by ideology but also by the extremely low tax revenue. In fact gifts from individuals were a supplemental source of revenue in the early days of our country. The practice is being encouraged today by an organization called "Citizens for a Debt-Free America" which operates out of New Berlin, Wisconsin.[72] According to Kay Fishburn, the organization's National Coordinator, "$719,515.82 were contributed to reduce debt principal in the first half of fiscal year 1987." Contributions may be sent directly to: Bureau of Public Debt, Dept. G, Washington D.C. 20239-0601.

Under the urging of Franklin Delano Roosevelt, state and local government began actively using OBEs in the 1930s. In order to put people to work and get the country moving again, the federal government was providing grants-in-aid to state and local governments. As strange as it may sound in retrospect, FDR was very much afraid of leading the nation towards the dependency of a welfare state and so he made federal funds contingent upon the states providing local matching funds. In the depths of the depression states borrowed to their limits and many were even in default. In 1934 FDR suggested in a letter to the governors of each state that they establish public corporations which would get around their debt limitations.

In their highly recommended book *Underground Government: The Off-Budget Public Sector,* James Bennett and Thomas DiLorenzo have a great deal to say about this era. "Federal government prodding and the promise of various forms of largesse from the national Treasury has contributed significantly to the explosive growth of OBEs at all levels of government." Between 1952 and 1972 the use of OBEs by state and local government more than doubled. Current statistics concerning OBEs are incomplete. (Politicians prefer it that way.) OBEs go by a variety of names (authorities, trusts, boards, districts or commissions) and since local governments need no one's permission to establish them (they need only confer a "public benefit—a very broad requirement) data regarding them is sketchy and inaccurate.

According to Bennett and DiLorenzo,[73] although the federal government since 1952 has collected data regarding OBEs, it is not comprehensive, as it only includes one particular type of OBE known as a "special district" which, although off-budget, has taxing powers and may even have elected directors as opposed to the myriad of OBEs that are not so neatly documented and have no taxing authority and politically appointed managers.

Prior to the 1974 Budget Act there was virtually no off-budget spending by the federal government. However, by using the Federal Financing Bank and relying on grants and loan guarantees, federal off-budget activity multiplied faster than jack-rabbits. As more and more of the public sector moved off-budget the electorate lost more and more control to unelected managers. Although OBEs are supposed to support themselves via tolls and fees, the truth is taxpayers end up shouldering the burden, usually via massive grants and subsidies. To add insult to injury many of the activities of these quasi-corporations compete directly with private sector firms and have the advantage of borrowing at more favorable rates because they are allowed to issue tax-exempt bonds.

WHOSE MONEY IS IT ANYWAY?

Government officials play a cat and mouse game with citizens. Spending and distributing goodies to constituents enhances the power, prestige and popularity of the former whereas the later have attempted to hold on to their dollars via tax shelters or going underground (not reporting all income). In 1982 the government estimates a loss of $100 billion in revenue due to tax evasion via the underground economy. Although tax revolts have been with us as long as taxes (remember the Boston Teaparty) they have varied in intensity. During recent cycles politicians discovered their own underground in the form of OBEs and were delighted to find they could continue to borrow and spend out of sight and control of the voters. OBEs allow politicians to preach fiscal conservativism even while expanding the scope and size of government.

There is no limit to the ingenuity of an official who intends to spend. In November 1985, Los Angeles county became the first local government to refinance part of its own capital requirements by selling taxable securities. Normally a government would issue a new series of tax-free bonds at a low rate. To comply with IRS regulations to prevent arbitrage (making a profit by reinvesting in higher yielding securities) by tax-exempt issuers, the proceeds from the second sale would normally be invested in special Treasury securities set up for this purpose. Los Angeles county, however, offered $50 million worth of 3 year taxable notes which sold about four percentage points above the bonds. Because they weren't subject to the IRS rules, the county was free to invest the proceeds at whatever rate it could find in the marketplace.

It is not unusual, as we have seen, for local government to sell taxable debt for hospitals and school district but they had never been sold before for a local government's own account.

THE ALPHABET PROGRAMS

Between 1972–1986 general revenue sharing poured $83 billion into state and local coffers. The National League of Cities showed that 56 percent of the 660 cities surveyed in June 1986, anticipated operating loses in that year, no doubt in part due to the September 1986 congressional cut in general revenue sharing. The end of revenue sharing coupled with the damper put on tax-free financing by the 1986 tax reform, was reason for pessimism. There was an alphabet of other federally subsidized programs (CDBG,ADEA,UDAG,REA) and they were not without their flaws.

In the name of regional economic development the federal government unwittingly spent money to pit one locality against another. The Department of Housing and Urban Development (HUD) gave Jersey City a couple grants to help construct major commercial complexes a few years ago and really opened up a can of worms. The next thing it knew it was being sued by New York City. It seems Jersey City was soliciting tenants from across the river. HUD froze the funds only to be sued by Jersey City. (Taxpayer v taxpayer!)

Urban Development Action Grant programs (UDAG) have a reputation for being among the most flawed. UDAGs cost the taxpayers about half a billion dollars a year and instead of helping the poor, more than half of the funds get channeled to commercial projects such as luxury hotels, shopping centers and high priced housing. Only two-thirds of the promised new jobs usually materialize, mostly for the not exactly poverty stricken construction worker. They are supported mainly by large city mayors, unions and developers. A 1982 HUD study purported to show that without grants 21% of the projects undertaken with UDAGs would have been accomplished anyway. (Unsubsidized).

Ronald Reagan, in his first term, proposed to wean state and local governments from federal funding over a period of five years. Congress thwarted those plans (UDAGs are still in force) but nevertheless, in response to the federal budget deficit, cutbacks will be felt in 1987. As a consequence, local politicians are scurrying around looking for ways to replace those funds and are finding private capital to fiance public assets makes sense. Political entities don't want the hassel of owning and operating if they don't have to. They would much prefer to lease the asset and finance it on a pay-as-you-go basis rather than have to come up with all the capital required to build the asset in the beginning.

A WORD TO THE CITIES

David Rosen, a consultant from Oakland, California, addressed the National League of Cities at their meeting in San Antonio, TX at the end of 1986. He spoke about creative ways for cities to raise capital for their social agendas in an attempt to replace funds withdrawn by the federal government. He suggested setting up trust funds to subsidize low income housing with PVE funds (Petroleum Violation Escrow funds—from oil overcharges in the past) or fees generated from title transfers or mortgage recordations.

U.S. CONFERENCE OF MAYORS

The U.S. Conference of Mayors met in January (1987) and produced a statement which said, among other things, that "programs that are essential to the domestic and economic strength of our nation are being cut." A member of the press asked Joseph Riley, Mayor of Charleston, South Carolina and President of the Conference why the states couldn't replace the federal government in helping the cities acquire revenue. Riley answered that the states don't have the money (the federal government always does because of those darn printing presses) and furthermore there is a commonality of problems among the cities which demand a national response. When pressed he gave examples such as universal inner-city decay which is a natural consequence of the poor streaming in as the rich pour out.

Mayor Riley was rather critical of House leadership because HR 1400, the continuing resolution for revenue sharing, was removed from the House agenda (not voted on). The mayor insisted that a return of a portion of the national tax base to local communities was a "sound, fair, and prudent program" and terribly modest compared to programs of other countries. (Aggh—*that* argument again!). A logical unsophisticated ten year old might ask why we don't tax less in the first place and then we wouldn't have to bother with a sound, fair and prudent program for the return of tax dollars. Such a child wouldn't have completely absorbed the "free lunch" attitude. How could he be expected to understand that everyone anticipates receiving more than he put in when it comes to the return. The more political clout the more reasonable is the hope for an extra portion.

Diane Feinstein, San Francisco's mayor, headed the Urban Economic Policy Committee which met later in January, 1987 in Washington DC. She saw no support for revenue sharing in Congress and counseled that in order for mayors to avoid further reduction in their perceived power, they should not push the issue. She admitted cities were facing a $30–$40 billion loss in the years ahead and joked that the idea of renaming "revenue sharing," calling it "mandated reimbursement" might be helpful. Another participant picked up the idea and suggested applying for funds again, for the "mandated reimbursement program." (Clever rascals, aren't they?)

Senator Pete Domenici, former Mayor of Alburque, New Mexico, pushed his way through one of Washington DC's worst snow storms to address the group. He agreed with Sam Purses that revenue sharing should not be championed but rather used in a trade-off with congress against the possible loss of other programs.

Senator Domenici expressed grave concern about "the black cloud of debt"; not just government debt but corporate and private debt. He did not believe government could put millions of citizens to work, at least not alone. He is a strong believer in the private sector. He contradicted the popular belief that the level of taxation on the American people is down. He pointed out that we're paying the same level of taxes as we did fifteen years ago but 3% of GNP is being spent on Social Security and Medicare. As other taxes fluctuate payroll taxes always go up. The 3 percent of GNP which is spent on senior citizens is in the unified budget and as a consequence when cuts have to be made they are made in other programs.

Then came the surprise of the meeting. Mayor Feinstein said that since so little of the federal budget is discretionary, Congress should attack Social Security and other entitlements like Medicare. (Yipes—she uttered the unutterable; she NAMED the programs—yes, she did!)

Senator Domenici answered, "you are preaching to the choir" and admitted he had been beaten without mercy for trying three times in the past and he absolutely refuses to try again. The good Senator did not appear in the least bit ashamed of his stand, perhaps because he could point to good company, and in fact he went on to say that even Ronald Reagan won't listen to a freeze on Social Security or any changes in Medicare; he insists they are unalterable commitments. Senator Domenici said Social Security is such a hot issue that it can't be touch without absolute SIMULTANEOUS BIPARTISANSHIP. He then added he thought it might happen, to which Mayor Feinstein replied under her breathe, "I think it will one day."

Then the conversation took off. There was disbelief expressed that if someone is making a million dollars they are still entitled to a COLA increase. Robert Isaac, Mayor of Colorado Springs, admitted we will have to cut Social Security and Medicare. He called for a means test and discredited the folk wisdom that Social Security recipients are all below the poverty level. He told his fellow conferee there is less poverty among the elderly than found in the rest of society. (So what else is new?)

AN ADMITTEDLY BIASED LOOK AT CALIFORNIA

In 1979 Californians passed Proposition 4, sponsored by tax reformer Paul Gann and known as the Gann amendment, which limits growth in local and state government appropriations each year to the increase in population plus inflation. It says any tax revenues collected over the limit must be refunded to taxpayers within two years.

In 1987 increased tax revenue due to an expanding economy and low inflation means California's politicians are going crazy—like fat ladies in a pastry shop who are suddenly put on a diet. The money is coming in; they want to spend the money; they are required to return the money. At least one California state senator can't stand it and is hoping to get a measure on California's June 1988 ballot that would allow the spending limit to increase each year, not by the change in population plus inflation, but rather by the change in personal income. In other words, all those people who are making more and getting a break because of lower inflation should share their good fortune. "I do well you do well"—it has a nice ring. Government moves right in like one of the family, a dependent with an insatiable appetite making certain no matter how hard you work you'll pretty much stay in the same place.

There are of course politicians who conscientiously attempt to do a good job along with those who are only interested in their own present prestige or future gain; ones with whom I agree and disagree, as with people in all groups. California politicians have managed to cut 2 percent from the state's budget (ending June 30, 1987) by using early retirement plans estimated to save $900 million. The Governor has asked each department to cut its spending 4 percent during the last half of the fiscal year in order to meet the 2 percent overall reduction goal. (We're talking about $100 million dollars.) All agencies were expected to participate in the cuts with the exception of those carrying out 24-hour care programs.

California is investing more than at any time in its history in schools, transportation, job creation, public safety, toxic cleanup and children—all without raising the general taxes of her citizens or businesses.

Is California perfect? Close maybe, but do you recall that $4 billion inflation windfall that Secretary Weinberger overlooked for awhile in the defense budget?[73] Just drop a zero. In the spring of 1986 the Deukmejian administration discovered $400 million in "overlooked" fees. That's a lot of fees to "overlook"! However officials pointed to computer and administrative problems at the Department of

Motor Vehicles, an explanation which was readily bought by most Californians.

Individual legislators have to be watched like hawks. One left a rental car in an airport parking lot for several weeks and the state had to pick up the tab. In another instance an outgoing State Controller moved most of his staff to office space which would cost 107% more than his old offices. That came to about $8.4 million in higher rent over the life of the state's five year lease for the new offices. So, in the tradition of great government leadership, the incoming Controller recommended that a part of the controller's staff move back to the old digs in the Capitol and lease the space thus vacated. Savings over the remaining 4.5 years of the lease would amount to $436,000. Should we applaud? Can waste of $8.4 million be overlooked since *they* now plan to save taxpayers $436,000? And it's not over—guess who is going to be the chump to pick up the sublease when some of the Controller's staff makes that cost-saving move—the Department of General Services (a taxpayer's nightmare).

Waste is one thing but there is legitimate spending which can only be undertaken by the state. I know, I know—according to *whose* priorities?

"Japan spends $107 per person for earth quake preparedness whereas California spends between 65¢ and $1."[74]

Last year (1986) the state legislature created a task force which is suppose to take three years, the time of 25 people, and spend $735,000 in order to find ways Californians can improve their self-esteem and prevent social problems.

WHOSE PRIORITIES?

The Deukmejian Administration is in the process of eliminating or reducing 20,000 state rules and regulations. There have even been attempts to limit the number of bills introduced into the state legislature each year. No wonder when it is understood that during the 1985–86 session 7,041 bills were introduced at an average cost to the taxpayers of approximately $4,000 each. In 1986 Governor Deukmejian signed 1,514 bills and permitted another six to become law without his signature. The Governor vetoed 224 bills in 1985 and 316 in 1986. Not bad when you consider the second most populous state, New York, in 1980 introduced 24,292 bills—an all time record (We hope)!

"THERE OUGHT TO BE A LAW"

Over the past ten years, according to the Commerce Clearing House in Chicago, which compiles these statistics on an annual basis, nearly one million bills were introduced in all the state legislatures combined with almost a quarter of a million of them approved. Just think—250,000 new state laws in this country—just what we *don't* need.

Gunnar Myrdal, the Swedish Nobel Laureate, once pointed out, Americans will say practically in the same breath, "No one can tell me what to do" and "There ought to be a law against that."

Section Three

Who We Are And What We Want

Who We Are And What We Want

AMERICANS IN THE EIGHTIES

Arbitrary generalized categories fail to do justice to the incredible diversity in America today but nevertheless give us a handle for discussion purposes. Never before has American society been less homogeneous. The oldest segment of the population is healthier than ever before in history and also wealthier on the average, than the younger groups in the country. The baby boomers, those born between 1946–1957, are the largest in size and complexity. They are followed by their children, an educated and materialistic generation, working like crazy just to stay in place. Then we have the newest generation, bright, energetic and eager. Unfortunately this group also encompasses the disillusioned kids on drugs, school drop-outs, the younger latch-key children and infants being raised by surrogate mothers. All these groups had vastly different childhood experiences, morals and values.

NO ONE IS ORDINARY

Calvin Coolidge once remarked that he had yet to meet that elusive character, the common man—never once had he met the man who considered himself or his loved ones to be ordinary.

Baby boomers have been described as individualists, abhorring the label "ordinary". Anti-conformist values, however, can only be catered to in an affluent society which can afford to offer increased freedom. Ironically, the mass-media television shows and advertising that developed the middle-class cohesiveness of the sixties is now helping to undo that orientation in the eighties with specialty magazines and cable-TV shows for every conceivable taste. More and diverse opinions will help splinter the old middle-class conformist values. The new middle class consists of groups—"investors", "gardeners", "golfers", "socially conscious", "intellectuals", "health enthusiasts" anything you can think of—the number of groups are infinite. There is even a "conformists" group. The "conformists" tend to be both religious and family-oriented and are the core of the old homogeneous middle-class. Twenty years ago they accounted for at least 60 percent of the middle-class population, but today, although they are still the back-bone and stereotype of the middle-class, they are only 38 percent of the whole.

Old middle-class morality—living for others with the emphasis on loyalty and self-sacrifice—has given way to middle-class independence. There is no need to impose a common mold on people; the America of the eighties is more tolerant than ever before.

THE HEROES OF WW II

Memories of the Great Depression of their childhood plagued our citizens who are currently over age 55. To make certain they would never go through the ordeal their own parents suffered, most determined to make security their number one priority. After the Second World War it was possible to work one's way to the top since there was a crying need for middle and upper level managers.

Between 1947–1957, the median-family income increased 64 percent (to just under $5,000/year), inflation was in the 2–3 percent range and unemployment stood at approximately 5 percent. We had budget surpluses except for the small, relatively speaking, $7 billion deficit during the 1953 recession.

According to the Census Bureau, the median income in the U.S. in 1985 was $29,152 for White families, $27,735 for all families, $19,027 for Hispanic families and $16,768 for Black families. Living standards are hard to judge because they are arbitrary. The problem is what to include and what not to include. However, the standards issued by the Commerce Department showed that while the economy is still slowly expanding, real per capita income has been declining since the second quarter of FY1986.

Thirteen percent of Florida's residents are over age 65 compared to just under 12 percent found in that category nationwide. By the year 2020, 17 percent of the nation will be over 65 years old. Those under age 18 who comprised 36 percent of the population in 1960 and are expected to account for only 20 percent by the year 2030 are decreasing as the number of persons over age 65 is increasing. Some people fear that the needs of the young could be overshadowed by the politically vociferous older segment of society and their needs. One more reason for people to look after themselves instead of relying solely on Social Security in the future.

At their peak in 1980, federal transfers to the poor amounted to 2.4 percent of the GNP; they were 2.2 percent of GNP in 1984. One-half of such transfers go to the elderly and disabled through Medicaid and SSI. These programs, which together account for $42 billion annually, have helped produce a rapid decline in poverty among the elderly just in the past decade.

Families headed by someone over age 65 owned homes with equity valued at $724 billion in 1984 according to Census Bureau reports. The per capita income of Americans over 65 is 7 percent higher than the national average whereas the 28 million citizens over age 55 have per capita incomes 26 percent higher than the national average. With a $416 billion annual income, this group has twice the spending power of those under age 35. Those 45 and over spend 60 percent of all income on consumer services, everything from leisure and recreation to health, medicine and travel. Remember security has been their number one priority and many of them have achieved it.

BABY BOOMERS

Things have been very different for the baby boomers. With an oversupply of managers and just about everything else, fierce competition made it extremely difficult to move to the top in any field. Many had to turn to other outlets for fulfillment. It has become a cliché to say that baby boomers are essentially more liberal on social and cultural matters and more conservative on economic issues. Some claim baby boomers are anti-New Deal in terms of their suspicions about the size of government and of government solutions to economic problems.

The free-spending habits and extravagant tastes of some baby boomers give the appearance of affluence, but the truth is many are worse off than their parents were. You might well ask "worse off in what way?", and the answer would unfortunately be in terms of fulfilling both material *and* spiritual goals. Their spending could well be motivated by the desire to stand out from the crowd and gain recognition.

Although America has created 30 million jobs over the past 15 years, a 1985 research report prepared for a Congressional Joint Economic Committee by University of Maryland Professor Frank Levy and the Urban Institute's Richard Michel, found that between 1975–85 ". . . neither wages nor family incomes have grown." In fact the median income of men age 25–34 fell 26 percent between 1973–83 according to the Census Bureau. Average family income (even with two incomes) fell 14 percent, adjusted for taxes and inflation, and although wages rose 80 percent, costs rose faster. The highest rises were for home mortgages and day-care. Seventy percent of all 30–35 year olds owned their own homes in 1983, down from 75 percent in 1979, but not homes like their parents had.

The Levy & Michel study also found that the average 30 year old in 1949 paid 14 percent of his income on mortgage payments and 44 percent in 1985. Not surprisingly, (*numbers-numbers*-everyone's got their own source of *numbers*) this information differs from a Wall Street Journal report offered a few weeks earlier on December 11, 1985, in which it was claimed mortgage payments in 1949 took 25 percent of income and in 1985 absorbed 33.3 percent—a rise less alarming. Many boomers marry late, have children late and are still buying homes late compared with other generations. There is a delayed impact as these experiences finally occur, as the boomers enter their 40s—their acquisition years.

In an impassioned speech to the Industrial Unions of the AFL-CIO in May 1987, presidential hopeful Joseph Biden of Delaware, himself a baby boomer, spoke of boomers having reached what is known as the conservative-age (entering the 40s) and "being ripe for Republican pickings". Senator Biden's appeal to the boomers in the audience was to remember the Kennedy era when there was a collective sense that great things were waiting to be accomplished. The Senator and other politicians who understand that the votes lie with this largest segment of the population, will continue to appeal to what they call the boomer's collective social conscience. They apparently have no trek with the evaluation of boomers as a group of individualistic nonconformists. Senator Biden, for one, hopes the boomers have not forgotten about ". . . commitment, compassion and willingness to make sacrifices."

REDISTRIBUTION

In the 1960s all things were believed possible. The USA was considered rich enough to withstand any damage to the nation's productive or financial capacity that might result from a government directed redistribution of wealth. The Washington elite banked on continued strong economic growth and inflation that would automatically push taxpayers into higher and higher brackets to keep the coffers full. They had not anticipated the tax revolts of the early 80s nor the sudden slow down in economic growth. Unfortunately, the decrease in anticipated revenue was not accompanied by a decrease in zeal for the redistribution of wealth. Our elected officials tried to soften the impact of slow growth and its by-product, unemployment, by expanding the safety net of social programs. As the entitlement programs grew, their true cost was masked by inflation.

CRANSTON'S SOLUTION

A few years ago Senator Cranston of California did some figuring. He claimed if we put the almost 17 million (at that time and according to him) unemployed to work, based on a salary of $10,000/year their taxes would equal approximately $1,343 per person or in the neighborhood of $22.5 billion dollars/year. The Senator further stated that for each one million workers who returned to work the nation would save $30 billion in assistance that would no longer be needed. He claimed a balanced budget could be achieved by reducing unemployment from 10.5 to 5.5 percent.

With tax reform the numbers may be off (aren't they all?) but the idea is sound. Raising taxes, expanding government borrowing or welfare are all part of the problem. Any politican who is not all talk but is serious about the unemployment problem will *cut* not expand government. (I wish he or she would please step forward!)

FULL EMPLOYMENT

Full employment has been defined as the level of unemployment that would exist when demand was adequate to keep the inflation rate stable. All unemployment at full employment would be voluntary in the sense that anyone who wanted a job would be able to find one by reducing his nominal wage enough to make employing him profitable to someone.

Partly to get away from the implication that full employment meant zero unemployment, economists adopted the term "natural rate of unemployment". The natural rate changes over time with changes in the age-sex composition of the labor force as well as for other reasons. In the 40s and 50s employment was "full" if no more than 3 to 4 percent of the labor force was out of work. By the 1970s the acceptable level was 6 or 7 percent because the baby-boom generation was entering the labor market in droves along with an influx of women.

New York's Governor Mario Cuomo, early in 1986 addressed the newspaper publishers in San Francisco: "(The current prosperity) has been purchased at the expense of the well-being, the hopes and expectations of a large part of our nation, by the acceptance of such things as a level of unemployment that this nation would have considered a scandal only a decade ago." George Will astutely pointed out[1] that at the time of Governor Cuomo's speech unemployment was 7.1 percent and a decade ago it was 7.7 percent.[1] As I write, halfway through 1987, it is under 6.5 percent. Sorry Governor, maybe later.

In the 1960s economist and Nobel Laureate Milton Friedman endorsed the theory that claims at some point attempts to obtain further gains on the employment front simply result in an acceleration in wages and prices. In 1986 some economists thought an employment rate of 7.1 percent might just about be the inflationary flash point.

In the 1950s a jobless rate below 5 percent was considered safe; by 1980 most economists thought the danger zone started at just under 7 percent. The natural rate rises when skills offered by the pool of unemployed and new workers fail to match new openings. This causes business to bid up wages. For instance wage and fringe benefits rose by 7.2 percent in 1982, but the gain was only 4.3 percent in 1985 and was about a point lower in 1986.

LENIN'S FORESIGHT

In this country we are presently consuming more than we're producing but not more than we could produce under full employment. Consumer sales are responsible for production and employment; when there isn't enough demand for goods and services, production slows and unemployment rises. Most production used to be consumed by the producers themselves—now it takes fewer producers to make the same amount of goods and services and the non-producers can't break into the cycle. That is the problem Lenin foresaw. But Lenin failed to understand that consumers are of less consequence in a free market than are traders who have first been producers in order to have something to offer in trade.

There are several reasons why consumers don't buy all that is produced. First the non-producing consumers' inability (no work—little $$), secondly the government takes a portion in taxes, then personal savings take a little and finally businesses pay out less than they take in. This is not the exploitation Lenin foresaw, it is merely prudent business practice to set aside dollars for depreciation, obsolescence and in anticipation of possible future downturns in the economy.

So who buys the GNP consumers cannot because of the reasons just given? Government and business! (See discussion on page 10.) When consumers cut spending, government and business must make up for the slack—they must spend more than they take in. (The federal government has shown a real talent for doing so.)

JOB MOBILITY

William Niskanen of the CATO Institute claims involuntary unemployment occurs when prospective employers and employees are prevented from agreeing because of interference, restraints and social restrictions imposed by government institutions.

The unemployment rate, both voluntary and involuntary, for people under 35, even though about 2 out of 5 have had at least some college training, is 9.3 percent—twice that of older workers. Only a small minority of these young unemployed are union members. Not surprising since union seniority rules often protect older workers at their expense. However the fear of foreign competition and recession has led to less use of the last-hired-first-fired system of allocating job cuts. A Labor Department study showed 25 percent of workers aged 25 to 34 who lost their jobs tried to start again in a new location whereas only 6 percent of those over age 55 moved on.

For the information of those who like to compare the USA with other countries, the European job markets are only beginning to thaw from decades of labor legislation and welfare state policies that have frozen labor mobility. In the U.S. the labor market has never been anywhere near as unionized or as regulated as it has been in Europe. The United States has been noted for its job mobility—the freedom of employers to hire and fire and the freedom of workers to move easily from one company to another around the country in pursuit of jobs. Labor mobility has been one of America's traditional strengths, but Americans have been moving less over the past 20 years. With two earner families it has become much more difficult to move and the high cost of housing is another reason to stay put. In areas with dying industries property values drop and it becomes impossible to sell and move on. Losing money on the sale of a house isn't so bad if a salary increase in a new job will offset the loss but that is seldom the case now days.

UNEMPLOYMENT INSURANCE

The Federal Unemployment Insurance Act and the State Unemployment Insurance Acts were originally designed to increase consumer spending in order to help the economy. Employers are required to purchase the insurance for their employees via a payroll tax. (In NJ, AK, & AL employees pay a little bit also.) The federal government pays administrative costs and the states pay the benefits. The employer's tax rises as the number of former employees collecting benefits increases. Many liberals are opposed to this feature of the law claiming it gives employers an opportunity to contest claims. (So is it right to let only one side be heard?)

Most states allow benefits even if the claimant is working part time as long as he/she is making less than the weekly benefit amount. Even part-time workers get extra dollars for dependents. All in all the system is a marvelous incentive for unemployment! In fact studies have shown that jobless benefits discourage people from seeking new work. Attorney General Edwin Meese said in an interview with CBS on November 26, 1982, "We do know that when unemployment benefits end, most people find jobs very quickly after that point."

Generally showing "good cause" such as health-safety violations or poor working conditions, will qualify persons who were fired or quit their job for unemployment insurance benefits.

In an article for *Public Interest* magazine, Martin Feldstein, then economics professor at Brown University, noted that most states set unemployment insurance benefit payments at about half the gross income a worker was earning before losing his job. In the absence of a tax on jobless benefits, Mr. Feldstein thought a worker could fare nearly as well on government relief as he could on the job after income taxes and social security payroll levies were deducted from his check.

THOSE STATISTICS AGAIN

Unemployment statistics are not reliable regarding gains and losses. The Department of Labor conducts a survey based on households which double counts people who have more than one job. No wonder non-farm job gains were less than half those reported in a payroll survey. Sometimes a job training graduate need merely obtain an interview to be listed by the government as successfully employed. Roughly 60 percent of the 11.6 million unemployed Americans live in a household where someone else is working.

Approximately 4 million people reach age 18 every year in this country and many become statistical "have-nots" even though their minimum or low wage jobs are temporary and for "pin-money". Many so-called dead-end employers such as fast-food restaurants are luring young workers with scholarship programs. Many of the teenage girls who work in the mall are still living at home while they attend local community colleges and their wages go to pay for school clothes and books.

Professor Frank Levy (University of Maryland) did a great deal of research into income distribution for his recent book, *Dollars and Dreams.* He found that wages increased at an annual rate of 2.5 to 3 percent from the end of the Second World War until 1973. In 1985 dollars an average 40 year old made $15,300 in 1947, $28,300 in 1973 and $24,000 in 1985. The decrease was due to a variety of circumstances, many going back to 1973.

During the 1973–74 oil crisis, purchasing power was transferred overseas which hurt this nation's productivity record as measured by the Commerce Department. According to the Bureau of Labor Statistics between 1965–85 union wages outpaced cumulative inflation by 1.4 percent. Those in auto assembly lines were paid more and thanks to union pressures, $30,000 was not an unheard of wage for sweeping floors! It wasn't until 1984 that union pay hikes fell below the CPI for the first time. Growth in the labor force was a little over 2 percent during those years and during the seventies alone approximately 20 million net new jobs were created! The projection for labor-force growth from now to 1990 is 1.6 percent annually and is only 1 percent a year between 1990–95, with fewer teenagers included until 1992. Between 1972–78 real after tax income per capita was flat but since then it has risen about 11.3 percent or $1,000 (in 1982 dollars) for every man, woman and child in the nation. However It's true that many new jobs don't pay as well as old. In 1983 the average employee in domestic industries made $16,000—in export industries he made $19,000. The new high-tech industries seem to pay either minimum wage for assembly line skills or high salaries for technical knowledge and training—no middle ground.

So what you've got on one hand is the loss of $28,000/year jobs and the increase of jobs paying under $7,000, or so says Professor

Levy. More adult males were unemployed than females for the first time in history in 1987. According to the good professor the middle class is decreasing and the wealth-poverty pockets are shifting. Due to mistakes made in computing Social Security benefits back in 1972 (tying benefits to CPI at a time when wages were about to decline) the elderly are no longer at the bottom of the poverty heap but women and children have taken their place.

JOBS PROGRAMS

There has been some improvement in job programs. No more dollars are being paid for attending ballet classes, or to aspiring rock climbers for hurling themselves over gigantic artificial boulders built for that purpose with $30,000 from the already employed taxpayers. However decentralizing authority from the federal government to local areas may have been the biggest improvement. Nationwide, in FY 1981, under CETA (Comprehensive Employment Training Act) $5,222 was spent per trainee and only 15 percent ever found jobs. $4,245 per trainee was spent using PIC (Private Industry Council) programs according to the Labor Department's figures and many PICs offer training only if there is a job waiting. There are 624 PICs which administer the programs under the Job Training Partnership Act (JTPA) which was initiated in 1983. If training is given on the job, the federal government provides up to half the workers' wages for up to six months and in many instances transportation and meals are thrown in as an additional incentive.

CETA received $9.5 billion in FY 1978 compared to $3.6 billion for JTPA in FY 1987. In many cases that is about $6 billion saved from the proverbial "drain"—as in "pouring down the". Some PICs have poorer records than Cincinnati's which places just under 80 percent of its graduates. Unfortunately in some areas money is used to train a population of non-employed for non-existent jobs. Some critics complain that providing too little time (CETA averaged 28 weeks and JTPA averages 14 weeks of training) will result in poor skills. But most complaints center on the cost effectiveness of various programs, pointing to examples like the $57/hour the government spent to train each potential bar tender. (198 of them between 1985–86)[2]

In 1982 the Office of Management and Budget (OMB) found that public works were a relatively high-cost way to create employment. It was estimated that only 12 percent of the jobs financed by the local public works programs went to the unemployed and on average unskilled workers kept their jobs less than four weeks. Those with motivation and incentive would have found work on their own and the others were mostly workers brought in by out-of-town contractors. They were paid in conformity with the Davis-Bacon Act which requires compensation to match the area's "prevailing" (read high union) wages. Such projects would simply put a lot of people to work for wages higher than those earned by two-thirds of the American workforce. Make-work programs raise the cost and reduce the supply of efficient production; another case of the inefficient driving out the efficient. Federal public works expenditures merely replace state and local government expenditures when there are no new private sector jobs. In some instances taxes may have to be raised causing displacement of private jobs also as businesses are forced to economize. Although financing public works via deficit spending may have worked once (the 'ol Keynesian solution), remember there is no longer the cushion we once had. The budget deficit has used up the margin of safety we once enjoyed—we are more vulnerable to domestic as well as global uncertainties.

Public service corporations, active in over 30 cities and 8 states as of 1987, are a step in the right direction. These are volunteer programs in which generally young people devote a year to community work receiving low wages and usually a bonus at the end of the service in the form of a scholarship or cash, at their option.

New York City invests approximately $10 million annually in its City Volunteer Corps (CVC) which has enjoyed the service of about 3,000 volunteers since its inception in 1984. The California Conservation Corps (CCC) is eleven years old and was made a permanent agency of the state in 1983. It costs the state $50 million a year and employs about 2,000 18–25 year olds. The idea is to get young people off the street and hopefully develop character, job skills and responsibility while at the same time providing a low-cost way to meet social needs.

Volunteer service is one thing but Congressman Robert Torricelli of New Jersey has a bill before Congress that would *mandate* one year of service for all 18 to 25 year olds. The military draft was abolished in 1973—there's not much chance that the nation will accept a civilian draft in its place.

One creative approach to the homeless problem which does not infringe upon *anyone's* rights was taken by the non-profit New York Coalition for the Homeless when it established Samaritan House, a shelter currently (1987) housing 10 women and 18 children in Brooklyn. Instead of city shelters with their rows of cots crowding both sexes, some mentally ill, some with drug problems, into a single room, Samaritan House offers bright cheerful rooms, one to a family, a playroom with donated toys, a warm airy kitchen and a generally up-beat atmosphere where those down-on-their-luck are allowed to stay for up to six months. Most of the women attend school in an attempt to get their job skills and life in order so they might strike out again on their own.

The shelter was bought by the coalition and renovated with private funds and a loan from Citibank. New York City pays $16 per adult and $11 per child for each night the coalition provides shelter. Samaritan House expects to make a "profit" of $20,000 to $30,000 after a year's operation which it will plough into another project.

Samaritan House is half-way to OK—that is it shows that a non-government entity can provide "more for less". Nevertheless it is using dollars "stolen" (via government coercion) from one group to support another. If the concept was carried one step further—letting voluntary contributions substitute for the money paid to the shelter by the city, it would be self-sufficient before long and still be able to expand, no doubt at a slower rate but on a more moral base. Today there are non-public-works programs competing for the attention of the underpriviliged, many who find illegal activities far more lucrative than anything government or non-profit organizations can begin to offer.

The "Youth Assistance Association" in Oakland California had the capacity in February 1987 to enroll 45 persons age 16 to 25 in an auto mechanics class but only two people enrolled even though the Association could claim a 100 percent job placement record with $1,000/month salary expected at the end of the program.[3]

Why, one might well ask, were there only two takers? Perhaps the restrictions were too tough. There was a $6,000 limit on family income for applicants and they were only offered $5 to get to and from the training center. Nevertheless, Oakland California is situated in the heart of the San Francisco bay area where hundreds of thousands of commuters could get to and from the center for $5 and more than a hundred thousand families had incomes low enough to qualify. A follow-up call to Fred Hansen, director of the program, revealed that the problem had been in reaching applicants. Visits to schools, parks and newspaper advertisements hadn't done the trick, but the publicity on TV and radio, albeit negative, netted the program 45 participants. Of the 45 only 15 were JTPA eligible and of those 12 finished the program and were placed in jobs. (2 of the 30 "JTPA ineligible" also finished the program and were placed.)

On the other hand some government programs are too cost inefficient to survive. In the spring of 1986 a program training 75, mostly single mothers for jobs closed down supposedly under the Gramm-Rudman restrictions. The program was costing $1 million/year which translated into $14,000 each per trainee.[4]

The Job Training Partnership Act is a step in the right direction, just as Samaritan House is, but here also it would be even better with no government assistance, unquestionably so from a capitalist ideology and even so from a purely practical (non-ideological) point of view.

For example, J. C. Penny, American Express, IBM, MCI all have training programs for pregnant teenagers. CBS News (5/27/87) featured a Norfolk, Virginia business man, Herman Valentine of Systems Management of America, who invested $100,000 in a program to train pregnant drop-outs because it made good business sense.

Job training is another example of government rushing to fill a void which if government stayed out the free market would fill more efficiently, and best of all *freely*—without coercion nor incentives.

"SHE GAVE THEM SOME BROTH WITHOUT ANY BREAD . . ."

In March 1987, the Senate Labor and Human Resource Committee proposed legislation that would give $3,700 to each former recipient of assistance who finds employment and remains employed for at least 3 years. The funds would come from the money saved by removing the former recipients from the welfare rolls and would not be paid until the savings were realized. (The funds Senator Cranston had planned to use to reduce the deficit—deficit—remember the *deficit?*) During a former recipient's first year of employment the state would receive 75 percent of the benefit that would have been paid to the person had he or she still received AFDC money. That figure would drop to 50 percent during the second year and 25 percent in the third year of employment. After three years the average bonus per recipient would be almost $3,700. (Maybe a good time to quit and start the largess rolling again?) Also included in the target groups are the recipients of Social Security disability payments. The plan may ensure federal budget neutrality but what about the philosophy? The concern seems to be wholly practical with little thought to the ideals of the nation or whether it makes spiritual as well as economic sense. Does anybody care?

There are parents who *pay* their children for getting good grades or cleaning their own rooms—bonuses or incentives they call it. What about instilling self-respect instead? Do it to please yourself not so you can pick up a government check or parental approval. Who wants to live in a family of spoiled children or a nation with spoiled citizens? No back-bone, no self-motivation, no evidence of self-worth or character—ugh! But those in authority, whether parent or legislator, tend to get what they expect. Keep the expectations low and you won't be disappointed. On the other hand, I am certain people respond to challenges and are capable of far more than they themselves realize. Government should provide opportunity and inspire citizens to do their best.

DINKS AND YUPPIES

Recently, the term Dink, referring to double-income-no-kids couples came into usage to compliment the catchy term used to describe young urban upwardly-mobile professionals—Yuppies. Apparently yuppies can be dinks but not all dinks are yuppies. Yuppies are the ones the peddlers of prestige items hope to lure. Companies have begun offering ordinary products in fancy packages but at a premium price. It worked like magic for Amex who came up with the American Express Platinum Card for $200 offering the identical services as the $50 green card and got 50,000 takers on the first mailing. Prestige is everything!

One third of the women born in the 50s won't have children because of finances. Whereas dinks may be blue collar workers without enough money to start a family, yuppies are more likely to postpone families in favor of the pleasures of a career or to attain material desires. It is not uncommon for a working couple in the eighties to wait 5 to 10 years before having a child compared to the average one year wait while the wife stayed home prior to 1970.

THE TWO-EARNER PHENOMENA

From 1965–85, the number of women with jobs almost doubled. Today, two-thirds of wives age 25–34 are working for wages compared with fewer than half ten years earlier.

In her April 19, 1984 newspaper column, Sylvia Porter said ". . . the contribution women make to our nation's economic stability via the two-paycheck family completely overwhelms whatever harm has been done to an employable man here or there.

Couples in the 80s have a whole set of expectations which differ from those of an earlier generation. They have a certain feeling of security in the two-earner family. If one gets laid off there is security in the other income. The two-earner situation has increased expectations for a rising, not a decreasing, standard of living and unhappily those expectations aren't always met.

AID TO FAMILIES WITH DEPENDENT CHILDREN (AFDC)

Welfare measures could add $2 billion to $3 billion to the $80 billion a year the federal government now spends on the poor. AFDC benefits vary from state to state. Monthly AFDC benefits for a family of three are $118 in AL versus $389 in Maine even though per capita incomes in the two states are approximately the same. In order to correct this situation some policy-makers would like to see a national minimum AFDC standard indexed to inflation, similar to SSI and food stamps.

Jack Meyer of the American Enterprise Institute says the federal government should also require that states grant benefits to all impoverished families with children; 24 states refuse AFDC benefits to households with adult males. If benefits were extended to two-parent families and a national minimum of $443/month were adopted, total AFDC expenditures, $15 billion in 1985 ($8 billion provided by the federal government), would rise by an estimated $2 or $3 billion. So who can pass up a good deal? *They* continue to encourage what *they* claim *they* want to discourage. I give up!

CHILD SUPPORT

The need for AFDC could be reduced by strengthening the system for enforcing child-support. Germany and Norway have tough government child-support systems and poverty rates among female headed households are far lower in those countries. If the absent parent's payments fall in arrears, custodial parents get their child-support from the government.

Already the United States Office of Child Support Enforcement estimates that $20 billion to $30 billion of taxpayers' money is spent each year to support children whose non-custodial parent has failed to meet his/her support obligations.

The original child-support program was established in 1975 to help locate missing parents and determine paternity. In 1984, Congress passed an amendment requiring states to adopt legislation authorizing the withholding of child-support from wages (the burden is on the employer once again) and state tax refunds. At each state's option, payments may be withheld from other sources of income like commissions, dividends and pensions. If the noncustodial parent has no second family up to 60 percent of his disposable income can be withheld, only 50 percent if he has a second family. All states must provide a mechanism to offset state tax refunds of delinquent parents and provision is made for liens against real and personal property. In 1985, $3.31 in child support payments was collected for every dollar spent to administer the enforcement program. In FY 1985, states and local governments paid a little more than a quarter of the costs to run the program ($243 million out of $814 million) with the federal government (all taxpayers) picking up the bulk of the tab. In 1986, according to the Department of Health and Human Services, this program was responsible for the collection of over $3 billion in child-support.

Wisconsin designates a fraction of the absent parent's earnings to support a child under 18. That amount is withheld by employers as child-support and the courts distribute the money to the custodial parent. Wisconsin makes minimal payments if the absent parent falls in arrears and if the payments dip below the minimum, the state will also make up the difference. Working parents receiving child-support will receive a $1 an hour bonus payment. That would give a single parent holding a half-time minimum-wage job more income than he/she would get from AFDC, effectively removing the built-in disincentive to work that has drawn so much criticism lately. What can I say?

FAMILIES

Many of our younger people have been taught to live for the moment; to seek instant gratification, to denigrate the future as Belinda Carlisle says in a popular song, as "stuff and nonsense". More than one generation has grown up with little thought of right or wrong. They have learned to escape rather than face their problems. Addiction is rated America's number one health problem and teenage pregnancies cost taxpayers more than $15 billion annually.

Although there are fewer births than in the past decades due to birth control and later marriage, the proportion of babies born to unmarried women has increased from 1.7 percent in 1960 to 13.4 percent in 1986 (Whites) and from 16.8 percent to 51 percent Non-Whites. Twenty-one percent of all babies born in the U.S. in 1986 were born out of wed-lock. (A truly archaic term—there is obviously no "lock" on marriage anymore!) Naturally this means an increase in female-headed one parent families which in 1960 accounted for 5 percent (White) and rose to 15 percent by 1986; for Non-White the rise was from 21 percent to 48 percent.

Two out of three persons in poverty are women. The great majority of female-headed families, whence comes feminized poverty, are due to either unwed mothers or divorce. The divorce rate has tripled over the past 25 years leaving 73 percent of the women with lower living standards and 49 percent of the men with higher living standards after divorce. The well-meaning reforms of the 1970s contributed to this state of affairs. No-fault-divorce gave men an easy way out of their marriage contracts with distribution of assets substituting for the old promise of support (alimony). Half the assets is generally a small fraction of the value of the earning power of the male so the female, and often the children, end up receiving far less in settlement than in the "bad 'ol days" when alimony often meant a "meal ticket for life." However, there is a continual turnover; it's not the same people in poverty every year. Three out of four divorced women remarry within five years. It is not a problem that has been engendered by a harsh or sexist society but it is a problem nevertheless.

Surprisingly a 1986 National Health Interview Survey showed 67 percent of all children live with both biological parents; 20 percent live with one biological parent; 9 percent live with one biological parent and one step-parent and 4 percent live with neither biological parent.

The Census Bureau in 1984 reported that 37 percent of all children under 18 had mothers who worked part time—33 percent had mothers not working and 27 percent had mothers that worked full time. Probably the reason given most by women working outside the home is the need for money "to make ends meet".

Another study (studies and more studies) for the Joint Economic Committee, prepared by Sheldon Danzner of the Poverty Institute, found in 1973 families with children made up 61.4 percent of the population. By 1984 they made up only 53.3 percent of the population and income had dropped for these families.

OFFICIAL POVERTY LEVELS

Figures for "children in poverty" were first calculated in 1929. In 1959, the figures stood at 26.9 percent and in 1985 at 20.1 percent, meaning that although poverty had declined since the "happy days" (fifties) close to 13 million children were living in families below the 1985 government's official poverty line cut-off of $10,989 for a family of four. Of those 13 million children, 43.1 percent were Black, 39.6 percent were Hispanic and 15.6 percent White (that leaves .7 percent for Asians et al—why don't statistics ever add up to 100 percent of anything?)

Poverty was one of those subjective words until policy-makers stepped in and made it "whatever they want it to mean." Many people are counted as poor who are not deprived by any objective standard, because there is considerable disagreement as to what should be considered in determining poverty.

Poverty thresholds were first set in 1961 when the Social Security Administration, along with the Agricultural Department determined the income necessary to adequately feed the number of children and adults in any given household and multiplied by three. Of course adequately is a subjective term. If children and adults were evenly distributed there wouldn't be a difference in their poverty rates. But, according to Victor Fuchs, Economics Professor at Stanford University, 40 percent of all children and 9 percent of all adults live in households with three or more children and 57 percent of all adults live in households containing no children. That means even if incomes of adults are similar the per capita income is much lower in homes with children. We certainly didn't need anyone's study to tell us that. Nor is it a surprising discovery that non-labor income attributable to pension and Social Security benefits, has grown more rapidly than labor income which has in fact declined. Children are clearly more dependent on the labor income of their parents which accounts for the statistics showing an increase in childhood poverty in recent years.

NON-CASH BENEFITS

In 1985, non-cash benefits to the poor were valued at $56.2 billion; almost double the $30.2 billion cash benefits. If, according to a 1986 study by the Census Bureau, non-cash federal assistance were to be considered, the number of citizens living in poverty might be 11.5 million lower than officially estimated. Every year beginning in 1979, the non-cash portion of public assistance has resulted in a lower number of poor people than officially published.

But anything can be carried to extreme. To include even the insurance value of Medicare-Medicaid benefits in counting non-cash aid would lead to the ridiculous result that in 8 states the value of those benefits would make it possible to consider an elderly person with absolutely zero cash income living above the poverty level. Counting Medicaid could mean that "the sicker the richer".

Of course not all income is reported (remember the underground economy). If by reporting minimal earnings or unexpected increases in assets, a family would be disqualified from subsidized housing or lose their food stamps or reduce their Social Security benefits, most families are simply not going to report the income. Unwittingly government policy is a powerful incentive to dishonesty.

MALFEASANCE

In all my research, the following is the most hackneyed statement I have ever come across. "Children are poor mostly because their mothers are poor." (What's this "mostly" business—why else would they be considered poor as "poor" is defined?) It has been attributed to Miss Well-Meaning, Co-Director of an antipoverty group in New York (I didn't want to embarrass anyone by using a *real* name). Ms. Well-Meaning, the mistress of platitudes, offers the following: "Poverty is the No. 1 killer of children in the United States. It's murder by malfeasance."[5]

Malfeasance is misconduct or wrongdoing contrary to official obligations. Misfeasance is the improper performance of an act which is lawful to do. However, the feasance Ms. Well-Meaning was apparently looking for is nonfeasance, the omission of an act one *ought* to do. This seems to be clear from the rest of her statement describing "murder" as lead-paint poisoning, elevator-shaft deaths, apartment fires and inadequate nutrition. This logic (I'm using the word loosely) would imply that birth control would also be murder—look at all the children that are prevented from life by omission of unrestricted sexual intercourse; something that could just as easily and arbitrarily be argued as an "ought".

But looking beyond the inaccurate use of language and absence of logic, what would Miss Well-Meaning have society do? Afterall there are numerous alternatives. We could sterilize those *we* judge may become *unfit* parents (states did this not that long ago) or remove children from homes where *we* judge they may be endangered by lack of attentive parenting (still being done today). Ms. Well-Meaning's solution, "Apart from the obvious solution . . . more money . . .", is to *think* about the problem first of all, then we must educate (did I tell you this lady was the master of platitudes?) and third, find a way to keep the poor ". . . from feeling like an island apart, broken off from the mainland". There you have it!

WOMEN IN THE WORKFORCE

Women have made strides towards social equality along with Blacks.

From 1939 to 1979 women made approximately 49 percent of what males earned whereas in the mid-eighties they were making 65 percent of a male's earnings. OK—partly because male earnings had dropped about 8 percent, but that's still progress, and it's getting better as younger women pick up graduate degrees and professional designations. In 1987 women between the ages of 21 and 24 were making 86 percent of a male's earnings. In 1960, only 4 million women held professional, technical, managerial, and administrative jobs. Today there are 11 million women in those jobs. In 1960 women accounted for 1 out of every 3 college students and today they're on a parity with men. In fact the 1987 freshman class at Chapel Hill, North Carolina was 63 percent women!

New Choices in a Changing America, a report issued by the Democratic Commission in August, 1986, found the increase of women in the workforce to be positive overall. It presumed that women in the workforce would increase America's productivity and enable the country to better compete globally, especially because there may well be a shortage in workers ten or twenty years down the pike because of demographics. I believe increased technology will prevent that shortage and, as unpopular as my belief may be, I nevertheless feel quite certain women working in the home will increase America's productivity far more than in the labor force. But as it is more than likely a large number of readers disagree with me, you will be delighted to know the report calls for better day care, more parenting leaves, flexible work hours, pay equity and comparable worth. The later is not only to give single mothers a better living, but married women more leverage with their husbands. Supposedly, husbands will feel compelled to do more of the house and family chores because comparable worth will assure that men no longer contribute more financially to the family than women.

The Reagan administration issued a report about the same time as that of the Democratic Policy Commission. It called for increased tax deductions for dependents, the idea being to provide child allowances to encourage more people to stay home and take care of their children. Women's new-found wide-spread ability to work and support themselves has both pros and cons. The "pros" have been dealt with steadily by every magazine and talk show across the nation for the past 20 years. Independence and self-worth are worthy achievable goals and were the subject of my first book[7] which was directed to young people and women especially. The "cons" have been discussed less and for that reason I will concentrate on them here.

MARRIAGE IS HARDER TO MAINTAIN THAN EVER BEFORE

Because a women is more readily accepted and has more choices than ever before in the work place, it is easier for her to leave an unhappy relationship but it is also easier for her husband to desert with less guilt. When men and women are economically independent, one rivet to the relationship has been removed leaving one less reason to stay together and work things out. These are merely facts; by no means would I ever advocate dependence for its own sake. If a marriage works by choice as opposed to necessity, that is the best of all worlds.

Those that point to women's liberation as the cause of our increased divorce rate are likely to be jeered as are those who suggest that old fashioned "commitment" is the answer. Experienced people audacious enough to suggest that anything can be made to work if enough effort is put into it are called "self-righteous". It is easy and fashionable to dismiss the truth by donning an air of superiority.

The role of wife and mother are wonderful productive roles if understood, and nothing in the labor force can be as rewarding to man, woman, child or the whole of society if the home-maker role is given the effort and creativity it deserves.

CHOICES

Many qualified outstanding women have contributed to this nation's wealth outside the home for well over a hundred years and have sometimes been recognized above men when their abilities merited it—and sometimes have not been so recognized when they should have been. Look at Julia Morgan who designed many beautiful and lovingly kept buildings in the bay area and was the architect chosen from all others (surely cost was no factor) for the magnificent Hearst Castle in San Simeon, California, which was under construction from 1919 to 1949. Such women will, in the 1980s–90s and into the next century, benefit themselves and all of us by work in their professions. But I will remind you what you don't want to hear, and that is that many women chose career *instead* of children. I know women today think that is unfair—why should they be forced to choose when men have both children and careers at the same time?

WOMEN *CAN* HAVE IT ALL

According to the Census Bureau, one in every five wives earns more than her husband—obviously most earn less. Nevertheless, women, even more than men, are living more educated, longer, healthier lives and can have several careers in succession if they choose to do so. It is no longer an either/or choice—life can be lived in different stages. To choose to have everything all at once harms women (Super Moms), their husbands, their children (in spite of "expert" claims to the contrary) and makes society less productive. (see page 178)

I have worried about the youngsters of the 1980s; the people who will be in charge of this country forty or fifty years from now. I wonder when I read stories about latch-key children and hear people demanding dollars for child-care centers. I wonder even more when I see successful businesswomen on TV panels proclaiming that today's woman can "have-it-all-at-once"; happy intelligent children, successful supportive husbands and a brilliant career outside the home. I believe a woman can have it all but not only is it easier but it is far better for society for her to "have it" in stages.

SOMETHING TO LIVE BY

Society has to instill the idea in our young people that they are needed. You may have heard of the suicide note left by a teenager a few years ago that read, "You have given me everything to live with and nothing to live for". Obviously money isn't everything. We have heard stories about the early poor-in-dollars-rich-in-spirit years of Mario Cuomo, Leo Buscaglia and countless other prominent individuals, and can unhappily compare them to the shortened youths of teenagers who were given things to live with but no philosophy to live by.

Numerous polls and surveys have purported to show that children with working moms are more independent, responsible and a host of other good things and that the only problem with a mother working is the mother's guilt. People will believe anything if they want to badly enough.

CHILD CARE

In May 1987, the Census Bureau came out with a study, "Who's Minding the Kids", which estimated that families with mothers who work outside the home spend over $11 billion a year on child care. Child-care currently costs anywhere from $4,000 to $10,000 per year. One solution to the child-care problem is for the mother to work at home. It is far from a perfect solution and in fact its worth would depend on the age and demands of the children to be cared for and the demands of the job as well as the working mother's energy level and other obligations.

In the summer of 1986, the Labor Department proposed repealing the federal ban on commercial garment work done at home. If effected, the proposal would, for the first time in over forty years, permit work on women's apparel, jewelry, gloves, mittens, buttons, buckles, handkerchiefs and embroideries in the home. Naturally the International Ladies Garment Workers Union predicted the nation would be returning to the sweat shops of the Industrial Dark Ages. Now why do you suppose *they* would say a thing like that?

CONSUMER SPENDING

Many economists and even retailers feel that consumers can safely handle more debt. Certainly some folks are in over their heads already but by and large the average consumer is not in that bad shape.

In fact the total net worth of American households is on the rise and their overall financial condition should not be an impediment to future consumer spending. Since 1983, Americans have purchased more than 42 million automobiles, 24 million refrigerators, 84 million TV sets, 38 million microwaves, and so on. The problem may become what to buy tomorrow?

The federal reserve's monetary policy featuring easier credit has created a buffer against recession as the baby boomers are able to continue their spending spree which keeps the economy alive. In 1986, the mainstay of the economy was consumer spending and outlays for housing. When their houses continue to rise in value it makes the average person feel wealthy.

The average urban household, according to the Bureau of Labor Statistics in January 1986, spent almost $9,000 a year with the largest expenditures on housing—$5,784, transportation—$3,712, food at home—$2,204, personal insurance and pensions—$1,625.

TRIPPING THROUGH A MAZE OF FIGURES

It's interesting to note that consumer spending remained at just under two-thirds of GNP during the last 30 years, a fact which encourages many observers to believe the debt issue has been greatly exaggerated, at least when it comes to consumer debt. Borrowing in the 1980s is governed, these critics argue, by the same functions and relationships as in the 1950s. But if the relation to GNP has remained relatively constant, the relation to personal income has not. In 1956, consumer debt was 9 percent of personal income; by 1976 it had risen to 12 percent and was up to 17 percent by 1986. It is easy to become confused—almost as if there were a conspiracy to keep the average person from discovering the facts. In mid 1986 Wharton Econometric Forecasting found that house-hold interest expense had risen from under 5 percent in 1970 to approximately 10 percent in 1985. Nevertheless, according to Wharton, consumers were in the mood for and able to continue spending. Remember, it was consumer debt as share of personal income that had risen to 17 percent in 1986 and Wharton is talking about the ratio of "interest expense". Debt to income ratios are misleading measurements. Some debts are stretched out with low payments over a long time period.

Next we are given information about "disposable personal income" (83 percent of it went to household debt—that is *total* household debt) in 1985. What we need in this instance is a definition of "disposable"—what has the personal income already been used for before it gets to this "disposable" stage. And "total" household debt needs to be defined too—what is included in "total"?

BANKRUPTCY

Debt service took one-third of all after tax income in 1987 and an estimated 15 million households paid over 50 percent of their total disposable incomes to service debt. First the government and then the creditors—it may seem to some to be a repeat of their father's tale of working for the "ol company store".

In an effort to discourage borrowing the Tax Reform Act of 1986 made interest on consumer and other forms of debt nondeductible. It didn't take the adjustable American consumer long to realize home equity loans still permit borrowing on an interest-deductible basis. However, a sudden down-turn in the economy, which is not unlikely according to many economists, will have the unfortunate affect of putting a large percentage of people's homes at risk. The delinquency rate on home mortgages is at a historic high, helped perhaps by the increase in government sponsored financing with its lenient qualifications.

Another omen may be seen in the number of bankruptcies which jumped from 179,112 in 1978 to 523,825 in 1981. The change in the personal bankruptcy law which became effective in October, 1979, accounted in part for that increase. As I've pointed out in many instances, our policy-makers are skilled at encouraging what *should* be discouraged. No longer do borrowers have to give up their homes and cars to gain protection from creditors. Bankruptcies were up 35 percent for the year ending June 1986. Thirty-six percent of the 261,000 borrowers from the Farmers Home Administration are behind in their payments and 80 percent of these have been delinquent over three years. This rise in the segment of the population most likely to borrow (baby boomers) is only partially offset by a rise in the segment of the population least likely to borrow—those over 65.

Of course neither debtor nor creditor expects to pay debt back with current income. Both are optimistically looking to larger future incomes which will enable all future commitments to be easily met. (Where oh where has prudence gone?) Pessimists claim we're over-consuming now, which means we'll have to under-consume in the future, which we are warned, will lead to a lower standard of living ahead for our children (Yeah—but they're always saying that—right?)

DEBT TO NET WORTH RATIOS

Over the years the ratio of mortgage and consumer debt to an individual's net-worth has increased from 8 percent in 1952 to 18 percent in 1985. The outstanding credit balances on the nation's Mastercards have more than doubled from $11 billion in 1983 to $28 billion in 1986. The American Bankers Association, which represents 13,000 lenders, reported an increasing delinquency rate in consumer installment loans in 1986. But many people use the cards purely as a convenience, paying their bills at the end of each month which means the effective debt burden is less than the data implies—only 2.3 percent of such loans were over 30 days past due at the beginning of 1987.

A NBC/WSJ poll taken in 1986 reported that of 2,239 people nationwide, 44 percent said they were better off now than in the 1970s, 31 percent better than in the 1960s, and 27 percent better than in the 1950s. A Conference Board poll of 5,000 households in 1986 found that more than 70 percent of those under age 35 thought their standard of living was as good if not better than their parents'. (There was less room for nostalgia here as many weren't even around in the 1950s!)

SAVINGS OR INVESTMENTS?

Definitions are important. Autos and durable goods could be considered investments and therefore savings. This would make the reported savings rate that much higher. Automobiles are generally financed, at least partially, from past savings. Not taking this into consideration makes our savings rate look lower than it otherwise would. (Another instance where a conflict of numbers could be traced to a misconstrued definition.) Savings can mean net-private-savings (subtract depreciation), or gross private savings (add back depreciation), or gross savings (add federal, state and local governments, business and personal—around 15 percent consistently), personal savings (take after tax disposable income and subtract consumption). The personal savings rate, meaning the percentage of disposable income left after outlays, moved from 4 percent in 1985 to 5 percent in 1986. Does that surprise you?

CORPORATE DEBT

When we start talking about corporate instead of personal debt, the tables are reversed with American businessmen being more conservative than their foreign counterparts.

U.S. executives typically finance their companies with much less debt than do the Germans and the Japanese. From 1972 through 1982, the percentage of total debt in the capital structures of the Japanese and German manufacturers averaged 60 percent and 64 percent respectively, more than twice the 30 percent of U.S. manufacturers.

By using high leverage, foreign competitors have several advantages over U.S. manufacturers: debt financing (with tax deductible interest) instead of financing via equity (stock) lowers the cost of capital (after tax). At the same time it reduces the stock market's influence on managerial decisions which in turn allows for longer range planning by foreign businessmen. However, a firm could always lower dividends for awhile but interest on a bond issue comes due—ready or not!

The cost of capital for American companies was estimated at 16.6 percent compared to slightly more than 9 percent for West German and Japanese companies by a 1983 study conducted by the International Trade Commission. In order to compete in world markets American companies must find capital at lower costs.

Besides using more leverage (debt) it would help if investors would accept lower, immediate returns on their investments. Lack of investor pressure would also allow American management to think and act more long-range which would in turn provide an environment conducive to greater experimentation and expansion. From 1972 through 1982, the average before tax return on capital for American companies was 21.1 percent compared to a return of 15.7 percent for the West Germans and 14.2 percent for the Japanese. Japanese and German investors are used to receiving lower returns on other investments and it is therefore relatively easy for these companies to reinvest profits to increase growth.

But American companies have begun to use more leverage. 1985 saw all non-financial corporate debt at $1.3 trillion, with short term debt registering a record 52 percent of total debt. Companies in 1986 exhibited ratios of liabilities to assets of more than 50 percent; higher than at any time since the Second World War. In 1960, the total liabilities of Fortune 500 industrial companies averaged 35 percent of assets; at the end of 1984 that figure stood at nearly 55 percent. In 1960 total debt for manufacturing—$40 billion; in 1983 approximately *$400* billion! Even if we subtract two-thirds of the increase to allow for inflation, debt still skyrocketed!

Many observers find this situation dangerous not only for the companies burdened with debt, but also for the institutions holding that debt. With the decline in inflation, borrowers can no longer look forward to repaying that debt with ever cheapening dollars.

But opinions are as numerous as people. Boston University Professor Robert Taggart believes we need to look not at the ratio of debt to book value but with the ratio of debt to total capitalization at market value. This ratio was 27 percent in 1984 which is far below the post WWII high of 38 percent in 1974. Borrowing can in fact be healthy, especially when proceeds are used to replace and improve means of production. Many manufacturers have depreciated plant and equipment investment, leaving them well positioned for economic growth. That's contrary to popular knowledge which says business has recently been spending less in plant and equipment. Actually business spent 11 percent of GNP on plant and equipment in the 1950s, 9 percent in the 1960s and over 12 percent in 1986.[8] Many companies went into debt to buy back their own stock, often as a defense against possible takeovers. Almost every takeover fight features an actual or proposed increase in the debt of companies involved.

If we're going to talk debt we must also talk assets. Raiders are well aware that decades of inflation have left assets on corporate balance sheets enormously undervalued. The shareholders equity portion of capital is understated and the debt portion is exaggerated. At any rate, a large debt load compels companies to operate at peak efficiency or die. In fact Robert Clark of Harvard, believes corporate raiders are performing a needed service by keeping business managers on their toes.

Although, as we said earlier, growth of debt has been matched by growth in assets, income is a worry. The biggest fear is that in a downturn, a company with too heavy a burden might be forced to contract and lay off employees who would then default on their personal debt obligation continuing a domino-like reaction that could end in a massive global recession.

NO CUSHION

I heard Milton Friedman say during a speech to the Commonwealth Club in San Francisco several years ago, and others have said it since, we could handle large amounts of debt in the past without any trouble because we had plenty of room to maneuver. Right now our economy is so leveraged that there is no cushion to absorb the shock. The huge budget deficit deprives policy-makers of the fiscal flexibility needed if the economy were to slump. The government has already cut tax rates (temporarily at least) and citizens have put second mortgages on their homes—what's left for an emergency?

THE NOBLE CREDITORS—WISHFUL THINKING!

We have tried to convince other nations what has become a tenant of American business philosophy, that is, that strong consumer sales are the backbone of a strong economy. Now that we are a debtor nation with a mounting foreign debt it would be nice if Japan and Europe were to act the part of the noble creditor, the part we played so well for them for decades after the Second World War. It would be good for everyone if they would import and consume more.

Not long ago, MASTERCARD conducted a study in Europe which revealed that 45 percent of those surveyed thought it unwise to borrow for anything other than a house; 74 percent felt credit cards made spending too easy. Most Europeans would rather walk than borrow money for a car. This aversion to borrowing means that even were the government of West Germany to lower interest rates and cut taxes, any extra money would go into savings. Europeans do not consume the way Americans do and are not likely to provide the markets needed to sustain a large increase in American exports. There is no doubt that consumer spending can encourage economic growth, but even if other *governments* are convinced, their people will not change their habits overnight.

Of course one of the reasons West Germans spend so little is attributable to government incentives to save. The West Germans have memories of the economic hardships suffered after World War II. There is no doubt Europeans are less secure than Americans and save more to compensate for their insecurity. There is a definite social stigma against borrowing. (Many would like to import that "stigma" to America!)

One of the reasons given for the high savings rate in Japan is the high cost of housing. (Hear-Hear, Mr. Gonzales!) Even by saving an average 21 to 22 percent of his income annually, it is unusual for the average Japanese consumer to accumulate enough to purchase a home before he's in his mid-fifties. But times are changing. Despite media reports to the contrary, the new generation of Japanese don't want to work 12 to 15 hours a day. Like their American counterparts, they feel it is important to enjoy life in the present and that means access to money through borrowing. American consumers can usually borrow for several points over prime. In Japan in 1985, the interest rates quoted ranged from 20 percent to over 65 percent and were already on a five year declining schedule. Those rates were a bargain compared to 1983 when the maximum interest rates the "sarakin" (salary man's financing) could charge on unsecured cash loans was over 100 percent!

ALL DEBT! YOU'VE GOT TO BE KIDDING!

In 1986, total federal, state and local government debt plus business and individual debt—i.e. *all* debt topped $7.5 trillion! (You can bet your booty they didn't get *all* debt—read *Underground Government* published by the Cato Institute.) That $7.5 trillion was up $1 trillion over 1985. Amazingly the federal government accounted for only 25 percent of that total. But it doesn't get better. Debt in 1987 totaled approximately 1.7 times GNP, the highest ration since the depression. Business failures have averaged $3 billion each month. The number of AAA rated industrial and utility corporations has dwindled over the past 10 years.

THE BUCK STOPS . . .

There has been a lot of talk about poor corporate management, some of it justified, some of it just talk. A most dangerous trend is the growing lack of accountability in all phases of American life; from the auto mechanics that can't find your car's problem, to the teachers who can't get Johnny to read, to the politicians who can't follow their own directives; not surprisingly the corporate world is no exception. Mistakes are masked by restructuring and calling it aggressive management. If shareholder's suffer losses—too bad. Oh yes, and the CEOs continue to collect eight figure salaries with no relation to performance. Employees often get fired in restructuring cop-outs whereas incompetent managers are promoted to avoid suspicion of negligence.

But more laws and further regulation is not the answer. Stock holder savvy may be. Fewer corporations enjoy the AAA rating, as we have seen, and people are going to start paying attention to merit. Weeding out will occur via the market if government can only keep its hands off and be patient.

AMAZING GROWTH

The number of U.S. corporations grew 80 percent between 1970 and 1983 to almost 3 million from 1.7 million; corporate assets rose to $10 trillion from $1.8 trillion. After inflation that's still a formidable 73 percent increase. (As Peter Grace would say—trillion shmillion, we can't possibly have any conception of the enormity of the numbers we're discussing—oh well!)

Small corporations with sales under $1 million doubled in number during the period 1970–83. Analyzing assets and comparing the 1970 U.S. economy with that of 1983 is difficult if not impossible. Assets are affected by changes in production methods, competition, interest and exchange rates and a myriad of other interactions. On top of that, many assets are depreciable and their market value declines with use and time. What is a plus in one time period becomes a minus in another. Bigness was an asset in the high-tech economy a few years ago but may prove to be a hindrance in adapting to rapidly changing business conditions in the global economy of today. The advantages for the future may well be liquidity and mobility.

BUREAUCRATS OR PRIVATE FOUNDATIONS?

In some countries the government keeps and distributes all or most of the wealth. Many would like to see that happen here. So far the American government doesn't operate every university and hospital and doesn't determine the arts. As a results, I believe all Americans benefit from decentralization and competition. The individual, by his contributions, can choose which organizations are worthy of support and their need to survive makes them better than they would be in a socialist environment.

Philanthropic foundations had unexpected gains in their portfolios in 1986. Assets of the New York based Ford Foundation jumped 25 percent in a year, to a record $4.6 billion on September 30, 1986, whereas the W. K. Kellogg Foundation of Battle Creek, Michigan, saw its assets soar 60 percent making it the country's second richest foundation. Since such foundations are required by law to give away at least 5 percent of their assets every year, it looks like giving could rise from 10 percent to 12 percent in 1987. Budgets are set at the beginning of the year before the year-end value of assets can be ascertained, and therefore foundations are given a year's grace period to make adjustments in their grants.

THE CHICKEN OR THE EGG?

Does the government have the citizens' money because citizens don't want to care for themselves or are citizens unable to care for themselves because the government has their money? Harold Howe II, former Commissioner of Education under President Johnson says there has been a decline in the belief that the national government ought to do something about our social problems. Hooray if he's right. However, a 1985 poll by I. A. Lewis for the Los Angeles Times shows that 73 percent of Americans favor more government support for the impoverished and 57 percent of those polled said they would pay a 1 percent federal sales tax to provide this support.

VOLUNTEERISM AND CHARITABLE GIVING

Reagan alluded to volunteerism in his election campaigns and said "With the same energy that FDR sought government solutions to problems, we will seek private solutions". Ronald Reagan believes individuals have the primary responsibility to take care of their needy fellow citizens and presumably so do those who voted for him. The caricature of conservatives as selfish egotists is refuted by data showing Americans are giving and volunteering in greater numbers and to greater degrees than at any other time in our nation's history. In 1980, total giving in the USA totaled $49 billion and was falling due to inflation; in 1984 it was $75 billion and rising. Equating liberalism with compassion just doesn't bear out with statistics.

In *The Nonprofit Section & The New Federal Budget* written by Alan Abramson and Lester Salamon and published by the Urban Institute, the authors claim an elaborate partnership exists between nonprofit organizations and government at all levels. They view reductions in federal spending as a very real threat to the existence of "non-profits" fearing such organizations will be unable to attract the revenue in the amounts they were able to in the past as new demands will be placed on less revenue as a consequence of budget cuts. Indeed, there is some evidence that this has been happening.

In 1985, about 70 percent of the volunteer food-distribution groups in Dallas, Houston and San Antonio (50 percent of those in MA) claimed they would go out of existence if the federal government stopped paying their administration expenses. Apparently it cost $3.2 million in Texas and $859,000 in MA to store and distribute the food provided by the federal government. "Thanks" but "no thanks". Perhaps a change in management is needed for some non-profit agencies.

Private charity may never be a substitute for the welfare state but in 1985 the average American donated more than 2 percent of his income to charity. Those earning over $50,000 a year say they give away an average of 2.9 percent of their income but those who make the least (under $10,000) give 3 percent of their income. Those ages 30 to 34 gave 1.7 percent but then they have less disposable income than the older people.

It is nonsense to believe people give primarily for tax considerations because the facts show in America most of the giving is done by people of modest means, perhaps because there's more of them. Contrary to popular belief, 90 percent of all giving in America comes from individual citizens, only 10 percent from foundations and corporations.

There's no doubt people are most likely to give when the economy is doing well, but it's more than that. People give more when they have hope and an optimistic outlook on the future. President Reagan has persuaded people that they are needed, that they can make a difference and for that reason volunteerism is up.

But Americans were volunteers long before Ronald Reagan became President. Alexis de Tocqueville was impressed with America's philanthropic spirit in 1831, and that's before the government decided to tax the people. He would no doubt be delighted to know that in America, 150 years later, charity is still a function of the heart rather than the tax code. The bally-ho about tax cuts hurting charitable giving was just that. It is the amount of disposable income rather than tax rates that affects giving.

In West Philadelphia, Sister Falaka Fattah, has significantly reduced gang violence with her House of Umoja Boystown, where over the years she has provided shelter for about 600 gang people. Begun in her home 15 years ago, the program includes tutoring and training, operating small businesses and renovating more than 20 row houses.

Jethro Mann of Belmont, North Carolina runs a "bicycle lending library" for kids whose parents could not afford to buy them a bicycle. The 35 bikes he has lovingly collected and put together are teaching tools as well as fun. Kids learn a sense of responsibility by signing the bikes in and out and learn to care about one another as older kids are encouraged to repair the bikes of those younger.[9]

Residents of the Kenilworth-Parkside public housing project in Washington, D.C. have sent nearly 500 of their children to college since 1975 with the help of grants, fund raising events and simple encouragement.

"Covenant House", a shelter for runaways founded by Father Bruce Ritter in New York in 1972, is one more example of what can be achieved without government interference and with private leadership, philanthropy and volunteers.

At the Midnight Mission in Los Angeles, every year since 1982, an older man has been passing out ten dollar bills to about 500 indigents at Christmas time. He doesn't want his identity known as it would be "a form of advertising, not giving".

But who is to say "advertising" precludes "giving?" Pan Am gives away several hundred thousand dollars a year in air travel to individuals in need. So-called mercy flights create good-will in addition to providing a service. Pan Am can measure the return on gifts of airline tickets by the personal responses—letters from the public praising the company and vowing to fly Pan Am in the future. Is that wrong?

Professor Gary Becker of the University of Chicago gets upset by the fact that approximately 50 percent of all giving helps support churches, synagogues and other religious bodies resulting in, according to the good Professor, a government subsidy of religion throughout the tax system since charitable contributions are tax deductible. The Professor cites statistics in an effort to show the ordinary taxpayer is subsidizing the wealthy. After all, 15 percent of all giving goes to higher education which is used by the wealthy, and plenty of others, and 10 percent goes to museums and symphonies. Maybe if a sign were posted saying "NO RICH PEOPLE ALLOWED" the Professor would be mollified. Could Professor Becker believe that the state has first call on everyone's income; that only by the state's grace a producer is allowed to distribute the fruits of his efforts as he sees fit?

IS THE AMERICAN DREAM STILL POSSIBLE?

We are Americans and we want everything for everybody. Some would question the possibility of achieving the American Dream as we prepare to enter the 21st century. In Section Four, I will try and convince you there is still hope for America's middle class and that America is still the land of opportunity. The real question is are we willing to sacrifice to achieve our goals? The answers are as varied as we are.

Section Four

Was Lenin Right?

WAS LENIN RIGHT?

CAPITALISM

Karl Marx was certain capitalism would destroy the middle class because eventually the number of poor would increase. Because of the capitalists' exploitation of the workers, Marx claimed laborers wouldn't have enough money to spend on the goods made available by increased production. He foresaw the problem which occurred during the Great Depression—the problem every successful industrial economy faces—the problem of maintaining a level of consumption adequate to ever increasing levels of productivity. Marx loved capitalism for its unprecedented productive power but predicted the inevitable boom and bust cycles would bring about its eventual collapse.

Of course pure laissez-faire capitalism, like pure communism, has never existed anywhere but in the minds of men. Capitalism does not demand, and in fact could not exist under anarchy, but it must have a labor market more free than any government has thus far been able to permit as it requires that no man's interests be sacrificed to another's.

Lord Keynes advocated a partnership between business and government, an idea that is still being advocated by politicians and writers today. But as Ayn Rand pointed out in *The Fascist New Frontier,* "There can be no partnership between armed bureaucrats and defenseless private citizens who have no choice but to obey. What chance would you have against a 'partner' whose arbitrary word is law, who may give you a hearing (if your pressure group is big enough), but who will play favorites and bargain your interest away, who will always have the last word and the legal 'right' to enforce it on you at the point of a gun, holding your property, your work, your future, your life in his power? Is that the meaning of partnership?"

No one wants to be thought an extremist so most confused and often disillusioned Americans choose moderation—the middle-of-the-road. Although it offers little intellectual satisfaction the middle-of-the-road is practiced by educated tolerant men and women and it is generally believed that anyone who holds uncompromisingly to an ideal must be closed minded, ignorant and worthy of ridicule. Such tactics work and therefore intellectual honesty is a very rare thing today. Most so-called intellectuals fear absolutes, but those who refuse to compromise and insist on integrity and excellence come to see moderation as synonomous with mediocrity and lack of integrity.

Just as one cannot be a little bit dead or a little bit pregnant, one can also not be a little bit honest or a little bit just. How can a government with integrity provide subsidies for tobacco farmers and warn citizens against smoking, rant and rave about our trade imbalance and award government contracts to foreign over domestic contractors, protect innocent life and provide dollars for abortions, pay lip-service to private property and tell owners how it must be used, subscribe to "innocent until proven guilty" except when it comes to dealings with the IRS. Is a little freedom OK if balanced by a little regulation? A few special privileges for the rich overlooked if balanced by hand-outs to the poor? A wholesome respect for rights balanced by a reasonable degree of brute force?

During the Second World War Republican congressmen proposed a bill to induce labor for the "good of the country". Like those who fail to see the forest for the trees, these officials were concerned about the ethical considerations which might arise if citizens, not volunteers but draftees made to work against their will, were paid wages on a par with military draftees. Their worry was not that men were being used as slaves in a supposedly free state, but rather that union wages would be undercut and to avoid *this* immoral situation they proposed that the difference between military and union wages go to the government. What can I say?

Karl Marx's contention that workers are exploited by the capitalists is viewed from a different perspective by Lenin in *State and Revolution* in which he declares, albeit in a round-about manner, that *only governments* can exploit. "The exploiting classes require political rule in order to maintain exploitation." Capitalism, however, can function quite nicely, thank you, without government's interference. A capitalist government exists only to protect citizens from criminals at home and abroad and to settle disputes among its citizens. The people and *their* priorities "call the shots".

In a capitalist society diversity of opinion, values and beliefs are encouraged and lead to a special social resilience which becomes an incubator for innovation. Innovation, flexibility and creativity are the work horses providing the wealth that keeps America classless and mobile. America's affluence has always been a by-product of the genius of free men, who while pursuing their own private interests, provided others with higher standards of living in the form of more and better jobs, higher wages and cheaper more abundant goods and services. There are those, however, who for their own reasons, refuse to attribute these virtues to capitalism and claim instead these benefits were achieved by the intervention of government and unions. But somehow they are unable to account for the new machines and other innovations which made it all possible.

Under capitalism all who participate in society benefit but those on the bottom rung benefit most from the creativity and hard work of those on top. Not everyone would agree with that assessment of course. Professor Jonathan Wiener of the University of California at Irvine suggests that those that work the hardest and are most creative are not the most wealthy in America. However he offers no figures or other statistics which can be refuted but only what appears to be a hunch that the wealthy were merely lucky or had wealthy parents. On p 198 I offer profiles of the wealthy which refute the good Professor's "hunch". Of course there are different kinds of wealth just as there are different kinds of spending—productive and draining. The worst type of wealth is the wealth created by legislated privilege.

Capitalism is the only system of government which can protect individual rights. All other forms of government place society and society's rulers above moral law. Past governments derived power by appealing to the Divine Right of Kings, as did the Paraohs of Egypt; others, like the Greeks, succumbed to majority rule. Ancient forms of government regarded society as an end in itself and individual man as only a means to that end. Quite naturally it was accepted that therefore society could dispose of man, his talents, his labor, his property, the fruits of his labor and his very life and that what an individual man had was his by the generosity of society as a whole. America broke away from this kind of thinking and experimented with a bold idea. But the idea was never perfected in practice and has been sidetracked over the past 50 or 60 years. Today in the United States of America, at the drop of a hat *they* speak of what man *owes* his country, what it *costs* the government to allow an individual or group to keep some of what they have earned in the form of a deduction or credit, as if all dollars were by right the government's. But the truth of the matter is that government has no purpose other than to protect the rights of each individual and these rights are not to be sacrificed involuntarily for the good of the whole. That is why in spirit, though surely not in substance, the Internal Revenue Code embodies a volunteer system. (OK, OK—stop laughing! I admit it's a sham!)

When schools and knowledge are available to everyone in a society one who has availed himself of the various opportunities to accumulate this knowledge does not automatically "owe something back to society" as most collectivists suppose. The equality of men with regard to knowledge is a right to the opportunity to master it, use it and take advantage of it. Society cannot have a moral responsibility to see that those who take advantage of their opportunities share the proceeds equally with those who, having the same opportunities, failed to use them. Who would not agree that those who make use of their opportunities are entitled to the benefits derived from their efforts?

Our leaders ho and hem and offer one mealy-mouthed excuse after another. "To reward people commensurate with their effort is to revert to the uncivilized concept of 'the survival of the fittest'." Fill in the blank. "Mr. Unfortunate can't help it because____________." (poor environment—drugs—ill—better things to do with his time—lazy—other) Pick one, or several.

Let's look at the perversion of the clause in our constitution ". . . right to life, liberty and the pursuit of happiness". Because man must sustain life through his own effort, if he is denied the "right" to the product of his effort he is thereby denied right to life. Today the clause is often interpreted to mean a man has the right to the fruits of somebody else's effort. If he does not earn by his own effort the necessities to sustain his life then, according to these interpreters the state has an obligation to provide those necessities. But the "right" is only an opportunity—an opportunity to obtain an object and not the promise of the object itself. The government's only legitimate role in a capitalist society is to protect what man has earned and his right to attempt to earn it. For centuries rulers have proclaimed that rights are either gifts of G-d or society but, as our founding fathers so wisely proclaimed, man by his very nature has certain unalienable rights which were recognized, verbalized and legitimized in our American Constitution.

IS THERE A WIDENING GAP BETWEEN RICH AND POOR?

There are those today who point to statistics claiming that there is a widening gap between rich and poor and that the middle class, so essential to America as we know it, is fast disappearing.

In reviewing figures presented by the Census Bureau Report on Wealth in the summer of 1986, and all similar studies, it is well to ask questions like the following:

1) How was the *top 12%* determined?
2) What is it to *control?*
3) What is meant by *wealth?*
4) How does *household wealth* differ from *wealth?*
5) What is meant by *typical?*
6) Make sure you know the definition of *net-worth.*
7) Is *wealth* or *income* being discussed and what is the difference?
8) Are *individuals* or *families* being discussed?

9) Are the figures adjusted for inflation?
10) Know something about the time periods being compared—some years are chosen because of their unique ability to distort.
11) If employment is mentioned are the workers full or part-time?
12) Are pensions, profit sharing plans and other benefits included in wage comparisons?
13) Are income or wage comparisons before or after taxes?

Definitions are the Key!

The Census Bureau Report claimed the top 12 percent, defined as White, well-educated, owning their own business or employed in a white-collar job with an income of over $48,000 a year and with a median net-worth of $123,474 *controlled* (?) 40 percent of *household wealth* (?). Forty-eight percent had college degrees and 21 percent had some college.

The *typical* (?) American family had a net-worth of $32,667 in 1984—41 percent accounted for by equity in a home. Two-thirds of all Americans own their own homes with the *typical* equity being $40,600. The typical White family had a median net-worth of $39,135 in 1984 but married couples had a median net worth even higher—$50,120—whereas the median net-worth of a female headed household was a mere $13,890.

WEALTH

Wealth is a life cycle matter; the young accumulate debts, the middle-aged accumulate houses and cars and the older people have assets without mortgages and loans while accumulating medical expenses. This translates in numbers to a median net-worth of $5,760 for those under age 35, $73,660 for those age 55 to 64 and $55,180 for those over age 75 as they begin to sell off some assets in order to meet expenses and maintain their standard of living.

There has been a great deal of controversy surrounding the Joint Economic Committee's report on the concentration of wealth which was released in the summer of 1986. The last I heard Representative David Obey, Chairman of the Committee, was standing by the assertion that 90 percent of American families have experienced a 10 percent decline in their share of the nation's wealth. (As if the *nation* had wealth—only individual producers have wealth). The study, conducted by the Democratic majority staff on the committee, found that the 420,000 wealthiest households held at least $2.5 million in assets. Ten percent of the wealthiest households in the entire country held nearly 72 percent of the nation's $10.6 trillion in net privately-owned assets. The congressional study said the proportion of wealth held by the rich declined from 1929 to 1963 when it hit about 25 percent

(1929—32% level) then began to rise again with a sharp dip in 1976 to only 14 percent.

In the spring of 1987 the results of a Harris Poll were published in which 500 persons with a minimum household income of $100,000 or net worth of $500,000 (excluding the value of their home) were interviewed. It found the average income was $142,000—55 percent were men—most had working spouses—83 percent were married—only 3 percent were divorced or still single—85 percent had children—82 percent made their own wealth and 6 percent inherited it—half worked for themselves—only half identified with a political party. Their top priorities were: ". . . providing for their families (85 percent), applying their talent to the greatest extent possible (84 percent), educating their children (75 percent) and contributing to a charity (50 percent)."[1] Wealthy Americans are not necessarily evil people.

RALPH NADER

Consumer advocate Ralph Nader held a press conference on October 19, 1986 on the eve of the 1986 elections in which he presented a lot of questionable information including a map showing 27 states in recession and 3 on the borderline. Extrapolating from a national survey, a Pennsylvania pollster came up with a unique definition of "deep recession". It is generally considered that a nationwide recession occurs when two consecutive quarters show negative growth in the GNP. The Commerce Department reported personal disposable income rose 7.4 percent in the second quarter of FY1986 and 6.5 percent the first. The nation's unemployment rate fell from 7 percent in June to 6.8 percent in July, not a lot but hardly a "deep recession".

The Sindlinger poll surveyed 32 persons (out of 5 million) in order to call Missouri in "deep recession". It sampled 11 of Utah's 1.6 million citizens, 17 Oregonians and 28 citizens of the great northwestern state of Washington. It only took the responses of 3 people to plunge Wyoming into "deep recession".

Mr. Nader spoke about the widening gap between the rich and the poor, declaring a healthy debate was needed and the President's words should not simply be accepted "per se". He said we now have distortion, deception and fantasy spewed to us regarding the economy. (No question about that!) He spoke of a decline in family income, and real hourly wages of workers, higher insurance premiums (not what caused these things, mind you) higher rents and unemployment. He thought there had been, during Ronald Reagan's terms, an abdication of anti-trust legislation. Mr. Nader claimed that under Ronald Reagan the economy is getting worse and worse. There is, according to Mr. Nader, increasing hunger, unemployment and an overall general decline in the standard of living. He says it is "shameful" the way the President ignores the working poor and turns his back on millions of unfortunate Americans. In a burst of pre-election zeal Mr. Nader quipped, "Happy talk and Miller Time politics along with money to televise it, is a winning Republican tactic." He went on to outline six weak areas in the 1986 GOP agenda:

1) GNP growth
2) Poverty and hunger
3) Trade deficit
4) Budget deficit
5) Factory workers' real hourly pay
6) "Gap" between rich and poor

Mr. Nader spoke of "maldistribution of economic and political power" leaving the distinct impression that any distribution which was distributed more fully toward the Democratic camp would be A-OK!

ERRONEOUS STUDY

Mr. Nader could have been influenced by an article in the September 22, 1986 issue of *Insight* in which Warren Brookes referred to a 1986 study reportedly showing that the share of national family net-worth held by the top .5 of one percent of the nation's wealthiest families had gone from 25.4 percent to 35.1 percent over a 20 year period (1963–1983). The Wall Street Journal had featured this information in an article on August 15, 1986 and who knows how many other places it had appeared, but on August 21, 1986 the Joint Economic Committee press office admitted the Federal Reserve Board had made an error in its data. The corrected data showed that over the 20 years mentioned, the wealthiest .5 of one percent had increased its share of the wealth only 1.5 percent which is an amount considered within normal statistical sampling error and therefore was statistically no change at all!

The error was caught by the Assistant Secretary of the Treasury for economic policy, Michael Darby. (Applause)

A similar, though more recent (March 1987) study by the Federal Reserve found that the top 10 percent (income over $50,000/yr) controlled 34 percent of total assets in this country. Those aged 35–44 in this high-earner group had median net-worths of $122,000, those over age 65 in this group had median net-worths of $866,000 and the average or mean for the older *families* (?) in this group was $2.5 million.

THE DISAPPEARING MIDDLE CLASS

In May 1987, the Harvard Institute for Learning and Retirement had members of an illustrious panel voice their opinion concerning "The Disappearing Middle Class" (topic). Alan Reynold of Polyconomics in

Morristown New Jersey told the audience that the Federal Reserve study in March 1987 had found that 54 percent of the family heads earning over $150,000/year had graduate school educations compared to 10 percent of the population as a whole. Only 1 percent of the high income families were headed by someone younger than age 35 compared to 31 percent of the entire population. In fact 31 percent of all family heads didn't work at all whereas in the high income group 56 percent had 2 spouses working. Mr. Reynolds concluded that the educated older families with 2 earners are likely to earn more than the uneducated younger families with one worker or less. If this is shocking or unfair, he joked, one might consider passing out a Harvard MBA to everyone in order to equalize things.

Mr. Reynolds went on to needle the other members of the panel, all in good humor. He expressed amazement that Professor Barry Bluestone of the University of Massachusetts was concerned that manufacturing's decline had forced people into "mediocre service jobs on Wall Street and Madison Avenue". He claimed not to share Professor Frank Levy's (University of Maryland) dismay that young people are not doing as well as their parents when due to computer skills and new technology, 30 year olds are constantly making more than 40 year olds in today's market place. He quipped that Lester Thurow (MIT) thought that there weren't "enough high paying jobs but too many people are getting high pay" and regarding the venerable John Kenneth Galbraith (Harvard) Mr. Reynolds reminded the audience that even in 1948 Professor Galbraith thought everyone was *too affluent*! As for himself, Mr. Reynolds had to admit that he had twice disappeared from the middle class—once in his struggling youth (dropped below) and now in his high-earning middle years (*too* high).

Mr. Reynolds cautioned the audience about being mislead and offered the following as examples of distortion:

Measuring incomes of households may be appropriate where everyone owns their own home, or at least sets up housekeeping on their own, but when things get tough households merge; younger or older people move in with either parents or children. Statistics would show a smaller number of households with higher incomes thereby making a bad situation look like an improvement.

Professor Levy's charts which show the top 20 percent of the population *control* 43 percent of total income fail to account for taxes. In Sweden, for instance, the top 20 percent *control* 41.7 percent but with their high tax rates they actually receive a lot less. What these statistics say is that one-fifth of the population receives two-fifths of the income (which taxes bring down to a lot less) whereas one-fifth of the population is responsible for producing a lot more than their income share. In fact the top one percent of the population is responsible for the production of wealth vastly disproportionate to their income share. That is because capital produces more than labor in today's society. Included in that one percent are entrepreneurs who provide plants and equipment which support thousands of jobs which directly and indirectly contribute to the productivity of millions.

Lester Thurow's paper[2] compares 1969, the 9th year of a boom with 1982, the trough of a 3 year recession, which is obviously not a reasonable comparison. Mr. Reynolds confided to his Harvard audience that 1969, 1973 and 1979 are favorite years for those who wish to skew the facts as they "were inflationary blow-offs followed by immediate declines." 1973 featured price controls and so is often chosen as a base year whereas 1984 is favored by those who can make use of the high unemployment which occurred as the nation emerged from a recession.

MORE "OTHER COUNTRIES"

There are many things to be aware of when comparing the United States with other countries. Other countries pay more cash but the United States pays more "in-kind" which is often not included in statistics. Over the past four years industrial production has grown 5.8 percent a year in this country—faster than in Germany or Japan, with manufacturing productivity up more than 30 percent from the recession and 20 percent from the previous peak. Since 75 percent of our productivity comes from services, if such activity could be measured properly American productivity would probably be higher than the numbers indicate. In 1981 Canada, the United States and Europe all had the same rate of unemployment, 7.5 percent to 8 percent, but since then Canada's rate has climbed to 9 percent, Europe's to 11 percent and ours has dropped to 6.5 percent. Allowing for compounding, GNP has increased 4 percent a year in this country, interest rates were cut in half and the stock market tripled. Taxes and the regional cost of living must be considered when evaluating compensation per hour over a period of time and people should realize that single entry bookkeeping often makes things look bad because liabilities are highlighted and assets are ignored.

STATISTICS

One of the most blatant distortions to the statistics regarding poverty is the fact that so many unmarried teenagers intentionally have children they cannot support. (Children in poverty.) To blame the resulting statistics on the economy is ridiculous.

Statistics concerning wealth are tricky as it is not always clear what is and is not included. Therefore most researchers feel it is more accurate to talk about income. There is little evidence of any substantial change in the concentration of income over the past 25 years. According to the Census Bureau, the range has remained 40 to 43 percent for the top 20 percent of earners; in the 15 to 16 percent range for those in the top 5 percent and those in the bottom 20 percent have shared in 4.5 to 5.5 percent consistently over those same years. All Americans have seen their real (after inflation) income double since 1950 and despite constant rhetoric to the contrary, citizens have benefited with amazing consistency. Why?

Some economists explain the phenomenon by pointing to the theory of the decreasing marginal utility of money. When a certain degree of wealth is reached, each additional dollar becomes increasingly less important; some people find they would prefer more leisure time. Of course this so called saturation point varies from society to society but it is certain that low tax rates tend to encourage people in all societies and in all income classes to earn more than they might otherwise for the simple reason that they will be able to keep more.

SAYS WHO?

I guess it's safe to say when it comes to something as arbitrarily defined as poverty, you choose whomever you prefer to believe. Columnist Carl Rowan on May 27, 1986 quoted heavily from the questionable "Physician's Task Force On Hunger In America" which purportedly found that "the problem of hunger in the United States is now more widespread and serious than at any time in the last 10 to 15 years". And here is James J. Kilpatrick's offering a few days later (6/2/86) "There is not a scintilla of valid evidence to prove that serious malnutrition is a widespread problem in the United States today."

NO "COLD TURKEY"

Americans have been led into dependency on and by government over the last fifty years. It would be irresponsible to call for the nation to go "cold turkey" and regain its independence and integrity in one fell swoop. But it can be done gradually over time by educating the younger generation. The San Francisco based National Center for Financial Education (non-profit—though why that should be a virtue and a selling point I will never understand) has courses for use in secondary education as do numerous other organizations. In March 1987 the Phil Donahue Show featured a discussion concerning the need for financial education and the audience expressed a desire to see it required in public schools to ensure the country's economic viability in the competitive future. Meanwhile we must target our programs more carefully so that the truly needy receive the help they have been taught to depend upon.

POOR BUT NOT STUPID

It may be significant that states which offer the lowest benefits to welfare recipients have made the most progress in eliminating poverty. Or, on the other hand, it may simply mean the poor are not stupid and have moved to states which offer better benefits!

In February 1986, the National Center for Policy Analysis in Dallas presented a report that attempted to show the more we pay people to be poor the more poor people we get. "At least 5.7 million people are living in poverty by choice as a result of the generosity of public welfare. Each additional $1 billion in welfare spending increases the poverty population by 250,000."[3]

Almost half our population was poor in the 1930s, using the poverty line deflated for 1930s dollars. By 1950 the poverty rate had fallen to 30 percent; to 20 percent by 1964 and to 12 percent by 1969 thanks to the Great Society's anti-poverty programs. However, by 1984 poverty was up again, this time to 14.4 percent with the Census Bureau classifying 34 million Americans as poor. During the 1970s the Census Bureau used a consumer price index which overstated inflation and included high interest mortgages, all effectively exaggerating the poverty rate. If food and housing benefits and the vagaries of the consumer price index had been taken into consideration, the number of poor Americans would have been 8 million less than the official count. Instead of 14.4 percent the poverty rate in 1984 would have been 11 percent, and in 1985 only 9 percent. That's without including Medicaid and under-reported income which would have brought the rate down even lower. (See pp 176–7.)

"ONE POTATO, TWO POTATO, THREE POTATO . . ."

Professor Galbraith got a round of applause when he professed his belief that "a broad movement to greater equality in income distribution is something which the good society should still value". Admittedly it was the good professor's personal judgment that "equality in income distribution" is an attribute of the "the good society" but a judgment which was apparently appreciated and shared by his audience. It was strange, however, that Professor Galbraith, who in 1958 defined poverty as $1,000 income, the equivalent of $3,800 today, failed to mention that we have come a long way and raised our sights many times in the process. It is hard to commend when one has made a long career of denigrating, but Professor Galbraith is wise enough to know no matter what the productive elements of society do for the non-productive it will NEVER BE ENOUGH!

PROXIMATE CAUSE?

Who has not wondered what would have happened if one had chosen a different path at some stage in his or her life? Married B instead of A? Chosen a career in X instead of Y? Settled in Bustle Town instead of Sleepy Hollow? Life would have been different—and yes—even better or worse but there is no way to prove the theory. America has progressed over the last 200 years as much *in spite of* as *because* of government's mandates. There are as many that believe it was the second world war not FDR's programs that helped us out of the Great Depression and that indeed we might have recovered faster and stronger if the free market had been allowed to work without interference. President Roosevelt never really succeeded in doing anything about the Depression—his charismatic personality made everyone believe he was in there trying! He sustained the spirits of the American people throughout the thirties just as Churchill did for the British throughout the forties. Unemployment peaked in 1933 at 24.9 percent but in 1939 at 17.2 percent it was even higher than it had been in 1931 despite all FDR's meddling. Furthermore, critics claim that it was government's interference that prevented market forces from doing their job in the first place and that was the cause of all the trouble. How much better off would America be without the infamous Interstate Commerce Act of 1887? The Act was not a response to the abuses of a free market but rather was an attempt to correct the distortions earlier government interference had caused. Those who claim the railroads and oil industry were out of control and needed taming are unaware of the historical facts. The railroads in the Eastern section of the nation evolved without government's help and were kept in check by free market forces i.e. competition. Extending the railroads to the West was unprofitable in the 1860s because of the small population in that part of the country so public policy prevailed over the market and the rails to the West were heavily subsidized. The railroad monopoly was *created* by government. Subsidy and monopoly inevitably lead to regulation and disallocation. Free enterprise works differently. Historically several small firms struggle along in the first stages of a new industry. In the second stage mergers take place resulting in higher profits for the larger still surviving firms which in turn attracts other to the field bringing the competition of the third stage which reins in the profits (prices) without government lifting its little finger. In a similar manner the 1890 Sherman Act did far more harm than good. Before the age of the automobile the oil industry accounted for less than one percent of GNP and was controlled by one heavy weight, Standard Oil. There was only one main player, not because of some evil intent but because it was efficient and would have been unprofitable for more players—in other words, it made economic sense. With the advent of the automobile and the demand for more oil, you can bet other companies would have scrambled for their share of the profits without a "by your leave" from the government or Standard Oil either.

Instead our political ancestors whipped up the anti-trust laws which should be judged unconstitutional on the basis of their vagueness and the bewilderment they pose to businessmen due to their retrospective qualities. What seems to be OK turns out, after the fact, not to be! It seems that restraints by private parties are taboo whereas government (elevated with each new extension of power to an ever higher pedestal) has free rein. Competition is great—but not *too* much!

STILL MORE "OTHER COUNTRIES"

But then you've heard all this before and so what?! Let's first determine if the middle class is indeed disappearing and then if necessary we can get into the *why* and propose either capitalist or socialist solutions. For the moment let's stipulate that America's character and reason for being is dependent upon her large middle class. Relevant then is Professor Thurow's assertion that income distribution is twice as unequal in the United States as it is in Japan. The ratio between top and bottom in this country is 13 to 1 compared to a ratio of 6 to 1 in Japan. "In West Germany, before taxes and transfers, 28 percent of the population have less than half the median income; in the U.S. the figure is 27 percent. After taxes and transfers, however, West Germany is left with only 6 percent of its population in that predicament, whereas the U.S. is left with 17 percent."[4]

SOAKING THE RICH

Those enamored with the idea of using other countries as a role model consider this to be a valid argument for higher more progressive taxation whereas the facts show that the best way to "soak the rich" is by cutting their tax rates. In 1981 before the Reagan tax cuts (ERTA) the top one percent paid 18 percent on average and in 1985 after the tax cut and when they stopped hiding their income they paid 22.1 percent. ERTA was not a unique situation. History shows that whenever marginal tax rates have been reduced the results have been increased productivity, jobs, real disposable income and overall impressive economic growth. This was true of the Kennedy tax cut which took place in 1963 and going even further back it was true of the Coolidge/Mellon cuts of the 1920s.

In 1987 a book forecasting the *Great Depression of 1990* advocated, as a solution to our deficit problem, slapping a 5 percent surtax on Americans with incomes over $200,000 a year. As Peter Grace (as in "Grace Commission"), co-chairman of "Citizens Against Waste", likes to point out to his audiences, putting a surcharge of 10 percent on all incomes over $60,000 will yield only $1.65 billion or .8 of one percent of the deficit. Even if 100 percent surcharge was put on incomes over $75,000 the government could only be run for 7.3 days with the resultant revenue. The truth that is seldom told is that less than 10 percent of all tax revenue is collected from those citizens with incomes over $35,000. To put it another way, over 90 percent of all tax revenue is collected from citizens with incomes under $35,000. Promises to tame the deficit on the backs of the rich are popular but ineffectual.

George Guttman, a tax attorney with the Research Institute of America, supposes that a role of government is not the confiscation of wealth but seeing that wealth is spread more evenly over society. (In a *capitalist* society, already?!) To accomplish this goal he suggests a tax on recipients of wealth—that is an inheritance tax at income tax rates. (Since when is a tax *not* a confiscation of wealth?) There would be less need for expensive estate-tax lawyers to devise elaborate schemes to avoid death taxes. The country as a whole would benefit, according to Mr. Guttman, because wealth would be less concentrated and probably put to more productive use. There are pros and cons enough for a good debate on both contentions but such a debate would be missing the real issue (as usual)—what right does the state have to "spread" anyone's wealth? A capitalist society functioning under the old-fashioned commonly understood meaning of the words used in the American Constitution can not justify such action by saying it might be "good for the country" (debatable), might be "put to more productive use" (Once government gets its hands on it? Oh yeah, and how many bridges have you bought today?) or the "spreading" might put some "expensive estate-tax lawyers" out of work.

THE PASTORAL LETTER

The Pastoral Letter written by the catholic bishops on the 40th anniversary of the Employment Act of 1946 challenged the nation to come up with options. It discussed the way the economy affects the dignity and opportunity of each person in America. The Reverend Rembert Weakland, Archbishop of Milwaukee testified on December 22, 1986 before the Joint Economic Committee's hearing on "Poverty, Ethics & Economics" that in his opinion government has a duty to intervene where "hurt is apparent" (rather ambiguous) and must take its "rightful role" (also not defined). He spoke a great deal about the rights of workers and duties of employers with emphasis on some rather unusual rights which he referred to as "Economic Rights": the right to *income* (Oh boy—I want some of that), *food* (uh huh), *shelter* (great! No sense spending income on rent or mortgage payments like suckers without these nifty rights), *medical care* ("America is the only industrial nation . . . we know, we know!) and *employment* (who is to employ *whom* to *do what* to be paid *by whom, with what, for what*—oh yeah—*when* and *how*?).

Gary Burtless of the Brookings Institute testified before the Committee as to the moral implications of the Pastoral Letter and its emphasis on alms giving and social obligation for economic well being. He declared that most efforts to reduce poverty and unemployment are expensive and may even be counterproductive but nevertheless advocated sacrifice on the part of the non-poor and employed. It will depend on society's willingness to tax itself to pay for the programs Mr. Burtless believes are necessary. He suggested that giving up a little economic growth might not be too much to ask in order to help the poor. As an economist he should realize that nothing could help the poor more than economic growth and the jobs and general prosperity that are its by-product. He ridiculed the theory that claims the best way to help those in need is to reduce aid so they will learn to achieve on their own. ("Fun With Dick & Jane")[5] Such a response, he feels, requires only light obligations on the non-poor; they are only required to give advice and examples and perhaps applaud when the job is done. The Pastoral Letter speaks of the "cost to the affluent majority" implying there is "no gain without pain", reminiscent perhaps of the self-flagalation prevalent in Roman Catholicism in the middle ages.

Professor Lawrence Mead of New York University introduced a semblance of level-headedness into the discussion claiming that the Pastoral Letter mistakes the very nature of poverty by denying the role of the poor in creating poverty as if they were merely passive victims. The Letter, according to Professor Mead, has medieval overtones and ignores the fact that in twentieth century America we enjoy civil liberties, rights and education, that opportunities are available which it is the responsibility of the poor to use to better their situation. The bishops, who talk so incessantly about dignity, deny these individuals any semblance of dignity by making them appear utterly helpless. The order of the day appeared to be "all show and no substance"—truth only if it sounds good or as Professor Galbraith has been known to say, if "all inconvenient facts have been ignored". For instance the bishops spoke as if to claim welfare mothers don't work would show prejudice—the "holier than thou" kind. So what if statistics show welfare mothers in fact, work about half as much as their counterparts who are not on welfare? And you must understand what is meant by *unemployment*. It is not simply the inability to find a job, it is the inability to land a *good* job! Lesser paying and unattractive jobs are plentiful but they wouldn't keep a family out of poverty as the government defines poverty so let the taxpayers "do their thing" until the *right* job comes along.

In 1940 FDR was surprised to learn that a neighbor's daughter, a Vassar graduate, was counted among the unemployed because she was after a very special job—she wanted to be an editor of *Vogue* magazine. As Herbert Stein said, "We not only do not consider it wrong for her to behave in this way or wrong to count her as unemployed, we are also willing to pay her unemployment compensation if she has been previously employed and now rejects all jobs other than editing *Vogue*."[6] The bishops don't put obligations on the poor just the non-poor, in Professor Mead's opinion. There is, he says, such a thing as Christian duty, just as there is parental duty. Jesus didn't treat the poor as victims; he held them accountable even though there was less opportunity in Judea 2000 years ago. An indulgent society which insists on taking care of its poor leaves them helpless like an over-indulgent parent who neglects his duty. (More "Fun With Dick & Jane" philosophy for Mr. Burtless to make fun of!) Professor Mead maintained that Americans are not against welfare; only against welfare abuse. The Professor believes the public is not seeking relief from responsibility to the poor, but that they want to see the poor reciprocate with responsibility to themselves, their families and society.

Welfare, as used by the Professor, is a state mandate, others believe, however, that comfort and aid to one's fellow man should come voluntarily from the community so that both the giver and the recipient can be nourished by the humaneness of the act. Charity is a moral obligation and should not be legislated. It is not the business of a handful of men to order but of all men to do voluntarily of their own free will and on a personal level. No one wants to face the fact that mandated altruism and capitalism are mutually exclusive. It should be apparent that since economic life does not exist in a moral vacuum, what is done of man's free will is of higher consequences than what is done through coercion. Higher ethical values are a natural by-product of capitalism.

THE HOMELESS PERSON'S SURVIVAL ACT

In June, 1986 the Homeless Person's Survival Act (known as Survival Act) was the first piece of federal legislation specifically addressing homelessness to be introduced into Congress—the 99th Congress.

At the beginning of the 100th Congress it was suggested that $50 million be given as emergency aid to the homeless; then $250 million; then $500 million; then adding the $500 and $250 *they* got $750 million. Going from a suggested $50 million to $750 million in 60 days is ludicrous!

House Minority Leader Bob Michel of Illinois claimed that already the federal government had provided $6 billion in block grants. He and Representative Penny wanted to see a "pay-as-you-go" plan adopted. The Michel Amendment said OK, emergency funds for the homeless but only if the plan is revenue neutral.

The opposition argued that such an amendment would mean before they can have a warm bowl of soup or a blanket and a cot the homeless would have to take it from someone else. Where have these Congressmen been? Do they live in a magic kingdom where everything grows on trees and automatically rejuvenates? In the real world every program takes from someone; someone else's priorities are jeopardized anytime Congress allocates more money. If not from current taxpayers, then from future generations. The piper must be paid by someone, sometime and we have politicians making sure it happens not only in the future but preferably to voters outside their own districts. But I guess Americans are satisfied—they keep returning incumbents to office.

The following are notes from a C-SPAN viewing of the March 5, 1987 session of the House of Representatives:

Representative Barney Frank of Massachusetts was "appalled at the compassion gap. . . . We can afford in this wealthy country to provide the money; let the funds come out of foreign appropriations." Mr. Frank preferred to borrow new money and add to the deficit in order to help the homeless, but if Congress wouldn't go along with that he offered his amendment "to take funds out of foreign appropriations" so that no American poor should suffer.

Representative Stewart B. McKinney of Connecticut asked "What kind of America do you want? The question is priorities—what are your priorities? Are you for people or are you for the budget?" A quote which I thought revealed the fact that he hasn't the foggiest idea what he is doing on Capitol Hill. Does he make any connection between the people and government being the same entity or does he really think government is a separate being, like the toothfairy or the godfather maybe? He carried on about our need to take care of the people that are the citizens of this country. He wants to cut back on defense so we can take care of the people. He fails to understand that the only fair method of allocating a finite number of resources among a infinite number of wants is to allow each man to support his own priorities with the fruits of his own labor. To do otherwise, as by compelling a man to use his own product contrary to his own priorities is unjust. It may not be illegal but there is no doubt such compulsion is immoral. We are living under immoral laws if morality is to be judged in a capitalist society and that will only change when we change our legislators.

Congressman Obey was extremely sarcastic and claimed the Administration was seeking $1 billion 100 million in additional foreign aid, $3 billion additional for the Pentagon, $12 billion additional in the total Reagan budget. In answer to his rhetorical question of how the administration proposed to raise the additional revenue he said $5.7 billion would be cuts in domestic programs. He agreed with the Pastoral Letter that the government has a moral obligation to the poor. But in truth our Constitution only provides for a government whose sole duties are to prevent force or fraud upon its citizens (defense and foreign aid are in pursuit of that legitimate purpose) and to oversee a system of settling disputes (court system)—the rest is to be left to the free choice of the people and their priorities.

Robert Walker of Pennsylvania, in his plea for fiscal responsibility asked "Are you more willing to add to the deficit or take it out of foreign aid?" The questions that should have been asked and the arguments that should have been made were never uttered. There was no thought that government should not provide funds for this purpose.

The House voted to add to the deficit. Yea—203, Nay—207 against the amendment to find funds without increasing the deficit.

A NEW RIGHT TO SHELTER

The first "right to shelter" suit was filed in New York City in 1979 by the Coalition for the Homeless. It successfully established a right to shelter under the New York Constitution for New York City's homeless. Since then similar suits have established rights in local jurisdictions around the country.

California's Welfare & Institutions Code #10000 et seq. and 17000 et seq. require counties to relieve and support indigent citizens. The Homeless Litigation Team which consists of lawyers from 8 public interest law firms in the Los Angeles area have expanded the application of the code and in the process may have established a new right—the "right to shelter".

Prior to 1984 identification was needed to obtain shelter. Identification is something most homeless people don't have and even *with* an ID an application for shelter could take weeks to process. In 1984 the Litigation Team won its first case, Eisenheim v Bd Supervisors[7] which ended the identification requirement and mandated that benefits begin immediately. A series of cases followed including Ross v Bd of Supervisors[8] in which the court ruled that the previous housing allowance "was not enough" and in response the county began issuing vouchers for *approved* (whose got more power now?) hotels. That practice led to Paris v Bd of Supervisors[9] which required higher standards for homeless hotels. In Blaire V Bd of Supervisors (1987)[10] the court ruled that in determining "minimum subsistence needs" what it actually takes to live in a given area must be taken into account. *Blaire* means that over a two year period there will be a 25 percent increase in relief checks which amounts to a $33 million increase in allotements to the homeless. Who is to pay? (Californians might want to ask the citizens of Massachusetts about that!—see p 95)

In the words of the Team's chief trial lawyer Mark Rosenbaum, "The rights of the poor have frequently been treated as largess by the government, or as charity by the public. This litigation has proved that indigents have significant and enforceable rights."[11] Doubletalk—words obviously with their own special meaning. "Largess" and "charity" as used by the ordinary layman fit exactly the concept of general welfare relief. Rights, on the other hand, are rights to action only, not to objects. Rights are moral principles and impose no obligations on others.

"Any alleged 'right' of one man, which necessitates the violation of the rights of another, is not and cannot be a right. No man can have a right to impose an unchosen obligation, an unrewarded duty or an involuntary servitude on another man. . . . The right to life means that a man has the right to support has life by his own work (on any economic level, as high as his ability will carry him); it does *not* mean that others must provide him with the necessities of life."[12]

There can be no right to shelter—only the right to acquire shelter—if not through purchase or rental as a result of one's own labor then the shelter is obtained through the charity of others either willingly elicited or coerced (by government edict).

The "significant and enforcable rights" of indigents that Mr. Rosenbaum speaks of are nothing more than a theft sanctioned by government. One group (working taxpaying individuals) are being forced (what choice are they given?) by government to provide for those who are not capable of providing for themselves. Fault has absolutely nothing to do with the analysis nor does compassion. When a beggar asks for a dollar on the street you can either say yes or no. When a charitably minded organization asks for a contribution to set up outreach programs for the unfortunate to save them the embarrassment of "begging" you can help or not as you *freely* choose. But where government is not asking it is taking by force.

Some would argue that individuals give tacit permission to have the fruits of their labor distributed to others by electing legislators whose records suggest that they will redistribute the income of producers to non-producers. To an extent that is true, however in more and more instances lawyers and so-called activist judges usurp the legislators' role as illustrated by the cases brought by the Homeless Litigation Team. Nobody gets a chance to vote for lawyers and not often for judges (Methods of seating judges varies throughout the country.)

Even media editorials are quick to speak "for the people". On February 9, 1987 the Wall Street Journal said "We're sure Americans don't want to 'turn their backs'." If we're all so sure then why is the "taking" from Americans mandated by law. Surely no one believes the federal government can serve the needs of the unfortunate better than local non-government organizations. No—the truth is they are afraid they will not get the money if they ask, so they take. Perhaps what they would get if they didn't take is something from local communities more valuable than money—concern, participation of the citizenery and some creative new approaches to our problems. As the Wall Street Journal said, "Many Americans remember when Congress thought poverty was caused by a lack of money, so it provided money. It thought unemployment was caused by a shortage of jobs, so it created work. Congress thought hunger was solely attributable to lack of food, so it made food freely available. But each problem proved to be far more complicated than originally thought. Three decades and more than a trillion dollars later we are seemingly no further along on these social problems than when we started."[13]

CONSUMERISM

Since the Second World War we have been taught to idolize a new sect—consumerism. Lenin may be right—it is not communism but consumerism that in the end may bury us. One cannot belong to consumerism without the ability to consume. But have no fear—as we saw in the example of Massachusetts (discussed on p 95) the Coalition for Basic Human Needs won a ruling which could make everyone a consumer. The 1987 ruling could result in monthly welfare benefits for a family of three in Massachusetts increasing to over $11,000 per year. The judgment was based, as you may remember, on a 1913 state statute ensuring adequate shelter. "Adequate" is a subjective term. In this case a judge decided (no matter what the ruling actually said) that as a matter of compassion one group of citizens should be forced to make another group comfortable. Ultimately what those advocates in Massachusetts were fighting for is the "right to consume" of every American. Somewhere along the line the right to private property—to the fruits of one's efforts has been discarded, or traded-in.

IMMIGRATION

It's easy to get the idea that we are cutting back on immigration in this country but the facts show otherwise.

During the 1980s the U.S. will admit approximately 5.7 million immigrants legally, up from 2.5 million legal immigrants during the fifties. Not only that, the percentage of foreign-born residents in the U.S. increased in only the last decade from 4.8 percent to 6.2 percent of the total population. Approximately 2 million illegal aliens were included in the 1980 census but some population experts in 1987 claimed the number of illegal aliens could be as high as 20 million. The 270,000 immigration slots available each year have in the past been filled by people with special preferences, skills or with relatives already in the U.S. In 1987 a sweepstakes was offered under a law designed to help people in 36 countries where immigration to this country had fallen off since 1965. Irish applicants won 3,112 of the 10,000 slots available over the next two year to people who wouldn't otherwise have qualified. The State Department advertised in the 36 countries that anyone sending entry forms to a P.O. Box in Washington D.C. would be selected on a first-come, first-served basis after the stroke of midnight on January 21, 1987. It was one more piece of evidence attesting to the fabled "luck of the Irish".

Does it make sense to allow illegal aliens (those who have broken our laws) who can prove they have resided here continuously since

1982 to be given amnesty despite the millions of would-be immigrants who have obeyed U.S. laws by waiting patiently to enter? Amnesty programs always encourage the very behavior they pardon. Punishing, instead of granting amnesty to illegal aliens would be far more effective in deterring illegal immigration. Simply returning those caught to their own borders so they can try to enter illegally another day is pure nonsense. American citizens are the only ones who lose in such a game.

The Simpson-Rodino bill, which was passed by Congress in 1986, grants amnesty to those who have spent at least 90 days working in the agriculture industry in this country during the 12-month period ending May 1, 1986 and to those who can prove they have lived in the U.S. prior to January 1, 1982.

Illegal aliens seeking legalization under the new immigration law will be charged a fee for the paperwork involved. According to an Associated Press release on Christmas Eve, 1986 "The INS will continue to apprehend and deport aliens who arrived after 1982, although enforcement agents will not have access to rejected amnesty applications." We're playing childish games! We are giving criminals a head-start, a sporting chance which makes one wonder seriously about our policy makers. Legislators decided to make these acts illegal—freedom of movement is not inherently bad nor forbidden except by governments.

Many U.S. employers, who in June 1987 will face jail terms and fines for each illegal alien hired after November 6, 1986 are dismissing all undocumented employees, including some hired before the cutoff date. If an employer inadvertently rejects a legal job applicant he could face anti-discrimination suits with fines starting at $1,000. Beginning June 1, 1987 employers must ask for identity and work authorization documents in order to fill out the I-9 form. It sounds like we're talking about another country—work papers and IDs are distasteful to Americans. But anywhere a business turns there is a potential trap. There are fines for employers who *knowingly* employ illegal aliens and at the same time refusing to hire legal aliens is an actionable violation which may well result in the loss of time, energy and money in courts. (Score another one for the lawyers!)

I have never been able to understand those who insist that illegal aliens should be expected to pay taxes and also be allowed access to our schools. If they are illegal they should be deported—period. The illegal aliens who receive amnesty will be eligible immediately for Medicaid and will become eligible in five years for welfare, food stamps and other federal benefits. Already these programs are in trouble. Are we electing folks to come up with *solutions* like this?

In November 1986, the Border Patrol apprehended 76,431 illegal aliens compared to 92,658 in November 1985. It was unclear whether the drop was due to the Simpson-Rodino legislation or stepped-up

Border Patrol efforts or the higher than usual water level of the Rio Grande. On the other hand, the Center for U.S.-Mexican Studies at the University of California at San Diego claims there are no documented cases of employer-sanction law ever being used successfully to reduce the number of illegal immigrants to any country.

The very thought of people fleeing this country in fear is contrary to everything America stands for in the world. It is ironic that a nation built by immigrants and a symbol of hope and opportunity for the oppressed is now rounding up people like cattle and ejecting them.

Most economists agree free movement of the factors of production enhances economic welfare. Why limit a set factor of production—labor—by restrictive immigration policies, all the while claiming economic self-interest? Our eventual goal should be open borders with our neighbors to the North and South with the flexibility and opportunity a single capital and labor market would provide. Immigration is and has been beneficial to our economy and could be instrumental in keeping jobs in the United States that might otherwise go abroad.

What's wrong with opening our borders to workers as long as they remain employed, not on welfare and obey our laws? The main argument seems to be the fear of losing jobs for Americans. The Government Accounting Office (GAO) reported on April 21, 1986, after reviewing 51 studies, that it couldn't comment conclusively on the supposed displacement of American jobs by immigrants.

Keeping cheap labor out is the same protectionist theme used by those who would set up a system of tariffs to keep inexpensive goods out of this country. In the end the country benefits from competition and an infusion of inexpensive goods. Inexpensive labor will also breed competition and make the nation stronger, more productive and will in the long run result in a higher standard of living for everybody. I disagree with Governor Lamm of Colorado who said in an address before the Commonwealth Club in San Francisco on October 17, 1986, "We cannot make the rest of the world wealthy nor can we absorb its surplus population. We can only make ourselves poor." The Governor favors restricting immigration to this country, claiming that we already take twice as many refugees as the rest of the world combined.

The idea that America is running out of room, jobs and all good things is a rerun of the identical fears expressed when our grandparents arrived in this country. In fact the entire world has been "running out" of wood, fresh water, air, land, fuel, food and every other necessity since the middle ages and even earlier!

Thomas Hobbes once defined liberty as "an absence of the lets and hindrances of motion." The right to freedom of movement implies a duty to permit immigration. Permitting people to leave a country freely, but preventing others from coming in is human mercantilism—

the 18th century economic theory which held that exports are good, imports are bad. (Many members of Congress seem to share that view today.) That was the fallacy which Adam Smith destroyed when he laid the foundations of modern capitalism.

The European Economic Community (EEC) permits all its citizens to work and live in all its member countries. As for refugees, Europe is less than hospitable. West Germany prevents those seeking asylum from taking a job for 5 years (1 year for East Europeans) restricts their movements and obliges them to live in camps, even if they have relatives in Germany. Belgium sends armed police onto arriving aircraft to check papers and turn doubtful cases around so there is no chance of having to deal with asylum-seekers later on. (Get them *before* they land!) Belgium, Britain and West Germany fine airlines for each dubious asylum seeker they carry. The airline employees do the "dirty work" for government officials and that allows the countries to preserve their reputations. After all, public opinion is not in favor of expulsions.

THE OXFORD ANALYTICS STUDY

Fortune magazine (4/24/86) ran a book review by Andrew Hacker, Professor of Political Science at Queens College, New York City, critiquing *America In Perspective* which was a study undertaken by Oxford Analytica, an international research and consulting organization based in Oxford, England.

The report said that America's main import was people and that of the entire world's migrants half are migrating to the United States of America. Sixty percent of all legal immigrants listed no occupation and of those who did list an occupation 80 percent were unskilled. Cellist Mstislav Rostropovich, one of the Soviet Union's most privileged citizens, was allowed refugee status in the United States several years ago. He now makes about $2 million a year, including $600,000 for 15 weeks' work as conductor of the National Symphony Orchestra, an amount, according to Michael Kinsley, "about equal to the Symphony's annual government subsidy."[14] Even more outrageous is the fact that Mr. Rostropovich has carefully avoided becoming an American citizen for tax reasons. "He carries a Swiss passport and 'travel papers' from Monaco, and takes care to spend most of his time abroad." Guess who has played America for a chump once again?

Admittedly Mr. Rostropovich is a unique case having little to do with the Oxford study. The study noted that all recent growth in the populations of California, Texas and Florida has been due to an influx of Spanish-speaking immigrants and suggested that a class system will become apparent as the gap between the rich and the poor widens. (Such insight!) Commenting, as the report does, that the large group of poor are less educated minorities and the rich are more often educated Caucasians is to miss the point that education, which is available to all, provides the mobility which is the attraction of America in the first place. Professor Hacker states that the report is unabashedly Marxist. It retells the old story that capitalism will enrich the already rich and hurl the masses into poverty, but offers little support for these contentions.

Has family income, for instance, really gone down in some meaningful sense? Remember families are smaller than they were in 1973. Also there is all the unreported income lost in the vast underground economy. The report sees U.S. immigrants as expensive public charges and explosive social tinder. But the fact is most immigrants come to America very much imbued with the work ethic; many hold two or more jobs, often in family enterprises. Instead of taking jobs from Americans, these and other immigrants have created their own employment, largely by catering to unmet needs. They have renewed neighborhoods and revitalized the city's middle class. In Marxist terminology, they look more like candidates for the bourgeoisie than for a revoluntionary proletariat.

SOCIAL MOBILITY

Social Mobility is sometimes dismissed as Horatio Alger hokus-pokus. Nevertheless free economies here and in other countries suggest that far from being remarkable the movement of people up and down the income scale is common place. The 1984 University of Michigan's Panel Study on Income Dynamics, summarized by Gregg J. Duncan in the book *Years of Poverty, Years of Plenty* found that between 1971 and 1978, about 52 percent of the families who began in the top bracket dropped to a lower bracket, and of those who started on the lowest level, 45 percent moved up. "Only a little over one-half of the individuals living in poverty in one year are found to be poor in the next and considerably less than one-half of those who experience poverty remain persistently poor." However, Charles Murray, author of *Losing Ground,* found that *cooked* definitions were responsible for the rosy scenario. "Dependent on welfare" was defined as receiving at least 50 percent of a family's income directly from welfare and without counting food stamps, housing assistance, medicaid, unemployment insurance and other supplementary programs. Also the "directly from welfare" definitions had to hold steady for eight out of ten years making it almost miraculous that even 2 percent of the population qualified as welfare dependent under such restrictions. In effect the definition fit only the totally disabled and elderly poor. Instead of finding dramatic increases in income due to the Horatio Alger syndrome we were offered examples of students about to enter the professions and start drawing the healthy salary of a doctor, engineer or attorney. The reason for jumps in other family income was traced to the addition of a second wage earner via marriage or just through the normal advancement from low man on the totem pole to gradual advancement through experience on the job.

But regardless of the Michigan Study, social mobility is almost synonomous with America and it is a persuasive justification for free enterprise. Under what other system can people in extremely unequal starting positions fully utilize varying drives and talents?

It has been said that *equality* is a luxury good that is sought during good times and ignored during down turns in the economy. But a great deal depends on one's interpretation of *equality.* The only meaning consistent with our Constitution is *equality of opportunity* which implies the social mobility which is so much a part of and necessary to a democratic capitalist nation. What can be more just than a system which offers the fruits to the laborer? And what can be better for the nation?

Marx and Engels derived their conception of the alienated proletariat from observing the British working class. England's class system resulted in poorly trained unimaginative workers who produced even during the war, (WW I) shabbier products far less efficiently than their German counterparts. In fact it took three times the number of man hours to build the British Spit Fire than to complete the Messerschmidt 109G. British unions even hindered the war effort with constant strikes and attempts to delay innovation—even though England's survival depended on their efforts.

Education has always been the great equalizer but Barry Bluestone, Professor of Political Economy at the University of Massachusetts sees an inherent injustice in the fact that the United States is becoming a meritocracy, more like Japan, where the dollars one is likely to acquire over a lifetime are more and more dependent upon the school and the number of years one puts into education.[15] He cites statistics which show that in 1963 high school drop-outs were 1.7 times (or 10 percent) more likely to be low wage than graduates and that by 1983 the likelihood was 2.4 times (38 percent). In the 1984 Census Bureau Study in all categories householders with a college education had twice the net-worth of those with only high school—$60,420 v $31,890. Professor Bluestone appears to be unhappy that as race and gender become less a factor in the job market, education is becoming more important. One wonders what Professor Bluestone would like to see as an overriding factor in determining employment. He certainly is against what he calls "Social Darwinism"—the survival of the fittest as defined by market concepts. Equating free enterprise with selfishness and greed and government interference with a sense of humaneness and compassion is his bromide.

Our own minority preference programs are the foundation for an ethnic spoil system—a caste system where one benefits by the circumstances of birth. It sets Blacks against Asians, Hispanics, other minorities and the White majority. Affirmative action is a terrible idea.

The Commerce Department's inspector general recently reported that insiders are more likely to gain from special awards given by the Minority Business Development Agency and that these benefits are inordinately expensive. According to Jack Anderson's April 15, 1987 column, "One shocker was a grant of $288,389 for five one-day seminars to make young Latinos aware of private enterprise's possibilities. This amounted to $1,068 for each student's day of instruction." Apparently similar seminars are offered from $50 to $195 by private sources. It looks like Uncle Sam is there and everywhere to be fleeced. (Mr. Anderson, in the same column, also reported on some $7, original cost, wastebaskets being leased for $29 each per year to *Guess Who?*)

The recent worsening position of Blacks is not due to excessive welfare incentives, drugs and ghetto culture or even racism according to William Wilson, sociology professor at the University of Chicago and author of a new book, *The Truly Disadvantaged: The Inner-City, The Underclass and Public Policy.* He blames the economy with its swing from manufacturing and high paying industrial jobs to the service economy with its choice of either low-pay low-skill opportunities or high-pay high-skill white collar jobs. He also notes a situation, while blaming no one, that has benefited some Blacks at the expense of others. ". . . desegregation laws allowed Blacks with stable jobs to flee the ghettos in great numbers, knocking the props from local institutions. Those left behind formed an increasingly homogeneous underclass whose members suffered from the 'concentration effects' of isolation from mainstream education, job and social networks."[16]

Fewer men with stable jobs or prospects means many Black women will have decided to forego marriage. Thirty years ago more than three quarters of Black families were intact meaning that a husband and a wife were present in a household. By 1986 only 40 percent could make that claim. Fewer than 20 percent of Black births were out of wedlock as recently as 20 years ago but in 1986, according to the Census Bureau, 74.5 percent of Black births were illegitimate.

In early March 1987, 30 Black scholars collaborated and came up with a study published by the Washington D.C. based Joint Center for Political Studies, titled *Black Initiative & Government Responsibility.* It concluded that a combination of government assistance in educational areas that would encourage economic independence and get working support within the Black community itself would be the best way to attack the disportionate poverty among Blacks.

On February 20, 1987 Tony Brown, chairman of the Council for Economic Development of Black America, told the Commonwealth Club in San Francisco that Blacks need to take charge of their lives and start charting their own course. "It's time to do as well in finance and economics as we do in football and basketball." he said. The Council is promoting a campaign which they refer to as "Buy Freedom" which stresses the importance of Blacks helping one another by patronizing Black enterprises. According to Tony Brown, "There is nothing complicated about success in this country. You outwork other people, work longer than they do, save money, sell at a good price, and sell a quality product or service. There are no short cuts."

Education has always been regarded as the latchkey into the middle class. One-quarter of a million Blacks attended college in 1960; by 1970, half a million Blacks were attending college—the number doubled in one decade. By 1980, 1.1 million blacks were attending college—it doubled again. So, in one generation the number of Blacks attending college increased by 400 percent. You may not have known that but I bet you are aware that the number of Blacks enrolled in college in 1987 is down from 1986. We hear little about the overriding upward trend—the number of Black elected officials and number of of Blacks included in the top echelon of income earners due mainly to their expertise in the high-paying sports and entertainment fields. Our information is biased and progress is not often acknowledged. Witness the remarks of Hodding Carter III who apparently wants us to believe that Lenin was right—the American Dream is over: "a class-ridden society abounds" and ". . . we are structuring a country in which Third World conditions coexist side by side with prosperity; in which too few have far too much (12 percent of American households control 38 percent of all personal wealth) and too many have far too little."[17] Who is to decide what is "too little" and "too much"? We know how it is done in other countries, countries whose citizens are falling all over themselves for an opportunity to enter this heartless, uncaring nation teeming with "social dynamite". (Carter's term.)

I have heard Blacks take offense at being referred to as a spokesman or leader for their people. They like to point out that Whites have no spokesman. While that may or may not be true, I think it might be more interesting to see if you can come up with the names of five Hispanic or Asian so-called leaders?

I doubt if many Hispanics would consider Cesaer Chavez as leader or spokesman and although he has undoubtedly improved the conditions of farm workers, especially in California, he is probably still too militant for most. When he told a Commonwealth Club audience a few years ago that the only hope for his people was organizing, I thought at the time that education might be the better hope. It has served other minorities in the past and is being used extensively by the Vietnamese in the eighties. Of course he knew education was the tool his people were using as he spoke about tens of thousands of the children and grandchildren of farmworkers—and of poor Hispanics—moving out of the fields and out of the barrios and into the professions, business and politics. Nevertheless he gave the credit to "organizing". The following words have haunted me: "Like the other immigrant groups, the day will come when we will win the economic and political rewards which are in keeping with our numbers in society. The day will come when the politicians will do the right thing for our people out of political necessity and not out of charity or idealism."[18]

Why are people like Mr. Rosenbaum (of the Homeless Litigation Team) and Mr. Chavez so adamant about refusing to call charity by its rightful name? They mistakenly think false dignity is better for society to maintain than integrity. Recipients and givers both know the truth no matter what "leaders" choose to call it. It would be interesting to discuss the "right thing" with Mr. Chavez but probably not revealing. It is almost certain he is demanding a piece of *the pie* for his people—*or else.* How else would you interpret *political necessity* in the quoted statement? There are simply no special privileges due certain groups. As Ayn Rand put it, there are political or economic rights but they cannot co-exist; one destroys the other. There are in fact, she maintained, "no 'economic rights', no 'collective rights', no 'public interest rights'. The term 'individual rights' is a redundancy: there is no other kind of rights and no one else to possess them."[19]

The census statistics which showed minorities were not getting the same portion of America's *Economic Pie* as Whites surprised no one. But I *was* surprised by the testimony of Secretary of Labor William Brock before the House Education and Labor Committee on Welfare Reform on May 5, 1987. The Secretary's observation that "classes" in America have remained rather stable since 1945—as if that were a good thing—was distressing.

We pride ourselves on being a "classless" society in America. Our forefathers went to great lengths to ensure that titles of nobility would not be granted here but we may have gotten away from that ideal and substituted designer labels and gold cards for titles. A little thing like flying first class—a few more inches of space and separate compartment—can tempt one to look down on one's fellows. We broke with England and nobility but not with elitism. A certain degree of pretentiousness is, I'm afraid, lurking in every man and he must do the "breaking" daily within himself. I hope the notion of classes in America is as distasteful to you as it is to me. Rolls-Royces, exclusive clubs, and "first-class" are not bad in themselves—they are, after all, only things—but they can turn a weak person into a elitist which few would consider "good".

If we take as a given the premise that there is a recognizable social strata in every society then it is important to recognize that it does not exist in nature but is manmade. The social strata reflects the values and morals of the society. It can and usually does change over time as the population changes.

Sociologists generally agree that an individual's place on the social scale can be based on many things. People can be valued for things purely beyond their control, like good looks, height, agility or the family they are born into. In a caste system such as India's, little can be done to change one's social position. India is an immobile society, although not nearly as immobile as it was once. Some societies put the greatest value on learning and others most honor their holy men. America has always been a mobile society where people, with effort and persistence, are able to move up in the social strata—"up" being almost as individualistic as everything else about America and Americans.

Dr. Rainwater, Professor of sociology at Harvard, and other sociologists might correct me and point out that money determines position in this country. I would not be so foolish as to deny this, but I would say although it is perhaps the most popular determining factor it is not the only one by a long shot. Ralph Nader, Jesse Jackson, numerous environmentalists, journalists, artists and educators are held in an esteem not necessarily matched in dollars. Denying this leads one into the comparable worth trap. If esteem is based on money alone and people get money from their work then it becomes very important that society determine how work should be renumerated. It seems unfair to many that value (determined in a capitalist society by a free market, i.e. what individuals, uncoerced, are willing to pay other individuals) should determine compensation. They argue that a person then would be rewarded simply because he was born smarter, prettier, stronger and so forth and that effort and need should play a part in deciding compensation. Those who claim disdain for the dollar could end up reducing everything to a dollar sign if they get their way. These same critics would scoff at the idea that "virtue is its own reward".

FOR FREE!

On May 5, 1987 Congressman Pat Williams of Montana, a member of the House Education and Labor Committee on Welfare Reform, expressed concerned about taking a whole generation of kids away from their parents by enrolling those parents in workfare programs. Secretary Brock said "not to worry" because AFDC children currently sit in front of a television set with their mothers and when these mothers are trained and put to work "they will be lively and ready to help with homework and give their kids quality time". (The Secretary has obviously never been a working mother!) Also, the Secretary explained, the children will be getting quality time while their mothers are at work. He went on to say that in the suburbs kids above 3 (and that's the age the Administration is talking about) often go to *paid* pre-school and the 1987 proposal is that poor kids get the same thing *for free*. (That should ease somebody's conscience—forget that it is blatantly unfair. What about families that struggle to give their children what others are now to get for free? Another instance of the government's morally bankrupt policy, not unlike the amnesty offered to immigrants that have broken the law while the law abiding stand patiently by.

Evelyn Moore of the National Black Child Development Institute testified on behalf of the 40 percent of the 7 million AFDC families that are Black. Ms. Moore claimed they *want* child-care teachers trained so they will be more than custodial. They *want* intellectual stimulation, cultural stimulation and emotional stimulation. They *want* a super quality program for these kids. (Don't we all?) Ms. Moore says the federal government *must* (??) pay the going rate for this program—$2,500 to $3,500 JUST LIKE THE WEALTHY!! (I told you it's NEVER ENOUGH!) According to Ms. Moore, apparently California and Massachusetts have already set aside significant funds for this. (Remember the right to consume?) The Program should be run by the Department of Labor to emphasize that child-care is an *Economic Support System* for working parents (full of clever little gimmicks, aren't they?). And Ms. Moore continued, "It could be as large as Social Security so of course we'll need a Commission to oversee it." Aaaaagh!

Ms. Moore attempts to justify the program by the same 'ol appeal—"It costs $8,000 to $12,000 to keep one child in foster care, instead let's provide $3,500 each for this program." THE NATION IS GOING BANKRUPT FROM SUCH ATTEMPTS TO SAVE MONEY!!!

Shortly after Ms. Moore's testimony, a staff attorney for the Child Care Law Center in San Francisco suggested there is a "RIGHT TO PAID CHILD CARE"—Here we go again! (As You Know Who might say.)

If you can identify the following political platform and its date you won't get a free book, but you can give yourself a pat on the back and a stern warning. It is very similar to much of today's political rhetoric.

> "We ask that the government undertake the obligation above all of providing citizens with adequate opportunity for employment and earning a living.
>
> The activities of the individual must not be allowed to clash with the interests of the community, but must take place within its confines and be for the good of all. Therefore, we demand: . . . there be an end to the power of the financial interests.
>
> We demand profit sharing in big business.
>
> We demand a broad extension of care for the aged.
>
> We demand . . . the greatest possible consideration of small business in the purchases of the national, state, and municipal governments.

> In order to make possible to every capable and industrious (citizen) the attainment of higher education and thus the achievement of a post of leadership, the government must provide an all-around enlargement of our entire system of public education. . . We demand the education at government expense of gifted children of poor parents. . .
>
> The government must undertake the improvement of public health—by protecting mother and child, by prohibiting child labor . . . by the greatest possible support for all clubs concerned with the physical education of youth."[20]

ALRIGHT ALREADY—WAS LENIN RIGHT OR WHAT?!

Lenin's prophecy is in the balance. He was right in the sense that if anything brings about our down-fall as a nation it will be consumerism not communism.

I urge you to watch your Congress in action for at least an hour a day for two weeks via C-SPAN. You will see that the spending habit is addictive and contagious, spreading from the top down to the rest of our society. Trying to obtain more things, be it health care, education, shelter, jobs or whatever, for more people by government mandate is robbery—a taking by force from producers for non-producers. So what *should* (what an ugly word) government do? Provide opportunity! (Talk about platitudes.)

Opportunity—ah, there's the rub. To those who advocate a welfare state it is the extended hand of government helping citizens meet life's day to day challenges in the form of government jobs (*opportunity* to work), educational grants (*opportunity* to learn), subsidized housing (*opportunity* to live in a better dwelling than would otherwise be possible), subsidized health care (*opportunity* to benefit from the knowledge and skill of others without the trade required by a free market), and security in old age (*opportunity* to participate in highly subsidized Social Security).

One person's idea of opportunity is what another would call dependency, i.e. opportunity for a hand-out. Government cannot give to some without taking from others. More often than not the taking is a raincheck on the production of future generations.

Embodied in the colloquial phrase "There's no such thing as a free lunch" is the realization that if the government gives a helping hand (welfare) it will determine the recipient's life style in some manner. In the past the receipt of welfare meant that a man could not be in the home. There were directives as to the placement of children, how food stamps were to be used or what dwellings qualify for subsidy and so on. Acceptance of a government job proscribes wages and numerous other conditions with no room left for private agreements between employer and employee.

As John Chamberlain said in his *Roots Of Capitalism* in 1968, "Even if state planning offered more material goods, people who have known and cherished liberty would rather live as free human beings on a more modest standard of living than sell their birthright for a mess of totalitarian pottage."

Spending in itself, as we have discussed, is not necessarily bad and in fact has been partially responsible for our affluence as a nation. It is the mind-set that goes with a compulsion to spend which is destructive. Well meaning people with high and noble aims make the mistake of believing morality can be legislated even though they have heard the idea denigrated often enough. I have heard demands similar to the following voiced many times in the past months. "We ask for a changed set of values so that looking after people may become as valued and therefore equally well paid and respected as looking after machinery and money now is." A changed set of values is not something that can be legislated. Of course these same people also want things that can and have been the subject of legislation such as better wages, child care and maternity leave.

The erosion of values that emphasize the future, the orientation towards redistribution rather than growth, loss of confidence and national goals are all to be viewed with alarm for the future of this country.

Consumer credit, by encouraging individuals to live beyond their means, robs them of dignity and self-respect. It encourages them to live from hand to mouth and forget about tomorrow, to live on the level of animals without control over their existence. The motives which drive people toward economic success are as varied as the people themselves. Profit and power do move people but so does the satisfaction of professional accomplishment, the desire for recognition and the urge to improve one's performance—the impulse to help and to give.

People inherently know there is more to life than making a living and gratifying material desires, that there is something which gives meaning to existence.

THE UNITED STATES OF AMERICA—THE GREAT EXPERIMENT IN GOVERNMENT

America has been changing according to some people's guidelines, but they are not mine and I wonder if they are the guidelines of the majority of Americans. America, or any country, starts off with the values of its founders, who were for the most part, radical tax protestors and people searching for freedom to express their deeply religious convictions. America in the eighties has come about 180 degrees on both these counts. Mostly the founders wanted Americans to be left alone—their fear of government meddling was so fresh and so intense that the Bill of Rights, including the tenth amendment were added to the Constitution—without them the Constitution may not have been ratified. Our newly formed government was the laughing stock of Europe. It was purposely as close to non-government (anarchy) as one could get and the Europeans were certain it wouldn't last a decade.

America has a purpose—a national purpose to bring to fruition the experiment that our founding fathers started; to show the world what can happen in a society where every single individual is free to pursue his own course and is beholden to no other man or group except by his own choice. We have the opportunity—no, the charge—to discredit for all peoples and for all times the idea that man is a sacrificial animal.

Ronald Reagan spoke of America as an experiment in his State of the Union address in January 1987: ". . . we were meant to be an endless experiment—with no limit to our reaches, no boundaries to what we can do, no end point to our hopes."

Professor Robert Reich of the John F. Kennedy School of Government refers to the self-made man as an American myth that must be discarded for the future well-being of the nation. Like so many academicians who never experience the real world except in theory, Professor Reich, in his new book *Tales Of A New America,* does not hesitate to give concrete business advice. According to the Professor, today's world ". . . requires of us a different and more subtle form of entrepreneurialism, which builds upon joint effort rather than individual conquest." It is fashionable in academia in the eighties, in the light of Japan's dominance in the global market place, to call for a "collective entrepreneurship".[21] But that is not what the American experiment is all about.

Pushing people around is characteristic of socialism. It is a product of the intellectuals (those who know what is best for you) and must be forcibly imposed upon others. Capitalism, on the other hand, occurs naturally if nothing or no one interferes.

GO AHEAD—*MAKE LENIN'S DAY!*

We have come a long way from the days when only white male landowners could vote, but our present addiction to spending has set us on a divergent path, away from our destiny as a nation.

I don't want to live in a country where "NO" is the answer to the following questions:

1) Would drug companies work on a cure for rare diseases without government subsidies?
2) Would women be treated fairly in the work place if employers were not forced to comply with laws?
3) Would Blacks, and other minorities get along with the White majority as well if they weren't *forced* to take specific actions?

4) Would the poor, sick and homeless be taken care of if there were no government programs?
5) Could workers get ahead if employers refused to pay them a minimum wage and provide standardized benefits?
6) Would people be able to come up with the money to pay their taxes if the government didn't take withholdings and thereby use their money all year without paying interest?
7) Would companies freely bend to public outcrys to care for the environment if they were not forced to comply with government standards?

Most people would agree that "NO" is the most likely answer to all of the above. Perhaps they would be right but I submit the reason is precisely because we have been "trained" to let government do it!

I am willing to bet with the power a free press wields in this country, coupled with a more limited government, people would know which companies spent resources altruisticly. Private organizations would raise money for projects as they do today, but with limited government there would be fewer taxes and more dollars available to give (free of coercion) according to what is *really wanted* not what *should* be wanted. Groups would be competing for funds, and just as Samaritan House outdid the New York City shelters, competition would mean dollars would go further with better results. Now government just about has a monopoly on charity. People tend to do less themselves when they are led to believe it is government's responsibility.

Imagine what it would be like to live in a country where people do things because they are enlightened, have good feelings towards their fellow men and are not only permitted to but desire and are encouraged to live a full life and stretch their abilities to the maximum; where citizens know they are entitled to the fruits of their efforts and they will not be robbed by government. A society where nothing gets done unless people who *care* take action. Isn't that infinitely preferable to a society where one small class makes all the decisions and does all the work for the large passive often lazy, unthinking and generally uncaring majority? Big Government is robbing American citizens of meaningful lives just as surely as a mother would harm a child by smothering him or her with too much attention.

Ronald Reagan came to office with the promise to get government off the backs of the American people. As we have seen, and without placing blame, it was an empty promise. Was the Reagan Revolution America's last gasp as many people believe? Only time will tell. Lenin's prophecy that America will spend itself out of existence, will fail or be fulfilled in the next decade. But were Lenin alive today he might stand there patiently and knowingly, much in the manner of one of my more famous neighbors, anticipating those already formulating the spending programs which they hope will pass Congress when the Reagan Administration is no more, and say, "Go ahead—make my day!"

Notes

PREFACE

A. *The Coming of the New Deal* by Arthur Schlesinger Jr.

SECTION ONE

1. Research Institute Recommendations, Vol 38, #2 Jan. 9, 1987
2. *Wall Street Journal* April 6, 1987
3. KGO Radio March 31, 1987
4. C-SPAN March, 1987
5. *Wall Street Journal* January 8, 1985
6. *Wall Street Journal* October 31, 1983
7. *Wall Street Journal* March 31, 1987
8. *Wall Street Journal* January 15, 1984
9. Senator Patrick Moynihan quoted in George Will's Column, November 20, 1986.
10. Ibid
11. *Business Week* January 26, 1987

SECTION TWO

1. *Wall Street Journal* September 5, 1986
2. *Social Security: An Idea Whose Time Has Passed* by Helen Rogers
3. Anglo-Irish Agreement Support Act of 1986 P.L. 99–415 Approved September 19, 1986.
4. *Wall Street Journal* March 23 1987
5. *Insight* November 17, 1986
6. *Wall Street Journal* August 8, 1985
7. *Insight* April 13, 1987

8. *Monterey Peninsula Herald* March 4, 1987
9. *Monterey Peninsula Herald* July 25, 1987
10. Ibid
11. First English Evangelical Lutheran Church of Glendale V. County of Los Angeles
12. *Wall Street Journal* March 13, 1987
14. *Wall Street Journal* April 2, 1987
15. Jack Anderson's column December 13, 1982
16. *Policy Review*
17. *Carl Rowan's Column* May 17, 1987
18. Ibid
19. Senate Labor Committee Hearings January 14, 1987 (C-SPAN)
20. Address by Senator Paul Simon January 19, 1987 to the Coalition for Higher Education (C-SPAN)
21. Counselor to the Secretary of Education viewed on C-SPAN January 19, 1987
22. *McNeil-Lehr Hour* November 20, 1986
23. *Associated Press* February 15, 1987
24. *Atlas Shrugged* by Ayn Rand
25. *Wall Street Journal* April 2, 1987
26. *The Ethics of Competition* by Frank H. Knight
27. Family in Piedmont, California with 20 plus children, many adopted and handicapped.
28. Article by Professor Kelman reproduced in the *Monterey Peninsula Herald* January 18, 1987
29. *National Underwriter* January 26, 1987
30. *Business Week* May 25, 1987
31. *Wall Street Journal* January 29, 1987
32. Names of those testifying before the Committee have been purposefully omitted to avoid any possible embarrassment.
33. *Time* February 16, 1987
34. *Wall Street Journal* March 18, 1987
35. FDR in 1934 from Arthur Schlesinger, Jr's book *The Coming of the New Deal*
36. Letter to the Editor of the *Wall Street Journal* February 5, 1987 by Governor Michael Dukakis of Massachusetts
37. *Wall Street Journal* January 19, 1987
38. Ibid #36
39. *American Bar Association Journal* January 1, 1987
40. Lochner v. New York (1905)
41. *The New Right vs The Constitution* (CATO 1986)
42. *Wall Street Journal* June 3, 1987
43. LPS Act—Lanterman-Petris-Short Act of 1967
44. *Wall Street Journal* October 8, 1986
45. Taken from "National Survey", a solicitation sent to households

in the spring of 1987 by the *American Farmland Trust*

46. Ibid
47. Dean Kleckner, President of the American Farm Bureau Federation supported Pete du Pont in 1988.
48. *Insight* July 14, 1986
49. *Wall Street Journal* October 3, 1986
50. *Insight* September 8, 1986
51. Article by William H. Peterson *Wall Street Journal* October 8, 1986
52. *Wall Street Journal* February 12, 1987
53. See page 106 for example of CA rice farmers
54. *Insight* April 13, 1987
55. *Wall Street Journal* article by Latique Jamel April 2, 1987
56. *The Coming of the New Deal* by Arthur Schlesinger, Jr.
57. Interviewed on KGO Radio April 25, 1986
58. *Wall Street Journal* March 10, 1986
59. *Jack Anderson's Column* April 16, 1986
60. *Wall Street Journal*
61. *Wall Street Journal* June 30, 1986
62. By the terms of the 1979 GATT Tokyo Round, nonmilitary procurements by govts must not discriminate against foreign suppliers in favor of domestic suppliers.
63. *Insight* March 9, 1987
64. *Wall Street Journal* November 25, 1985
65. Interview on KGO Radio April 25, 1986
66. *Insight* March 9, 1987
67. *Time* March 7, 1983
68. *Associated Press* February 1, 1983
69. *Fortune* March 4, 1985
70. *Associated Press* March 3, 1987
71. No. 10 of *The Federalist*
72. *Citizens For A Debt-Free America* 2550 S. Sunnyslope Rd. New Berlin, WI 53151 (414) 782-1305
73. *Underground Government: The Off-Budget Public Sector* by James Bennett and Thomas DiLorenzo (CATO Institute)
74. CBS Radio Editorial May 1, 1986

SECTION THREE

1. *George Will's Column* May 8, 1986
2. *Insight* March 9, 1987
3. KGO Radio News February 17, 1987
4. KGO Radio News May 10, 1986
5. Christian Science Monitor Service September 26, 1986
6. *Everyone's Guide to Financial Planning* by Helen Rogers

7. *Wall Street Journal* June 2, 1986
8. See "Backroads with Charles Kuralt" (film)

SECTION FOUR

1. *Associated Press* May 22, 1987 story by Mitchell Landsberg
2. *Scientific American* May, 1987 Vol 256 No. 5 "A Surge in Inequality"
3. Lowell Galloway & Richard Vedder, Ohio University economists in a paper published by the National Center for Policy Analysis (1986)
4. *Scientific American* May, 1987
5. "Fun With Dick & Jane" is the title of a Jane Fonda-George Segal humorous movie made in the 1970s in which wealthy parents refused the down-on-their-luck couple financial help "for their own good in order to build character". The couple succeeded all right—at crime! It was "tongue-in-cheek" but some people, like myself, *really* believe it works. One of my favorite movies because it makes fun of what I believe in. It reminds me that no one should take themselves or their ideas too seriously!
6. *The Coming of the New Deal* by Arthur Schlesinger, Jr.
7. L.A. Superior Court #C-479-453
8. L.A. Superior Court #C-501-603
9. L.A. Superior Court #C-523-361
10. L.A. Superior Court #C-568-184
11. *California Lawyer* May 1987
12. *The Virtue of Selfishness* by Ayn Rand
13. *Wall Street Journal* February 9, 1987
14. *Wall Street Journal* April 3, 1986
15. Professor Barry Bluestone was a panel member discussing "The Disappearing Middle Class" at the Harvard Institute for Learning & Retirement in May, 1987.
16. *Time* May 11, 1987 Book Review by Jack White
17. *Wall Street Journal* June 24, 1986
18. Cesaer Chavez at the Commonwealth Club (S.F.) November 9, 1984
19. *The Virtue of Selfishness* by Ayn Rand
20. Political Program of the National Socialist Workers Party of Germany (NAZIS) adopted on February 24, 1920.
21. See page 84

Bibliography
(Simplified)

A Primer on Government Spending by Robert L. Heilbroner & Peter Bernstein
Pork Barrel: The Unexpurgated Grace Commission Story of Congressional Profligacy by Randall Fitzgerald & Gerald Lipson
Working Toward A Fairer Civil Justice System by A Monograph The Insurance Information Institute
Social Security Reserves by James S. Parker
Social Security: Prospects for Real Reform edited by Peter Ferrara
Social Security: The Fraud In Your Future by Warren Shore
Social Security: An Idea Whose Time Has Passed by Helen P. Rogers
Underground Government: The Off-Budget Public Sector by James Bennett & Thomas DiLorenzo
The High-Flex Society by Pat Choate & J. K. Linger
A Greater Good: Potentials For An Intelligent Economy by Robert Zevin
The American Search: Expansion & Self-Assertion edited by Parman, Waltmann, Stickle & Fithian
America's Third Revolution: Public Interest and the Private Role by Irving S. Shapiro
A New Social Contract: The Economy & Government After Reagan by Martin Carnoy, Derek Shearer & Russell Rumberger
The Capitalist Reader edited by Lawrence Stepelevich
Capitalism: The Unknown Ideal by Ayn Rand
Making America Work Again by J. Morton Davis
The Conservators by Elliott Roosevelt
Profits and The Future Of American Society by S. Jay Levy & David Levy
America In Search Of Itself by Theodore White
The Neo-Liberals by Randall Rothenberg
Facets Of Liberty edited by L. K. Samuels
Washington: City of Scandals by Donald Lambro
Dangerous Currents: The State Of Economics by Lester C. Thurow

Zero-Sum Society by Lester C. Thurow
A Time Of Passion: America 1960–1980 by Charles R. Morris
Bright Promise, Dismal Performance by Milton Friedman
Loyalties by Daniel Patrick Moynihan
Black Economic Development by Fournoy A. Coles, Jr.
Spheres Of Justice by Michael Walzer
Wealth & Poverty by George Gilder
Burning Money by J. Peter Grace
A Taxpayer Survey Of The Grace Commission Report by William Kennedy, Jr. & Robert Lee
On The Road With Charles Kuralt by Charles Kuralt
In The Name Of Profits by Robert Heilbroner and others
The Good Years by Caroline Bird
The Truth About Supply-Side Economics by Michael Evans
Minding America's Business by Magaziner & Reich
Revolt Of The Haves by Robert Kuttner
The Next 200 Years by Herman Kahn
The Spirit Of Democratic Capitalism by Michael Novak
Who Bears The Burden? by Pechman & Okner
How Much More Equality Can We Afford? by Edgar Browning
The Other Generation Gap by Cohen & Gans
The Graying Of America by James Jorgensen
The Graying of Working America by Sheppard & Rix
Can We Afford Early Retirement? by Frank Kleicler
Atlas Shrugged by Ayn Rand
The Ethics of Competition by Frank H. Knight
The Coming of The New Deal by Arthur Schlesinger, Jr.
The New Right vs The Constitution (CATO Institute)
The Virtue Of Selfishness by Ayn Rand

Index